THE STAFF OF MOSES

Reflections on Islamic Faith,
and Divine Existence and Unity

THE STAFF OF MOSES

Reflections on Islamic Faith,
and Divine Existence and Unity

BEDİÜZZAMAN SAİD NURSİ

Translated by
Hüseyin Akarsu

Light

New Jersey

Published by The Light, Inc.
345 Clifton Ave., Clifton,
NJ, 07011, USA

www.thelightpublishing.com

Library of Congress Cataloging-in-Publication Data Available

ISBN 978-1-59784-254-9 (hardcover)

Printed by
Numune Matbaacılık ve Cilt San. Ltd. Şti. İstanbul - Turkey

Table of Contents

Preface

EDIÜZZAMAN SAID NURSI (1877–1960), WHO IS ONE OF THE MOST effective and profound representatives of Islam's intellectual, moral, and spiritual strengths, spent most of his life overflowing with love and ardor for Islam, pursuing a wise and measured activism based on sound reasoning, and following the Qur'an and the Prophetic example.

Said Nursi lived during a time of transition—the Ottoman State's dying years and the Turkish Republic's formative years. He traveled widely, seeing first-hand the ignorance, poverty, and internal conflict prevailing in Anatolia and the larger Muslim world. In the sermon he gave in the Umayyad Mosque (Damascus) in March 1911 to about 10,000 people, including 100 high-ranking scholars, he analyzed why the Muslim world was stuck in the "Middle Ages": growing despair, the loss of truthfulness in social and political spheres, the love of belligerency and ignorance of the bonds proper among believers, pervasive despotism, and egocentricity.

On the same subject and concerning the defeat and collapse of the Ottoman State in the WW1, he wrote in his *Sunuhat* ("Occurrences to the Heart") and *Lemeat* ("Gleams") as follows:

> Humankind's misguided thinking, Nimrod-like obstinacy, Pharaoh-like haughtiness grew and grew on the earth until they reached the heavens. Humanity also offended the sensitive mystery of creation. It caused the shudders of the last war to pour down from the heavens like the plague and deluge; it caused a heavenly blow to be dealt to the infidel. So the calamity was the calamity of all humankind. The common cause, inclusive of all humankind, was the misguided

thinking that arose from materialism, bestial freedom, and the despotism of carnal desires and fancies. Our share in it resulted from our neglect and abandonment of the pillars of Islam. For the Creator the All-Exalted wanted one hour out of the twenty-four. He ordered us, willed that we, for our good, assign one hour for the five daily Prayers. But out of laziness we gave them up, neglected them in heedlessness. So we received the following punishment: He made us perform Prayers of a sort during these last five years through a constant, twenty-four hour drill and hardship, keeping us ceaselessly moving and striving. He also demanded of us one month a year for fasting, but we pitied our carnal souls, so in atonement He compelled us to fast for five years. He wanted us to pay as *Zakah* either a fortieth or a tenth of the property He gave us, but out of miserliness we did wrong: we mixed the unlawful with our property, and did not give the *Zakah* voluntarily. So He had our accumulated *Zakah* taken from us, and saved us what was unlawful in our property. The deed causes the punishment of its kind. The punishment is of the same as the deed. (*Gleams of Truth: Prescriptions for a Healthy Social Life* [trans.], Tughra Books, New Jersey, 2010, pp., 47–48)

Two of the All-Majestic One's Attributes of perfection give rise to two sets of laws. One is the law of life or of the creation and operation of the universe, which proceeds from the Attribute of Will, and the other, the well-known Shari‘a, which proceeds from the Attribute of Speech. Just as the commands or laws of the well-known Shari‘a are obeyed or disobeyed, so too do people obey or disobey the law of life. The reward and punishment for the former is received mostly in the Hereafter, while the penalties and rewards of the latter are suffered mostly in this world. For example, the reward of patience is success, while the penalty for laziness is privation; and the reward of labor is wealth. The reward of steadfastness is triumph. The punishment of poison is illness and the reward of its antidote is health. (We neglected both of these laws and got our merits.) (*ibid*, pp., 69–70)

The crisis was a global crisis and the basic cause of this crisis was unbelief. As Collin Turner from Durham University of England notes, "Said Nursi saw that modern unbelief did not originate from ignorance, but from science and philosophy. Paradoxically, the Muslims' neglect of science and technology caused them to fall behind the West economically and militarily. But the same science and technology that enabled the West to achieve global military and economic superiority caused Western people to lose their belief and traditional moral and spiritual values, and fall into pessimism, unhappiness, and spiritual crisis. This was natural, because although the Divine laws of nature (the subject matter of science) are the counterpart of the Divine Scripture or Religion, they were separated from each other in the West. Secular morality and economic self-interest then replaced religious and other traditional values. Said Nursi viewed nature as the collection of Divine signs. Thus science and religion could not be in conflict, for they are two (apparently) different expressions of the same truth. Minds should be enlightened with science, and hearts need to be illumined with religion."

Having discovered the main problem of humanity, Said Nursi concentrated on belief, worship, morality, and good conduct. While, according to Turner, the numerous Islamic movements of the past 150 years have had little if anything to do with the resurgence of religious faith and most of these have actually been political movements, with leaders whose underlying goal has been to solve a specific problem: the problem of the perceived backwardness of the Muslim peoples and their subservience, politically and culturally, to the West, Said Nursi drew the attention to the following points as the main issue of all humanity:

> Creation's highest aim and most sublime result is belief in God. The most exalted rank of humanity is knowledge of God. The most radiant happiness and sweetest bounty for jinn and humanity is love of God contained within knowledge of Him; the spirit's purest joy and the heart's purest delight is spiritual ecstasy contained within love of God. All true happiness, pure joy, sweet bounties, and unclouded pleasure are contained within the knowledge and love of God. (*The Letters*, [trans.], Tughra Books, New Jersey, 2005, pp., 239–240)
>
> Belief is not restricted to a brief affirmation based on imitation; rather, it has degrees and stages of development. It is like a seed growing into a fully grown, fruit-bearing tree; like the sun's image in a mirror or in a drop of water to its images on the sea's surface and to the sun itself. Belief contains so many truths pertaining to God's Names and the realities contained in the universe that the most perfect science, knowledge, and virtue is belief and knowledge of God originating in a belief based on argument and investigation. While belief based on imitation can be refuted through doubt and questions raised by modern thought, belief based on argument and investigation has as many degrees and grades of manifestation as the number of Divine Names. Those who attain certainty of belief coming from direct observation of the truths on which belief is based study the universe as a kind of Qur'an. (*Emirdağ Lahikası* [Addendum of Emirdağ], Istanbul, 1959, vol., 1, pp., 102–103)

He offered his cure—hope, truthfulness and trustworthiness, mutual love, consultation, solidarity, and freedom in accordance with Islam—and stressed the following:

> History shows that Muslims increased in civilization and progressed in relation to how firmly they adhered to Islam. In other words, the strength they drew from Islam's truth was proportionate to their adherence to it.
>
> We Muslims, students of the Qur'an, follow proof. We do not abandon proof for blind obedience and imitation of the clergy, as do some adherents of other religions. Equipped with sciences, knowledge, and the virtues of true civilization, the human tendency to seek the truth, fairness and the feeling of justice in human nature, as well as love of humanity, are beginning to defeat and remove the obstacles before Muslims and all humanity.
>
> Since the tendency toward perfection is ingrained in human nature, if humanity does not suffer total destruction due to its faults and injustices, the truth of Islam will bring happiness to the Muslim world in particular, and the whole world in general, and will thus serve as atonement for the past and present vices of humanity.
>
> Look, time does not move in a straight line so that its beginning and end grow distant from one another. Rather, like the movement of the earth, time moves by drawing a circle. It sometimes displays progress as an embodiment of spring and summer and sometimes displays decline as an embodiment of winter and a season of storms. So, just as every winter is followed by spring and every night by the morning, so too humankind will, God willing, also live a new morning and spring. From the Divine Mercy we can expect to see the true civilization marked by a general peace in the sun of the truth of Islam. (*Gleams of Truth*, 125–128)

Though outwardly simple, many of Said Nursi's ideas and activities were wholly original. He embraced humanity; opposed unbelief, injustice, and (religious) deviation; and struggled against all kinds of tyranny—even at the cost of his life. His deep belief and feeling, when combined with his wise and rational ideas and problem-solving methods, produced an example of love, ardor, and feeling. His balanced thought, acts, and methods of acting made him a far-sighted man who assessed and judged surrounding conditions and solved problems.

Said Nursi died in Urfa on March 23, 1960, which may well have been the Night of Power in Ramadan. The coroner fixed his estate as a turban, a gown, and 20 lira. The real legacy of this hero of Islam was the 6,000-page *Risale-i Nur* Collection. This collection is a most widely read one after the Qur'an in Turkey and has so far been translated in several languages.

The Risale-i Nur and The Staff of Moses

Withdrawing from public life completely, Said Nursi devoted himself to defending and explaining Islam's main principles of thought, belief, worship, morality, and way of life through writing. His books are known as the *Risale-i Nur* ("The Treatises of Light"). It consists of 130 parts, which were collected in some ten or so books. In his *Risale-i Nur*, considered a classic of Turkish religious literature, he identified the cause of the Muslim world's decline: the weakening of belief's foundations. When joined with the unceasing attacks of scientific materialism, atheism, and material progress, he saw a great cloud of denial and doubt hovering over the Muslim world. To neutralize it, he undertook a *"jihad* of the word with the diamond principles of Islam" designed to strengthen—even save—belief by reconstructing Islam from its foundations of belief.

The *Risale-i Nur* explains Islam and belief to modern people in their own terms and according to their own worldview. Analyzing both belief and unbelief, he used clearly reasoned arguments to prove that the Qur'anic conception of God and His Unity, Prophethood and bodily resurrection, and all others are the only rational explanations for existence, humanity, and the universe.

Using easily understood stories, comparisons, and explanations, Said Nursi produced categorical proofs showing that modern scientific discoveries actually support and reinforce the truths of the Religion. He used the Qur'anic methodology of addressing each person's intellect, and all inner and outer facilities, to encourage people to study the universe and its functioning in order to understand creation's true nature and purposes. This, in turn, leads to learning the One Creator's Attributes and their own duties as God's servants.

Said Nursi explained the universe's true nature as being a comprehensive sign of its Creator, and showed via clear arguments that all fundamentals of belief can be proven rationally when the universe is read in this way. As belief is then grounded in modern science, it remains firm and immune to materialism, naturalism, and atheism.

Such believers view all scientific and technological advances as merely uncovering the cosmos' workings. Viewing the cosmos as a vast and infinitely complex and meaningful unified book describing its Single Author, all discoveries and advances reinforce, deepen, and expand belief. Thus their most fundamental needs—to worship God by recognizing His Most Beautiful Names and Attributes, and to obey His laws—are met.

Said Nursi himself describes the *Risale-i Nur* as a true commentary on the wise Qur'an that emanates from its miraculousness. In addition to proving the six pillars of Islamic belief through both concrete and rational arguments and producing the human conscience and basic nature as witnesses, especially through comparisons it vividly demonstrates the true natures of and difference between belief and unbelief. It demonstrates that in misguidance there is a sort of Hell in this world, while in belief there is a kind of Paradise. It shows the severe pains in sins, evil deeds, and forbidden pleasures, and proves that pleasures akin to those in Paradise are to be found in good deeds and virtues, and in the truths of the Religion.

'*Asa-yi Musa* ("The Staff of Moses") is a collection of his writings concerning many benefits of belief, worship, and good conduct, and the Existence and Unity of the Divine Being. Said Nursi named it after the Staff of Moses, which broke and destroyed the spells of the sorcerers as a miracle of Moses, upon him be peace (see, the Qur'an, 7:111–122; 20:57–70), because it breaks and destroys the "spells" of unbelief which especially scientific materialism casts on belief. It has two chapters. The first chapter is composed of fruits of belief, and the second one, which Said Nursi named The Treatise on God's Final, Conclusive Argument, after the Qur'anic verse, *Say, "(as against what you argue) God's is the final, conclusive argument."* (6:149), contains decisive arguments for God's Existence and Oneness, and other pillars of the Islamic faith.

The Publisher

The
First Chapter

The First Chapter

Fruits of Belief

This is the response of the *Risale-i Nur* to heresy and absolute unbelief. It is our true defense in this incarceration of ours, for it is this and this alone which occupies us here. This treatise is a fruit and souvenir from Denizli Prison, and the product of two Fridays.

Said Nursi

In the Name of God, the All-Merciful, the All-Compassionate.

So he remained in prison for some years more (12:42).

ACCORDING TO THE MEANING OF THIS VERSE, PROPHET JOSEPH, UPON him be peace, is the patron-saint or guide of prisoners: prison may be seen to be a kind of "School of Joseph." Since this is the second time that students of the *Risale-i Nur* have been sent to prison, it is necessary to study and teach in this school a number of matters connected with imprisonment, which are explained by the *Risale-i Nur*. In the hope that we may benefit from them thoroughly, we will explain five or six of those matters in brief.

The First Matter

As expounded in The Fourth Word, every day our Creator bestows on us twenty-four hours of life as a kind of capital with which to obtain that which is necessary for our lives in both this world and the next. If we spend twenty-three of these hours on this extremely fleeting worldly life and fail to spend the remaining one hour—which is sufficient for the five obligatory canonical Prayers—on the very lengthy life of the Hereafter, it is clear that we will have committed an error of the greatest magnitude. One can hardly imagine what a great loss this would be or the extent of the distress that our mind and spirit would be made to feel as a result of our short-sighted behavior. Not only would our future actions be ruined by our distress, we would also be unable to reform our conduct on account of the despair that would overwhelm us.

However, if we spend that one hour on the five obligatory Prayers, the profit to be had is inestimable. For each hour of this calamitous term of imprisonment will at times be equal to a whole day's worship, while the single hour devoted to the canonical Prayers will be transformed into many permanent hours. In addition, the despair and distress we feel in our hearts and spirits will begin to fade, and one hour's Prayer will serve as atonement for the errors that led to imprisonment in the first place, thus allowing them to be forgiven. Furthermore, it will also help us to receive training and improvement, which is the purpose of imprisonment. How beneficial this is and how pleasing a consolation it is for us and our companions in hardship!

As was written in The Fourth Word, let us suppose that a person gives five or ten liras out of his twenty-four to a lottery in which a thousand people are taking part in order to win the thousand-lira prize, but fails to give a single lira to buy a ticket for an everlasting treasury of jewels. See how he rushes to the former, even though the possibility of his winning the thousand liras in that worldly lottery is no more than one in a thousand. And see how he flees from the latter, even though according to the reports given by a hundred and twenty-four thousand Prophets, and the confirmation provided by countless numbers of truthful informers from among the saints and purified saintly scholars, the chances of a true believer winning that 'lottery', the prize of which is everlasting felicity in the Hereafter, is nine hundred and ninety-nine out of a thousand. Now think how irrational this is, to rush towards the former but to flee from the latter!

Prison governors and wardens, and indeed the country's administrators and guardians of public order, should be pleased with this lesson that is provided by the *Risale-i Nur*, for it has been witnessed and experienced on numerous occasions that the management and disciplining of a thousand religious people who constantly have in mind the prison of Hell is far easier than that of ten people who have no belief at all, who do not perform the obligatory Prayers, who care only about worldly imprisonment, who have no consideration for what is licit or illicit, and who have become habituated to living undisciplined lives.

The Second Matter

As explained in the treatise entitled *Gençlik Rehberi* ("A Guide for Youth") in the *Risale-i Nur*, death is as inevitable as night following day, or winter following fall. Just as this prison is a temporary guesthouse for those who enter and leave it one after the other, the earth too is a like a caravanserai on a long road; here caravans, rushing to get to their destination, stay overnight before moving on. Surely death, which has emptied all of the cities of the earth into the bowels of the earth a hundred times over, places demands on us far greater than those demanded by life. The *Risale-i Nur* has explained this awesome truth, a brief summary of which follows:

Since death cannot be eliminated and since the door of the grave cannot be closed, we must look for a way that can save us from being condemned by the executioner of death to the solitary confinement of the grave and eternal perdition in the world to come; surely this should be humankind's greatest concern and surely it is in our best interest to investigate this possibility. There is such a way —a way shown by *Risale-i Nur* and inspired by the teachings of the Qur'an. What follows is a brief summary:

Death is either eternal execution—a gallows on which a person and their friends and relatives will be hanged—or it is a kind of entrance ticket to another, permanent realm, a palace of happiness prepared for those who possess belief. As for the grave, it is either a dark, bottomless pit of solitary confinement or a door which opens outward from the prison of this world onto a permanent, illuminated garden and place of feasting. This truth has been expounded in the *Gençlik Rehberi* as follows:

For example: many gallows have been set up in this prison yard, and immediately beyond the wall a huge lottery office has been opened; everyone in the world has purchased a ticket. There is no doubt whatsoever that the five hundred people in this prison are certain to be called one by one, without exception, to that yard: there is no hope of escape. One can hear the announcements being made: "Come and receive your document of execution and mount the gallows!" or "Take in your hand the decree condemning you to eternal solitary confinement and enter through that door!" or "Congratulations! Yours is the winning ticket that is worth millions. Come and take it!" We see with our own eyes that people are mounting the gallows, one after the other. Yet, while some mount the gallows only to be hanged, we learn from the reports of the earnest officials who are working in the prison yard that some of the people are using the gallows as one would a ladder, and are scaling the wall to enter the lottery office that lies beyond.

At this juncture, two delegations enter our prison. One delegation brings musical instruments, wine and apparently delicious sweetmeats and pastries, which they endeavor to make us eat. But the sweetmeats are in fact poisonous, for demons in human form have put poison in them.

The second delegation brings papers of education and training, lawful foods and licit drinks. The members of this delegation present these things to us and say with great earnestness:

> The gifts brought by the first delegation are a test; if you accept and consume them, you will be hanged on the gallows over there, like the others that you have seen hanged before them. However, if you accept the gifts that we have brought you at the command of this country's ruler, and if you recite the supplications and prayers written on these papers of education and training, you will be saved from execution. Believe without a shadow of a doubt that each of you will receive the winning lottery ticket worth millions as a royal favor. But if you eat these unlawful, poisonous sweets, it is written in these decrees—decrees with which we all concur—that you will suffer the effects of the poison until the very moment that you are taken to the gallows to be hanged.

As in this comparison, for the people of belief and obedience—provided that they depart in a state of true belief—the ticket for an eternal and inexhaustible treasury will be drawn from the lottery of human fate beyond the gallows at the appointed hour, of which we are always aware. However, for those with no belief in the Hereafter and who persist in vice, unlawful actions, unbelief and sin, there is a hundred per cent probability that they will, unless they repent, be condemned by judicial decree to execution and eternal perdition. For those who believe in the immortality of the human spirit, yet still tread the path of vice and sin there is a ninety-nine per cent probability that they will be condemned to permanent solitary confinement. Certain news of this was given by one hundred and twenty-four thousand Prophets, all of whom were equipped with innumerable miracles as evidence of their truthfulness. The same news has been given by more than one hundred and twenty-four million saints, who discern and affirm through spiritual uncovering the traces and shadows—as though seen on a movie screen—of the news brought by the Prophets. Similarly, thousands of millions of exacting scholars, interpreters of the Islamic law and veracious scholars have, with decisive proofs and powerful arguments, established with rational and logical certainty the information provided by these two eminent groups of people.

Consider, then, the situation of someone who, on the advice of a single individual, abandons the safe path they have been following and opts for a longer and much more dangerous one, ignoring the collective wisdom of the people of truth mentioned earlier—those moons, suns and stars, those sacred leaders of humanity—who have pointed out the straight path which leads directly to eternal felicity.

The situation of such a person is this: having embarked on this journey, the wretch hears someone say that by taking the short path there is a one per-cent chance of danger and the possibility of a month's incarceration at the end of the road. So, on the spurious advice of a single person, our traveler abandons the short path and takes a longer route. They do this because it appears harmless, although in reality there is no benefit in this path. At the same time, innumerable wise and well-informed individuals warn them not to abandon the shorter and easier of the routes—the one which will, with utmost certainty, lead them eventually to Paradise and eternal happiness. However, they chose to ignore their words and opt for the rougher, more troublesome route—the one which, with ninety-nine percent certainty, will lead to incarceration in Hell and everlasting misery. Surely, such a wretch has lost their mind, their heart and their spirit, for only a drunken lunatic would flee from the slight sting of a few mosquitoes on the safe path and rush onto a route along which dragons hide, waiting to attack and tear the poor wretch limb from limb.

Since this is the reality of the situation, we prisoners should accept the gifts of the second, blessed delegation so that we may avenge ourselves completely for the calamity of our incarceration. That is to say, just as the pleasure of a minute's revenge or a few minutes of vice has condemned us to years of incarceration, making our worlds into a prison, in order to take revenge we should transform an hour or two of our prison lives into a day or two of worship. In this way we will be able to transform two or three-year sentences into twenty or thirty years of permanent life thanks to the gifts of that blessed delegation; in this way we will be able to turn prison sentences of twenty or thirty years into a means of forgiveness from millions of years of incarceration in Hell, thus allowing our everlasting lives to smile in retaliation for the weeping that has characterized our transitory worlds. Demonstrating that prison is a place of training and education, we should try to be well-behaved, trustworthy, and useful members of our nation and country. Prison officers, wardens, and administrators should also see that the men whom they considered to be bandits, vagrants, murderers, and men of vice—and thus harmful to the country—are in fact students engaged in study in this most blessed place of education. And they should feel pride and offer thanks to God for this bounty.

The Third Matter

What follows is a summary of an instructive incident that is described in *Gençlik Rehberi*:

I was once sitting by a window in Eskişehir Prison during the National Republic Day. The young girls in the school opposite the prison were playing and cheering in the schoolyard. Suddenly, I saw them fifty years on, their future conditions played out to me like a film on a movie screen. I saw that of those fifty to sixty girl students, forty to fifty had turned to dust in their graves and were suffering. The other ten were unattractive septuagenarians, despised by those from whom they might have expected love, on account of the fact that they had not preserved their chastity when young. Observing this, I wept at their pitiable states. Some of my friends in the prison heard my weeping and asked me what was wrong, but I had to tell them to leave me alone for a while.

You must understand that what I saw was real and not imaginary. Just as summer and fall are followed by winter, the summer of youth and the fall of old age are followed by the winter of the grave and the Intermediate Realm. If there were a device which could show future events in the same way that films can show the events of the past, then those of fifty years ago would be shown in the present, and the people of misguidance and vice would be shown their condition fifty years from now; they would cry out in pain and disgust, bemoaning bitterly their present state of apparent felicity and illicit pleasures.

While preoccupied with these observations in Eskişehir Prison, a sort of collective persona, which encourages vice and misguidance, appeared embodied before me like a devil in human form. It said:

> We want to taste all the pleasures and joys of life, and to make others taste them too; do not interfere with us!"

In response I said:

> Since for the sake of pleasure and enjoyment you do not recall death but, rather, plunge yourself into vice and misguidance, know for a fact that because of your misguidance all the past is dead and non-existent: it is a desolate and most dreadful graveyard, filled with rotted corpses. The pains that arise from those innumerable separations you have suffered and from the deaths of your friends—pains which, since there is no hope of reunion with your loved ones, have had a grievous effect on what remains of your heart and mind—will soon destroy those insignificant drunken pleasures which constitute your present. As for the future, well, because of your lack of belief, that too is nothing more than a dark, dead, and desolate wasteland. And since the unfortunate wretches who are destined to come from there to emerge in this realm of existence and in the present will also be beheaded by the executioner's sword of death and, according to your assumption, thrown into non-existence, on account of your concern and relationship with them which stems from your being a creature with intelligence, grievous worries will rain down continuously on your disbelieving head, devastating beyond recognition your petty, dissolute pleasure.
>
> If you abandon misguidance and vice and enter the sphere of true belief and righteousness, you will see through the light of faith that the past is neither non-existent nor a graveyard filled with rotted corpses; rather, it is a real, luminous world that has been transformed into the future: it is a waiting-room for the immortal spirits who will enter palaces of happiness in the world to come. Since it is so, it gives no pain; on the contrary, depending on the degree and strength of one's belief, it causes a sort of paradisiacal pleasure in the world. The future, too, when seen through the eye of belief, is not a dark, desolate wasteland, but a ground in whose palaces of eternal happiness banquets and exhibitions of gifts have been set up by an All-Merciful, All-Compassionate One of Majesty and Benevolence—One Who has infinite Mercy and Munificence and Who

makes spring and summer into tables laden with bounties. Since the movie screen of belief reveals the future to be like this and since belief also gives the awareness that people are being dispatched there through the door death, everyone can experience some sort of the pleasure pertaining to that permanent realm while still in this world, to the degree and strength of their belief. *In conclusion, true, pain-free pleasure can be found only in belief and is possible only through belief.*

Since it is related to our discussion, we will explain something which was included in *Gençlik Rehberi* as a postscript, namely a single instance of the thousands of benefits and pleasures that belief produces even in this world. It is as follows:

Imagine, for example, that your beloved only child is suffering the pangs of death and you are desperately worried about her painful demise. Suddenly, a physician like Khidr or Luqman appears with a wonderful medicine, which he gives to your loved one. Your dear, most adorable child opens her eyes, delivered from death. Can you imagine the joy and relief that you would feel at her recovery and escape from death?

Like the child in the example, countless people whom you love and for whom you are concerned are, in your view, about to rot away for all eternity in the graveyard of the past. Suddenly, like Luqman the Wise, the truth of belief shines a light from the window of the heart onto the grave, which is thought of as a vast place of eternal annihilation. Thanks to the truth and light of belief, all of the dead spring to life, as though saying, 'We did not die and will not die; we will meet with you again!' What boundless joy and exhilaration you would feel at experiencing this reality! By giving the same boundless joy and exhilaration in this world, belief proves that it is like a seed— a seed which, were it to be embodied, would grow into a private paradise, a veritable *Touba*-tree of eternal felicity."

Persisting in its obduracy, that devil in human form responded thus:

At least we can pass our lives like animals, immersed in pleasure and enjoyment, indulging ourselves with amusement and dissipation, and casting all thought of these subtle and delicate matters out of our minds!

My answer was as follows:

No, you cannot live like an animal, not least because neither past nor future exists for animals. They feel neither sorrow nor regret over the past nor worry or fear with regard to what is yet to come. An animal receives unalloyed pleasure. It lives and sleeps in comfort, offering thanks and praise to its Creator. Even an animal that is about to be slaughtered does not feel anything. It feels pain as the knife cuts its throat, but that pain is momentary and disappears in an instant. This means that keeping the Unseen unknown, without revealing what will happen there, is a great instance of Divine mercy and compassion; it is an even greater blessing for innocent animals. But on account of the fact that human beings are sentient, and because their past and future can be seen to emerge from the Unseen to some extent, what lies beyond the veil of the visible world cannot remain wholly hidden; as a result, O human being, you are unable to live as carefree and unconcerned as animals. Regrets about the past, the pain of separation and worries about the future reduce to ashes your fleeting present pleasures, making them a hundred times less appealing than those enjoyed by the animals. Since this is a fact, either abandon your intellect, turn yourself into an animal, and achieve salvation that way or, alternatively, come to your senses through true belief, pay heed to the Qur'an, and experience pure pleasure also in this transitory world, which is a hundred times greater than that enjoyed by animals.

For a while, these words of mine silenced my adversary. But in his obstinacy he turned to me once more and said: "Well, then, we can at least live like the irreligious people of the West."

I replied:

In the same way that you cannot live like animals, you cannot live like the irreligious people of the West either. For even if they deny one Prophet, they believe in others. Even if they do not recognize the Prophets, they may believe in God. And even if they do not know God, they may have certain personal characteristics and virtues through which they find fulfillment. But if a Muslim denies the final Prophet, the greatest of God's Messengers, upon him and them be peace and blessings, whose religion and mission are universal, to what can they turn? For they will be unable to accept any other Prophet and will even have to turn their back on God Himself. For their knowledge of God and all the other Prophets has reached them through Prophet Muhammad, upon him be peace and blessings; without him, how can other Prophets have a place in anyone's heart? It is because of this that while many people have, since the earliest times, abandoned other faiths to enter Islam, few, if any, Muslims have become true Jews or Christians. Muslims who abandon Islam tend rather to become completely irreligious: as a rule, their characters are corrupted and they become a danger to the country and nation.

Hearing this argument, the obstinate devil in human garb could find no further straw at which to clutch. Unable to respond, it disappeared and went to Hell.

So, classmates of mine in this School of Joseph! Reality is as I have described it, affirmed by the *Risale-i Nur* which, with its proofs, has worn down the obduracy of many an obstinate soul and caused numerous people to believe over the past twenty years. Since it is thus, we should therefore follow the way of belief and correct conduct—a way which is safe and easy, and which benefits our lives and those of the members of our nation not only in this world but also in the next. Instead of indulging ourselves with pointless and ultimately painful fantasies, we should spend our free time reciting the *suras* of the Qur'an that we have memorized and learn their meaning from friends who can teach them. We should make up for the canonical Prayers we have failed to perform in the past. And, taking advantage of each other's good qualities, we should try to transform this prison into a blessed garden in which the seeds of good character can be nurtured. With righteous deeds such as these, we should do our best so that the prison governor and those concerned may be kindly masters and guides charged with the duty of preparing people for Paradise in the School of Joseph and supervising their training and education, rather than dispensers of torment, like the Angels of Hell, who stand over criminals and murderers.

The Fourth Matter

Again, this matter has been explained in *Gençlik Rehberi*. I was once asked the following question by some brothers who were helping me:

> For fifty days now you have asked nothing at all, nor have you shown any curiosity, about this terrible World War which has thrown the whole world into chaos, even though it is connected closely with the fate of Islam and the Muslim World. However, some of the religious and the learned listen to the radio intently, and some are even distracted from congregational Prayers as a result. Is there some other event more momentous than this war? Or is it in some way harmful to be preoccupied with it?

My reply was as follows:

The capital of life is very little and the work to be done very great. Like concentric circles, everyone has certain spheres of concern which exist one within the other: they have the spheres of the heart and the stomach; the spheres of body and home; the spheres of the quarter in which they reside and the town or city in which they live; the sphere of their country, the spheres of the earth and humankind, and the sphere of all living beings and the world as a whole. Each person may have certain duties in each of those spheres, but the most important and permanent duties are those which pertain to the nearest, smallest sphere, while the least important and temporary duties pertain to the furthest, largest one. According to this standard, there may be duties, the importance and sphere of which are inversely proportional to each other. But because of the appeal of the largest sphere, those vital duties that pertain to the smallest sphere tend to be neglected, as people become preoccupied with unnecessary, trivial, and peripheral matters. It destroys the capital of their life for nothing and causes them to waste their precious time on worthless things. For example, someone who follows the events of the war may come to support one side in their heart, and as result may even look favorably on tyranny and become a part of it.

With regard to the first part of the question, all people—Muslims especially—are faced continuously with events more momentous than this World War, and an issue infinitely more important than that of world dominion. Indeed, if everyone had the wealth of the Germans and the English, plus an iota of sense, they would spend it all on finding a solution to this issue. This issue, about which hundreds of thousands of Prophets, saints, and purified scholars have informed us, relying on the thousands of promises and pledges given by the Owner and Disposer of the universe, is as follows:

For everyone there exists the possibility of winning, thanks to belief, an eternal property that is as vast as the earth, filled with gardens and palaces. Without belief, however, that property cannot be gained. In this age, many are losing because of the plague of materialism. A certain saintly scholar, who was capable of unveiling certain hidden realities, once observed in one district that out of forty people who lay on their deathbeds, only a few won; the others lost. Can anything, even power and dominion over the whole world, substitute for such a loss?

We *Risale-i Nur* students know that it would be foolhardy to abandon the duties conducive to felicity in the Hereafter, and to give up on that excellent lawyer who helps ninety-nine percent of the people to win their case, and instead preoccupy ourselves with trivia as though we would remain in this world forever. For this reason, we *Risale-i Nur* students are convinced that if each of us were a hundred times more intelligent than we are now, we would still use our intellectual capital on the same right cause.

To my new brothers here who share with me the calamity of imprisonment I would say this. You have not yet come to know the *Risale-i Nur* as well as my old brothers, who entered this place with me. Calling on them and thousands of students like them as witnesses, I assure you that the *Risale-i Nur* is the leading 'lawyer' of the age, inspired by the miraculousness of the wise Qur'an and able to help those who study it to win the most important case of their lives. Indeed, over the past twenty years it has helped twenty thousand people to attain true belief—itself a guarantee that their case will be successful. Although for the past eighteen years my enemies and various heretics and materialists have cruelly turned some members of the government against me and the authorities have imprisoned us in order to silence us, something they have tried to do before, they have been able to criticize only two or three of the one hundred and thirty pieces of 'equipment' which make up the steel fortress of the *Risale-i Nur*. In other words, the *Risale-i Nur* is enough for one who wants to engage an advocate to win the case of their life. Also, do not fear, for the *Risale-i Nur* cannot be banned! With two or three exceptions, its most significant treatises are circulating freely among representatives and other leading figures of the government. By God's leave, a time will come when venerated governors and officials will distribute these lights to the prisoners as though they were food and medicine in order to turn the prisons into truly effective houses of reform.

The Fifth Matter

As described in *Gençlik Rehberi*, there is no doubt that a person's youth will one day disappear: just as summer gives up its place to fall and winter, and just as day eventually becomes evening and then night, youth will one day become old age and end in death. All Divinely-revealed Scriptures tell us that if the young spend their youth on righteous deeds, behave chastely and act within the bounds of good conduct, they will eventually gain eternal youth. However, if they waste their youth and spend it on dissipation, they will lose it forever. Just as a murder resulting from a minute's fury brings in its wake millions of minutes of imprisonment, the illicit pleasures of youth will, as every young person may confirm from their own experience, prove to contain more pain than pleasure. As well as the regrets that one feels in this world with the passing of such pleasures and the penalties one often receives here as a result of sin, there is the torment of the grave to consider, as well as the fact that one will have to answer for one's misconduct in the Hereafter.

For example, the temporary pleasure to be found in illicit love is changed into poisonous honey on account of the pangs of jealousy, separation, and not being loved in return. If you want to understand why young people frequently end up in hospital with physical and mental diseases on account of their excesses, or in prison on account of their misconduct, or in bars and dens of vice, you only have to visit those places. And the graveyards are full of those who were destroyed as a result of the distress caused by the inability of young human hearts to find true nourishment through the performance of their proper duties. Visit the hospitals and prisons and listen to the sighs of regret and watch with pity the tears that are shed for a youth that has been frittered away on excess, misconduct, and illicit pleasure.

The Qur'an and all other Divinely-revealed Scriptures and Decrees inform us in many of their verses that if it spent within the bounds of good conduct, youth will be preserved in the Hereafter, where, as a Divine favor, it will become immortal. Since the sphere of the lawful is sufficient for human enjoyment, and since an hour of unlawful pleasure sometimes leads to years of punishment in prison, surely it is vital to spend the sweet bounty of youth correctly and within the bounds of righteous conduct as thanks for that bounty.

The Sixth Matter

The following is a brief indication of one of the thousands of the universal proofs of the pillar of belief in God, many of which, together with explanations, can be found in the *Risale-i Nur*.

In Kastamonu some high-school students asked me: "Tell us about our Creator, for our teachers do not speak of Him." I replied as follows:

All of the sciences you study speak continuously of God, the Creator, in its own tongue, and makes Him known. Do not listen to your teachers; listen to them.

For example, a well-equipped, well-designed pharmacy has many medicines and pills, composed of different, precisely-measured components.
This indicates, without a doubt, to the existence of an extremely skillful
and learned pharmacist. In the same way, the pharmacy of the earth is
stocked with countless life-giving cures and medicines. Through the science
of medicine, even the blind can know the All-Wise One of Majesty Who
is the Pharmacist of the largest pharmacy of the earth.

Let us use another example. A wonderful factory that produces thousands of different cloths woven from a simple material indicates without a
doubt the existence of a manufacturer and a skillful mechanical engineer.
Similarly, the factory of the Lord, which we call the earth, has countless
parts, and each part possesses hundreds of thousands of machines. Without
a doubt, the factory that is the earth makes known, through the science of
engineering, the existence of its Manufacturer and Owner.

Another example is a shop that has a well-organized storage place for
numerous varieties of provisions brought there from hundreds of different
places. The very existence of the shop indicates in turn the existence of a
shop owner who prepares, stores, and distributes those provisions. Now the
earth on which we live may be seen as a huge storehouse of mercy or a
Divine vessel which traverses a vast orbit each year, housing innumerable
species which require different foods: as it passes through the seasons on its
journey, it fills spring, which is like a huge wagon, with a great variety of
provisions and brings them to all the living creatures whose sustenance
was exhausted during the winter. This storage depot, which is the earth,
surely indicates, through the science of economics which you are studying,
the existence of the Owner, Manager, and Organizer of this depot that is
the earth and makes Him loved.

Or imagine, for example, an army that consists of numerous tribes and
nations, each one requiring unique provisions, weapons, uniforms, drills,
and demobilization. If its miracle-working commander meets all their
needs on his own, without forgetting or confusing any of them, surely the
army and its camp will serve as an indication of this commander's existence
and make him appreciated. Similarly, every spring a single Commander-in-
Chief provides a newly recruited army of countless animal and plant species
with uniforms, rations, weapons, training, and demobilizations in a perfect
and regular fashion. He forgets nothing and does not become confused. This
Divine army of spring indicates, through military science, the existence of

that most attentive and sensible Ruler of the earth, its Lord, Administrator and All-Holy Commander, and makes Him loved, praised, glorified, and acclaimed.

Or imagine a magnificent city illuminated by millions of mobile electric lamps with an inexhaustible fuel and power source. Such a set-up would evidently point to the talent of a wonder-working artisan and extraordinarily skilful electrician who makes the lamps, establishes the power source, and provides the fuel. And it would cause others to admire and congratulate this electrician.

Now many of the lamps—the planets and the stars—which adorn the roof of the palace that is the world, in the city that is the universe, are a thousand times larger than the earth and move with an amazing speed. Yet despite their rapidity, they move most precisely without colliding with one another; they are not extinguished, nor do they run out of fuel. The science of astronomy, which you study, tells us that our sun, which is like a lamp or a stove in the guesthouse of the All-Merciful, is hundreds of thousands of times larger than the earth and several billion years old. To keep burning each day, it needs as much oil as there are seas on the earth, as much coal as there are mountains, or as many logs and pieces of wood as exist on ten earths.

It is clear, then, that such lamps indicate with their fingers of light the existence of an infinite Power and Sovereignty Which, in turn, illuminates the sun and other similar stars without oil, wood, or coal, allowing them to travel at great speed without colliding with one another or being extinguished. Thus, the science of electricity and the testimony of those radiant stars indubitably indicate the existence of the Sovereign, Illuminator, Director, and Creator of the greatest light exhibition of the universe, and make Him loved, glorified, and adored.

Now imagine a marvelous book. Within each line of that book, another, smaller book has been written, and within each word, a whole chapter—a *sura*—has been inscribed with a fine pen. This book is most meaningful and expressive, and all of its topics corroborate each other. Such a book shows as clearly as daylight that it must be the product of a particular artist, who is possessed of extraordinary perfections, arts, and skills. It makes us appreciate the author and call down God's blessings upon him.

What is true of the book in the example is true of the vast book that is the universe. For example, we see with our own eyes a pen inscribing on the page of the earth hundreds of thousands of plants and animal species, each one of which is like an entire volume in itself. And they are inscribed all together, one within the other, without error or confusion; they are inscribed with such perfection and precision that an ode is compressed in a single word, like a tree, and an entire book is to be found within a point that is a seed. However much vaster and more perfect and meaningful than the book in the example mentioned above is this infinitely meaningful compendium that is the universe, this embodied 'macro-Qur'an,' in every word of which there are numerous instances of wisdom, to that degree—through the natural sciences that you study, it makes known the Inscriber and Author of this book of the universe with His infinite Perfections. Proclaiming "God is the All-Great," it makes Him known; declaring His sacredness with "All-Glorified is God," it describes Him; and praising Him with such expressions as "All praise and gratitude are for God," it makes Him loved.

Indeed, through its extensive measure, its particular mirror, its far-reaching view, and its searching and instructive perspectives, each of the hundreds of sciences makes the All-Majestic Creator of the universe known with His Names, Attributes and Perfections.

It is in order to elucidate the evidence explained above, which constitute a most convincing and magnificent proof of Divine Unity, that the miraculous Qur'an frequently describes our Creator in terms such as "the Lord of the heavens and the earth" and "the Creator of the heavens and the earth".

I told the students all of this and they accepted and affirmed it, saying: "Endless thanks be to God, for we have received a true and sacred lesson. May God be pleased with you."

I added as follows:

> A human being is a living machine subject to many sorrows and capable of knowing many pleasures. Although totally impotent, we have infinite physical and spiritual enemies. Although completely destitute, we have infinite internal and external needs, and we suffer continuously from the blows of gradual decay and separation. But if, through belief and worship, we can establish a connection with the All-Majestic Sovereign, we will find a source of support against all of our enemies and a source of help for all of our needs. Everyone takes pride in the honor and rank of those in high places with whom they enjoy a connection. Given this fact, if one establishes a connection through belief with the infinitely Powerful and Compassionate Sov-

ereign; if one enters His service through worship and, by so doing, changes the sentence of execution at the appointed hour of death into a most welcome acquittal and discharge, imagine the pride, joy, and contentment they will feel.

To the calamity-stricken prisoners I repeat what I said to the schoolboys: those who recognize and obey Him are prosperous, even if they are in prison, while those who forget Him are like wretched prisoners even if they live in palaces.

Once a wronged but fortunate man—fortunate on account of his belief and ensuing martyrdom—said to the wretched wrongdoers who were executing him: "I am not being executed; rather, I have been discharged from my duties and am going forward to eternal happiness. However, I can now see that you are condemned to eternal punishment; this suffices as my revenge upon you." And saying "There is no deity but God," he died a happy man.

All-Glorified are You! We have no knowledge save what You have taught us. Surely you are the All-Knowing, the All-Wise.

The Seventh Matter

This is the fruit of one Friday in Denizli Prison.

In the Name of God, the All-Merciful, the All-Compassionate.

The matter of the Hour (of Doom) is (in relation with the Divine Power) but the twinkling of an eye, or even quicker. Surely God has full power over everything (16:77).

Your creation and your resurrection are but as (the creation and resurrection) of a single soul. (31:28)

Look, then, at the imprints of God's Mercy—how He revives the dead earth after its death: certainly then it is He Who will revive the dead (in a similar way). He has full power over everything (30:50).

Those inmates of Denizli Prison who were able to have contact with me also read the lesson in The Sixth Matter that I had given to the high school students in Kastamonu—those who had asked me: "Tell us about our Creator." Having acquired a firm belief, they felt a longing for the Hereafter, and said to me: "Teach us about the Hereafter too, so that our evil-commanding souls and the devils of the age do not cause us to deviate from the Straight Path and end up in prison again." And so the request of the *Risale-i Nur* students in the Denizli Prison and the readers of The Sixth Matter has made it necessary to explain in brief the pillar of belief that is the Hereafter. Here I will offer a short summary of the relevant discussions on the Hereafter in the *Risale-i Nur*:

In The Sixth Matter we asked the heavens and the earth about our Creator, and they revealed Him to us as clearly as the sun through the tongue of the sciences. Having come to know our Lord, we will first ask Him about the Hereafter; we will then ask our Prophet, then the Qur'an, then the other Prophets and Scriptures, then the angels and finally the universe itself.

Our first step is to ask God Himself about the Hereafter. He replies through all the Messengers He sent, through the decrees He revealed in the form of Books or Scriptures, and through all of His Names and Attributes: "The Hereafter exists, and I am dispatching you there." The Tenth Word has explained the Hereafter with twelve decisive arguments based on a number of Divine Names. Contenting ourselves with these explanations, we will give only brief indications of them here.

There is no sovereignty that does not reward those who obey it or punish those who rebel against it. Therefore an eternal Sovereignty, Which is at the degree of absolute Lordship, will certainly reward those who adhere to It through belief and submit to Its decrees; similarly It will punish those who deny It through unbelief and rebellion. Reward and punishment will be meted out in a manner befitting God's Mercy and Grace, and His Dignity and Majesty respectively. Thus do the Names the Lord of all worlds, the Sovereign, the Supreme Ruler and the All-Requiting One reply to our question.

What is more, we see a universal Mercy and an all-embracing Compassion and Munificence on the earth as clearly as we see daylight. Every spring, for example, Mercy dresses all the fruit-bearing trees and plants like the *houris* of Paradise and fills their hands with every kind of fruit. And it is as if these trees hold out their fruits to us, saying: "Please help yourselves and eat!" Mercy, Compassion, and Munificence also offer us healing sweet honey to eat from the poisonous bee and dress us in the softest silk by means of a tiny insect without hands. They also deposit for us in a handful of minute seeds numerous kilos of food, making those tiny stores into reserve supplies. Surely such Mercy and Compassion would not annihilate for all eternity those lovable, grateful, worshipping believers whom they nurture so tenderly? Rather, they discharge them from their worldly duties in order to bestow on them still more radiant gifts of Mercy and Compassion. Thus do the Names the All-Compassionate and the All-Munificent answer our question, affirming that Paradise will truly come.

Also, we see clearly that a hand of Wisdom is at work in all creatures on the earth with such skill and that events take place according to standards of Justice with such precision that the human mind cannot conceive of any wisdom or justice superior to them. For example, that eternal Wisdom inscribes in the human memory, a human faculty from among hundreds of faculties and no bigger than the tiniest seed, the entire life-story of a human being, together with the numerous events that fill it, making it in effect a small library. In order to remind human beings continuously of their deeds—deeds which are recorded and will be published openly so that they can be judged in the Place of Resurrection—that Wisdom inserts this small library into the mind, as a note of the record of our deeds. As for perpetual Justice, It endows all creatures with organs and members in an exceedingly balanced and harmonious manner, from the microbe to the rhinoceros, from the fly to the eagle, from the tiniest flowering plant to the countless millions of plants and flowers that make up spring, and makes each one into a wonderful work of art. This It does according to a precise balance and order, with due proportion and exquisite beauty and with no waste at all. It also gives all living creatures their rights of life in perfect measures and makes good things produce good results and evil things evil results. And since the time of Adam, upon him be peace, this Justice has made Itself felt forcefully through the blows It has dealt to rebellious and tyrannical peoples. Certainly, just as the sun is linked inextricably with daylight, eternal Wisdom and everlasting Justice are linked inextricably with the Hereafter and necessitate its existence. It is inconceivable that they would allow the most tyrannical and the most oppressed to be equal in death, without true justice being dispensed; they would never tolerate such iniquity, unfairness, or such a lack of wisdom. Thus do the Names the All-Wise, the All-Judging, the All-Equitable and the All-Just give a conclusive answer to our question.

Also, whenever living creatures seek their natural needs, which are beyond their power, through the language of their innate capacities and essential neediness, which is itself a kind of supplication, these needs are provided by a most compassionate Hand from the Unseen. Moreover, approximately seventy percent of voluntary verbal supplications offered by human beings, and especially by the Prophets and other most distinguished believers, are accepted in a manner that lies outside the normal course of events. It can thus be understood clearly that behind the veil of the Unseen there is One Who is All-Hearing and All-Answering, Who listens to the sighs of every suffering creature and the prayers of every needy soul. He sees the most insignificant need of the smallest living being and hears its most secret sigh. Having compassion on them, He duly answers them and satisfies them.

There is one from among humankind, the most important of God's creations, who includes in his prayers the universal invocation of all humanity concerning the eternal life, which is connected with all the Divine Names and Attributes and, indeed, the entire universe. This being has the support of all the other Prophets, and the suns, stars and leaders of humankind, who exclaim, "Amin! Amin!" so that his prayer may be accepted. Also, every devout person in his Community of believers invokes God's peace and blessings on him several times a day, and adds an "Amin!" to his prayer. And all the other creatures also take part in his prayer, saying, "O Lord, give him what he asks for; we too ask for what he asks for!" While there are countless reasons why the Resurrection must of necessity come about, it is no exaggeration to say that a single prayer of Prophet Muhammad, upon him be peace and blessings, everlasting life and happiness in the Hereafter is sufficient for the existence of Paradise and the creation of the world to come, which is as easy for Divine Power as the creation of spring. Thus, do the Names the All-Answering, the All-Hearing, and the All-Compassionate provide an answer to our question.

Also, it is as clear as the daylight which indicates the existence of the sun that behind the veil of the visible world is an unseen One Who shows Himself in the control and management of the earth, in the deaths and revivals which take place as the seasons come and go. He administers the mighty earth with the ease and orderliness of a garden or even a tree; He tends to the splendid spring as though it were a single flower, and with the same facility, decoration, and sense of proportion; He displays the countless species of plants and animals as though they were hundreds of thousands of books exhibiting hundreds of thousands of examples of the Resurrection. The Pen of Power Which inscribes these things one within the other, all intermingled yet without the least disorder, confusion, fault, flaw, or error, and with perfect order and purposefulness—this vast, comprehensive Power operates with limitless mercy and infinite wisdom. The One Who possesses that Power has subjugated, decorated, and furnished the vast universe for human beings as though it were a house, and has appointed human beings as ruler of the earth, bestowing on them the "Supreme Trust"[1]—a trust which the mountains, sky and earth would not take on, and from which they shrank in fear. He has favored human beings with the rank of commander over other living beings to a certain degree, and honored them by making them the recipient of the Divine address and conversation, thus conferring on them a supreme status. Moreover, in all the revealed Decrees He has promised humanity eternal happiness and permanence in the Hereafter. From all this it follows that for humankind, whom He has so ennobled and honored, He will certainly open up that realm of happiness, which is as easy for His Power as the creation of spring, thus bringing about the Resurrection and the Last Judgment. So, the Names the All-Reviving, the All-Dealing One of death, the All-Living, the Self-Subsisting, the All-Powerful, and All-Knowing answer our question.

If one considers the Power Which every spring brings back to life the roots of all the trees and plants that have died in winter and creates hundreds of thousands of plants and animals as examples of the Resurrection, and if one visualizes the thousand-year period of each of the communities of Prophets Moses, upon him be peace, and Muhammad, upon him be peace and blessings, it can be seen that the two thousand springs display innumerable examples and proofs of the Resurrection to come. One would have to be completely blind and senseless to imagine that that bodily Resurrection is difficult for such a Power.

Furthermore, a hundred and twenty-four thousand Prophets, the most renowned of all humankind, attested unanimously to the truth of eternal happiness and permanence in the Hereafter; not only did they rely

---

[1] The Supreme Trust is human selfhood or being human or human nature as the focus of the manifestations of God's Names that are manifested throughout the universe. (Tr.)

on God Almighty's countless promises in this regard, but they proved it themselves through their own miracles. Also, innumerable saints have testified to the same truth through their illuminations and spiritual unveilings. Since this is so, surely this truth is as clear as the sun, and those who doubt it must be mad.

The opinions and judgments of one or two scholars or scientists concerning their particular field of expertise are sufficient to refute the opposing ideas of a thousand people who lack such expertise, even though they may be masters in their own fields. Similarly, two people who testify to the existence of something are able to defeat a thousand who deny its existence simply by producing an example of that thing. For instance, if two trustworthy people claim that they have seen the crescent moon which heralds, say, the lunar month of Ramadan, on a day when the sighting of the new moon is unlikely, although not impossible, their claim is accepted as veracious even if everyone else denies it. Also, if two people claim that there is a garden on the earth where coconuts resembling cans of milk are grown, their claim will be verified if they bring forth a single coconut or, alternatively, indicate the place where they can be found. Those who deny this claim, however, can prove their point only by searching all four corners of the earth in order to demonstrate that no such coconuts exist anywhere. Thus one who claims that Paradise exists can prove his claim simply by demonstrating a trace, a shadow, or a manifestation of it. Those who deny it, however, can prove their point only by scouring the whole universe and traveling throughout all time, from pre-eternity to post-eternity, in order to demonstrate its non-existence. It is because of this that scholars have agreed on the rule "Provided that they are not inherently inconceivable, denials or negations which are not concerned with a specific matter but which pertain to the whole universe, such as the truths of belief, cannot be proven," and accepted it as a fundamental principle.

Because of this undeniable truth, the opposing opinions of thousands of philosophers should not cast even the slightest doubt or suspicion on even one truthful and trustworthy individual who brings reports concerning matters of belief. You may understand, then, what lunacy it is to fall into doubt concerning the pillars of belief or faith—pillars upon which countless thousands of Prophets, saints, and scholars have agreed—on account of the denial of a handful of philosophers who rely solely on their physical senses and who have grown distant from all spiritual matters.

Also, it is as clear as daylight itself that working in ourselves and all around us there is a comprehensive Mercy, an all-embracing Wisdom, and constant Grace and Favoring. We also observe the traces and manifestations of an awesome sovereignty of Lordship, a precise and elevated Justice and the dignified activity of Majesty. Indeed, Wisdom, Which affixes to a tree as many instances of wisdom as there are fruits and flowers on that tree; Mercy, Which bestows favors and bounties and on every human being to the number of their members, senses, and faculties; and the dignified, gracious Justice, Which protects the rights of the downtrodden and punishes wrongdoers such as the rebellious people of Noah, Hud, Salih, and the Pharaoh, and the verse:

> And among His signs is that the heaven and the earth stand firm (subsisting) by His Command. In the end, when He calls you forth from the earth (with a single, particular summons), then (at once) you will come forth (30:25),

all state the following with consummate succinctness:

Obedient and well-disciplined soldiers in their barracks spring to their feet and rush to their duties as soon as their commander summons them and the bugle has been sounded. Similarly, when the dead of the heavens and the earth, which are like two well-ordered barracks for the obedient soldiers of the Eternal Sovereign, are summoned by the Trumpet of the Archangel Israfil, upon him be peace, they will immediately don the "uniforms" of their bodies and rise up. This is similar and testified to by the fact that those lying dead in the barracks of the earth in winter act in similar fashion every spring with the trumpet-blast of the Angel of Thunder. It is therefore impossible that the sovereignty of Lordship, which can be understood from this mighty event and which is explained in The Tenth Word convincingly, would allow the infinite grace and beauty of Mercy to change into infinitely ugly cruelty by not bringing into existence the abode of the Hereafter, the realm of the Resurrection, or the Supreme Gathering, all of which are most definitely required and necessitated by that Mercy, Wisdom, Favoring, and Justice. It is utterly impossible for that limitless perfection of Wisdom to be turned into infinitely worthless futility and wastefulness, for that sweet Favoring to change into utterly bitter treachery, for that precisely balanced and equitable Justice to be transformed into the most severe tyranny, for that infinitely majestic and powerful eternal Sovereignty to decline and lose all Its magnificence, and for the perfections of Lordship to be tainted with impotence or defect. Such a thing would be completely unreasonable and inconceivable; it is false, precluded, and completely beyond the bounds of possibility.

Anyone with consciousness would surely understand how cruel it would be if, having been nurtured so tenderly and endowed with faculties such as the intellect and heart, which long for eternal happiness and ever-lasting life, humanity were to be annihilated completely and consigned to nothingness. How contrary to wisdom it would be if the myriad purposeful faculties and endless capacities of the human mind were to be wasted completely through eternal annihilation; how utterly opposed to the magnificence and perfection of Divine Sovereignty and Lordship would it be if God were to be revealed—God forbid!—as impotent and ignorant due to His failure to carry out His countless promises. Thus do the Names the All-Merciful, the All-Wise, the All-Just, the All-Munificent, and the All-Sovereign answer with the above truths the question we asked our Creator concerning the Hereafter, proving it beyond a shadow of a doubt.

We also see clearly that a vast, all-encompassing Act of Preservation prevails over creation. It records the numerous forms of all things, beings, and events, the duties they perform throughout their lives, and their deeds, which are like the glorification of God in response to the Divine Names manifested in them, on the tablets that belong to the World of representations or "ideal" forms, in their seeds and in their memories, which are tiny samples of the Supreme Preserved Tablet, as well as in the capacious libraries that have been placed in the mind, and in other material and supra-material mirrors, where they are reflected. It inscribes, records and preserves them, and then, when the time comes It displays before us all these immaterial inscriptions in physical form: every spring, a mighty flower of Divine Power, proclaims to the universe an amazing truth of the Resurrection which is expressed in the verse: *And when the scrolls (of the deeds of every person) are laid open* (81:10), in billions of languages and with the force of millions of examples, proofs, and samples. In this way It offers the most powerful proof that created beings, humans in particular, are not destined for eternal annihilation and non-existence. Rather, they have been created in order to advance continuously toward and through eternity, to gain permanence through perpetual purification and refinement, and to embrace the everlasting duties necessitated by their endless innate capacities.

Every year we observe that the innumerable plants which die in the doomsday of fall, and all of the trees, roots, seeds, and grains which are resurrected in the spring, recite the verse: *And when the scrolls (of the deeds of every person) are laid open.* By carrying out the same duties as it performed in previous years, each interprets one meaning or aspect of this verse in its own language. In this way, they all testify to that vast Act of Preservation. By displaying in everything the four tremendous truths of the verse, *He is the First, the Last, the All-Outward and the All-Inward* (57:3), they inform us of this Preservation and the Resurrection with the ease and certainty of spring.

These four Names manifest themselves and act on all things, be they particular or universal. For example, receiving or being favored with the manifestation of the Name The First, a seed, which is a tiny case containing the precise program of the tree and the faultless systems of its creation and growth, proves indubitably the vastness of Divine Preservation.

Similarly, every fruit, which manifests the Name The Last, is a coffer that contains in its seeds the list of the contents of all the duties the tree has performed, together with the principles of the life of another tree identical to it. So it too testifies completely to the act of Divine Preservation.

The physical form of the tree, on which the Name The All-Outward manifests Itself, is a finely proportioned, skillfully decorated garment, resembling the multi-colored, gilt-embroidered robes of the *houris* of Paradise. As such it visibly demonstrates the tremendous Power, the perfect Wisdom, and the awesome grace and beauty of Mercy which are manifested in the Act of Divine Preservation.

The inner mechanism of the tree, which is favored with the manifestation of the Name The All-Inward, is like a an orderly, miraculous factory, a workshop where innumerable chemical processes take place and which possesses a precisely measured cauldron of food, which leaves none of its branches, fruits, or leaves without nourishment. So flawless is this mechanism that it proves beyond all doubt the perfection of the Power and Justice and the grace and beauty of Mercy and Wisdom that are manifested in the Act of Divine Preservation.

Similarly, with regard to the annual seasons, the earth resembles a tree. Through the manifestation of the Name The First, all the seeds and grains entrusted to Divine Preservation in the season of fall are like tiny collections of the Divine Commands and lists of principles that issue from Divine Determination or Destiny concerning the formation of the tree of the earth which will put forth billions of branches and twigs, flowers and fruits when it is eventually dressed in the garments of spring. These seeds and grains are also lists and tiny records of the tasks and deeds that the tree has performed in the previous summer. This quite clearly demonstrates that they work through the infinite Power, Justice, Wisdom and Mercy of an All-Preserver of Majesty and Munificence.

Then in the season of fall, the tree of the earth deposits in tiny cases all the duties it has performed, all the glorifications it has made in response to the manifestations of the Divine Names, and all the records of its deeds that will be published in the following resurrection of spring: these it submits to the hand of the Wisdom of the All-Preserving One of Majesty, reciting before the whole universe *He is the Last* in countless tongues.

By opening hundreds of thousands of different kinds of blossoms, which demonstrate hundreds of thousands of examples and signs of the Resurrection, and by spreading out innumerable banquet tables of Mercy, Providence, Compassion, and Munificence for living beings, the outer form of the tree offers praise and commendation, reciting *He is the All-Outward* in languages to the number of its fruits, flowers, and foods. And in so doing it demonstrates beyond all doubt the truth of: *When the scrolls (of the deeds of every person) are laid open* (81:10).

As for the inner face of this splendid tree, it is, as mentioned earlier, a kind of kitchen or workshop, operating numerous well-arranged machines and finely balanced factories with perfect order and in a regular fashion; these enable it to produce thousands of kilos of food out of one ounce to offer to the hungry. It works with such precision and balance that it leaves no room for chance. Like certain angels who glorify God with a thousand tongues, the inner face of the tree that is this earth exclaims *He is the All-Inward* in a hundred thousand ways.

In addition to resembling a tree with regard to its annual cycle, which makes the Divine Preservation manifested through those four Names a key to the door of the Resurrection, the earth is also a well-organized tree with regard to its entire worldly life; the fruits of this tree are sent to the market of the Hereafter. It is a place for the manifestation of these four Names which is so vast; it is a road that leads to the Hereafter which is so broad that our minds are incapable of comprehending them. All we can say is this:

The hands of a weekly clock which count the seconds, minutes, hours, and days resemble one another and indicate the nature and function of one another. Therefore, one who sees the movement of the second hand cannot help but admit the movement of the other hands and the other pieces of the clock's mechanism. Similarly, the days which count the seconds of this world, which is a vast clock of the All-Majestic Creator of the heavens and earth, the years which count its minutes, the centuries, which show its hours, and the eras, which make known its days—all of these resemble one another and indicate the nature and functions of one another. Finally, this clock of the earth, which counts the days, years, centuries and eras of the world, informs us with the certainty of night being followed by dawn and winter by spring that the dark winter of this transient world will be followed by the glorious spring of the everlasting realm. And so in this way, the Names the All-Preserving, The First, The Last, The All-Outward, and The All-Inward give truthful answers to the question we put to our Creator concerning the Resurrection.

Also, we see and understand that humanity is:

- the final and most comprehensive fruit of the tree of the universe and, with respect to the Truth of Muhammad, upon him be peace and blessings, its original seed;

- the supreme sign of the cosmic Qur'an and its Verse of Divine Supreme Seat[2], which bears the manifestation of the Greatest Name of God;

- the most honored guest in the palace of the universe and the most active official empowered with stewardship over the other inhabitants of the palace;

---

[2] The Qur'an's Verse of Divine Supreme Seat, to which Said Nursi likens humanity with respect to humanity's place in the universe compared with the place of this verse in the Qur'an, is as follows:

> God, there is no deity but He; the All-Living, the Self-Subsisting (by Whom all subsist). Slumber does not seize Him, nor sleep. His is all that is in the heavens and all that is on the earth. Who is there that will intercede with Him save by His leave? He knows what lies before them and what lies after them (what lies in their future and in their past, what is known to them and what is hidden from them); and they do not comprehend anything of His Knowledge save what He wills. His Seat (of dominion) embraces the heavens and the earth, and the preserving of them does not weary Him; He is the All-Exalted, the Supreme. (2:255)

- the official responsible for monitoring income and expenditure and for planting and cultivating the gardens in the quarter of the earth in the city of the universe;

- its most vocal and responsible minister, equipped with hundreds of sciences and thousands of arts and skills;

- a kind of inspector, a vicegerent appointed by the Sovereign of all eternity to oversee, under His close scrutiny, the country of the earth in the realm of the universe;

- the race which has been given the authority to control and deploy it, and whose actions, be they particular or universal, are all recorded;

- the division of living creatures which has agreed to bear the Supreme Trust, from which the heavens, the earth, and the mountains all shrank in fear;

- the kind of being in front of whom lie two roads, one of which leads to utter wretchedness, while the other to utter contentment;

- a universal servant of God charged with most extensive worship;

- the kind of being favored with the manifestation of the Greatest Name of the Sovereign of the universe;

- a comprehensive mirror of all God's Names;

- a special intimate and addressee of God, with the best understanding of His Divine addresses and speech;

- the neediest of all living beings in the universe: a wretched creature who, despite their endless poverty and impotence, has innumerable desires and goals and yet also countless adversaries and things which threaten to harm them;

- the kind of being who is most blessed in potential, yet the most prone to suffering with respect to the pleasures of life, which are made poison by the existence of ghastly pains;

- a most wonderful miracle of the Power of the Eternally Besought One;

- a most amazing product of creation who is both the most in need of everlasting life and the most worthy of receiving it;

- the kind of being who seeks eternal felicity with endless prayers—indeed, were they to be given all of the pleasures of this world, they would not satisfy their desire for everlasting life in the least;

- the kind of being who loves to the degree of adoration the One Who bestows bounties on them and makes Him loved and is loved by Him;
- the kind of being whose faculties, which are as vast as the universe itself, show by their very nature that they have been created to acquire eternity.

In short, humanity is bound to God Almighty's Name the Ultimate Truth through the above universal realities, and their actions are recorded continuously by the All-Preserving, Who sees the most particular need of the tiniest living being, hears its pleading, and responds to it. The deeds of humanity, which are related to the entire universe, have been written down by the noble scribes of that All-Preserving One, and it is humanity who, more than any other creature, receives Its attention. Given this, surely this noblest of beings will be granted a resurrection and a judgment. And at this judgment, in accordance with the Name the Ultimate Truth, humankind will receive reward for their duties or punishment for their crimes; they will be called to account for all their actions, universal or particular, which have been recorded by the Name the All-Preserving. The doors of the banquet halls of everlasting happiness in the eternal realm will be opened, as will the gates of the prison of eternal misery. The "officer" who has stewardship over numerous species of beings in this world, who intervenes in them and sometimes casts them into confusion, will not escape interrogation concerning their actions once they are in the soil; nor will they be allowed to lie down in hiding without ever being roused.

To hear the buzz of the fly and to answer it by giving it its rights of life, but to ignore the invocations for eternity which arise from innumerable human rights and are made through the language of the above truths—invocations which reverberate through the heavens and earth like thunder—would be pure injustice and a transgression of these rights. Similarly, to take into careful account the tiniest of creatures—the wing of a fly, for example—but then to disregard and waste the abilities, hopes, and desires of humankind, which extend to eternity, together with the countless bonds and truths in the universe which nurture these abilities and desires—this would constitute a tyranny and injustice so ugly and despicable that all beings which testify to the Names such as the Ultimate Truth, the All-Preserving, the All-Wise, the All-Gracious and the All-Compassionate would reject it, declaring it utterly impossible. Thus do these Names reply to the question which we asked our Creator about the Resurrection. They say: "Just as we are true and have substantial realities, and the beings that testify to us are also true, so too is the Resurrection true and certain."

I was going to write more, but since the above is enough to show that the truth of the Resurrection is as clear as daylight, I have curtailed the discussion here.

Thus, as also can be understood from the truths explained above, just as through their manifestations and reflections in beings, each of God Almighty's hundred, indeed thousand, Names that relate to and show themselves in the universe prove self-evidently the existence of the One Whom they signify, so too do they demonstrate the Resurrection and the Hereafter, and definitively prove them.

Just as our Lord and Creator gives us sacred, decisive answers to the question we asked Him with regard to the Resurrection through all of His revealed Books and Scriptures and most of His Names, He also causes His angels to answer the same question in their own language:

"There have been hundreds of incidents from the time of Adam that testify indubitably to your meeting both with us and with other spirit beings. There are also other innumerable signs and proofs of both our existence and the existence of those other spirit beings, and of our servanthood and obedience to God. In agreement with each other, we have told your leaders whenever we have met with them that we travel through the halls of the Hereafter and around some of its mansions. We have no doubt that these fine, everlasting halls and well-furnished, decorated palaces and dwellings beyond them have been made ready for important guests who are to be accommodated there. We give you irrefragable news of this." Such is the reply of the angels to our question.

Also, our Creator appointed Prophet Muhammad, upon him be peace and blessings, as the greatest teacher, the best master and the truest guide, one who neither goes nor leads astray, and sent him as His last Messenger. Thus, in order that we may advance in our knowledge of God and our belief in Him, progressing from certainty based on knowledge through certainty arising from vision and on to certainty arising from experience, we should first of all ask this master the same question that we put to our Creator. For, just as that person proved through his numerous miracles that the Qur'an is the true Word of God, the Qur'an, through its forty aspects of miraculousness also proves that he was God's true and rightful Messenger. As the tongue of the visible world, the Prophet declared the truth of the Resurrection throughout his life and was confirmed by all the Prophets and saints; the Qur'an, as the tongue of the Unseen World, also declared the truth of the Last Day and the Hereafter, and was confirmed in its declaration by all other Divinely-revealed Books and Scriptures. Given this, the existence of the Resurrection is proven beyond all reasonable doubt.

Such an awesome matter as the Resurrection, the understanding of which transcends normal reasoning, may be perceived best through the instruction of these two wonderful masters—Prophet Muhammad and the Qur'an—and thereby understood.

The reason the early Prophets did not explain the Resurrection in as detailed a manner as the Qur'an was that theirs were the eras of relative primitivism, or the "childhood" of humanity. There is little point in giving detailed and intricate explanations to those who are undergoing elementary education.

To sum up: since most of the Divine Names require the Resurrection, all the proofs which demonstrate the existence of these Names also demonstrate to some extent the existence and necessity of the Resurrection.

And since the angels inform us that they have seen the spheres and mansions of the eternal realm of the Hereafter, the proofs which establish the existence and worshipfulness of the angels, spirits, and spirit beings also help to establish the truth of the existence of the Hereafter.

And since after Divine Unity, the matter emphasized with the greatest insistence by Prophet Muhammad, upon him be peace and blessings, was the Hereafter, it follows that all of the proofs and miracles which testify to His Prophethood also testify indirectly to the existence of the Hereafter.

And since a quarter of the Qur'an concerns the Resurrection and the Hereafter, with approximately a thousand of its verses offering proofs of the life to come, all of the evidence and arguments which establish the veracity of the Qur'an also indirectly establish the existence of the Hereafter.

Now see how firm and certain this pillar of belief really is!

The Eighth Matter

In The Seventh Matter, we were planning to question numerous different beings with regard to the Resurrection. However, since the replies given by our Creator's Names were so powerful and convincing, we contented ourselves with them, seeing no real need to question anyone or anything else. Now, in this Eighth Matter we were planning to elucidate a hundredth of the benefits that belief in the Hereafter has for humanity and their felicity in both this world and the next. However, since the miraculous Qur'an leaves no need for further explanation concerning the benefits of belief in securing happiness in the Hereafter, and since the benefits of belief for humanity in this world have been discussed in detail in the *Risale-i Nur*, readers may refer to the Qur'an and the relevant sections of the *Risale-i Nur*. Here, we will summarize only three or four out of the hundreds of results of belief in the Hereafter concerning human individual and social life.

THE FIRST: Just as a person has relations with their home, they also have relations with the world beyond it. Similarly, just as they have relations with their relatives, they also have relations with the rest of humankind. And just as they desire a kind of temporary permanence in this world, they also yearn passionately for an enduring permanence in the realm of eternity. In the same way that a person strives to meet the need of their stomach for food, they are, by nature, compelled to strive to provide sustenance to the metaphorical stomachs of their mind, heart, spirit and humanity. Their desires and demands are such that nothing but eternity and everlasting felicity can satisfy them. As mentioned in The Tenth Word, when I was young I asked myself: "Do you want to live for a million years as ruler of the world but then be dispatched into eternal non-existence? Or would you prefer to have an ordinary and at times difficult existence, but live forever?" I saw that my imagination always opted for the latter, saying: "I want to live forever, even though it be in Hell!"

Thus, since the pleasures of this world do not satisfy the imaginative faculty, which is a servant of the human essence, it follows that the comprehensive essence of humanity is, by its very nature, attached to eternity. For despite being preoccupied with boundless hopes and desires, humanity has only an insignificant faculty of will as their capital, stricken as they are with absolute poverty. Belief in the Hereafter, then, is such a powerful and sufficient treasury, such a means of happiness and pleasure, such a refuge and source of assistance and benefit, and such a means of consolation in the face of the endless sorrows of this world that if the life of this world had to be sacrificed in order to gain it, it would still be a cheap price to pay.

ITS SECOND FRUIT AND BENEFIT PERTAINING TO HUMAN PERSONAL LIFE: This was explained in The Third Matter, and can be found in *Gençlik Rehberi* as a footnote.

The most constant and over-riding anxiety of humanity is that we will one day enter the grave, as our friends and relations have before us. The wretched human being, who is ready to sacrifice their very soul for a single friend, imagines that the countless millions of human beings who have entered the grave before them have been condemned to eternal annihilation, and this supposition makes them suffer the torments of Hell. Just at this point, belief in the Hereafter appears, opens our eyes and raises the veil. It tells us: "Look!" And looking with belief, we can see that our companions have been saved from eternal annihilation and are awaiting us happily in a light-filled world; realizing this, we receive a spiritual pleasure that is a reflection of the pleasures of Paradise. Contenting ourselves with the explanations of this second fruit in the *Risale-i Nur*, we will curtail the discussion here.

A THIRD BENEFIT: Human beings are superior to other living beings on account of their elevated characteristics, their comprehensive abilities, their universal ability to worship and the extensive spheres of existence which make up their life. However, the virtues which characterize the human being, such as love, zeal, brother and sister-hood and humanity, are acquired in accordance with the extent of this fleeting present time, which is constricted between the past and the future, both of which are dark and non-existent.

For example, a person loves and serves their father, brother or sister, their spouse, nation or country, none of whom they knew before; they will see none of these people once they have departed from this world. Since the fleeting nature of life means that it is highly unlikely that a person would be able to achieve complete loyalty or sincerity in any one relationship, their virtues and excellences are proportionately diminished. Then, just at the point where they fall to a level lower than that of the animals and become more wretched than they already are because they have intellect and reason, belief in the Hereafter comes to this person's assistance. It expands the present, which is as narrow as the grave, to the extent that it encompasses the past and future and manifests a sphere of existence as broad as the world, stretching from pre-eternity to post-eternity. Realizing that relations with one's spouse, parents and siblings will continue for eternity in Paradise, they love, respect, help and have mercy on them while in this world.

With this new realization, a person will not exploit such important duties based on the relationships that encompass this broad sphere of life and existence for the sake of the worthless affairs of this world and its petty interests. Being able to achieve earnest loyalty and sincerity, a person's good qualities and attainments begin to develop accordingly, and their humanity becomes exalted. While they cannot match even a sparrow in enjoyment of this life, they can become the noblest and happiest of guests in the universe, superior to all animals, as well as being the best loved and most appreciated servant of the universe's Owner. Since this matter has also been explained in the *Risale-i Nur*, we content ourselves here with this much.

A FOURTH BENEFIT OF BELIEF IN THE HEREAFTER, WHICH RELATES TO HUMAN SOCIAL LIFE: What follows is a summary of this benefit, expounded in the Ninth Ray of the *Risale-i Nur*:

Children, who make up a third of the human race, can live a truly human life and maintain truly human capacities only if they have sincere belief in the Hereafter. Without belief in the Hereafter, they are forced to compensate for the anxiety they feel over their eventual oblivion by filling their worldly life with trivia and meaningless distractions. For the constant deaths around them of children like themselves have such an effect on their sensitive minds and weak hearts, which cherish far-reaching desires, and vulnerable spirits, that it makes life torture for them and their reason a tool of suffering. If, however, they are brought to belief in the Hereafter, the anxieties they once felt at the deaths of their playmates, which they try to escape by immersing themselves in meaningless distractions, will give way to joy and exhilaration as they realize the truth. For supported by belief in the Hereafter they will say: "My sibling or playmate has died and become a bird in Paradise. He (or she) is now flying around and enjoying himself much more than we are. And although my mother has died, she has gone to the realm of Divine mercy. One day I will see her in Paradise, where she will take me into her arms once again." Such a realization will enable these children to live in a state which befits them as human beings.

It is only through believing in the Hereafter that the aged, who constitute another third of humankind, are able to find consolation in the face of what they see as the inevitable extinction of their lives and the fact that they too will soon be consigned to the bowels of the earth and their precious and lovable worlds have come to an end. Without belief in the Hereafter, those compassionate, respected fathers and those tender, self-sacrificing mothers would become so distraught and distressed in heart and spirit that their world would seem to be a prison of despair for them and life a heavy burden of torment. But belief in the Hereafter addresses them, saying: "Do not worry! A radiant, everlasting life awaits you and there you will enjoy eternal youth. You will be reunited in joy with your beloved children and the relatives that you have lost. All your good deeds have been preserved and you will be rewarded for them there." Belief in the Hereafter gives them such solace and joy that were they to experience old age a hundred times over, it would not cause them to despair.

A third of humankind is made up of the youth. With their turbulent passions and emotions and the difficulty they have in controlling their bold intellects if they lose their faith in the Hereafter and do not bring to mind the torments of Hell, the property and honor of the upright members of society, along with the peace and dignity of the weak and the elderly, will be at serious risk. One youth is able to bring down destruction on a happy home for the sake of one minute's pleasure, and the years of imprisonment that follow will turn them into a wild animal. But if belief in the Hereafter comes to their assistance, they quickly come to their senses, thinking: "It is true that the government informers do not see me and I can hide from them, but the angels of the All-Majestic Sovereign, Who has a prison known as Hell, see me and are recording all of my evil deeds. I am not free and left to my own devices: I am a traveler charged with duties. One day I too will be old and weak." Suddenly this person begins to feel sympathy and respect for those they would have assaulted before without thinking twice. Being content with the explanations of this truth which the reader may find in the *Risale-i Nur*, we cut the discussion short here.

Another important section of humankind comprises the sick, the oppressed, the poor, those like us who are disaster-stricken and prisoners languishing in jail, subject to severe punishment. If belief in the Hereafter does not come to their aid, their lives are bound to be filled with torment. For illness reminds them constantly of death; the haughty treachery of the oppressor, in the face of whom they are unable to save their honor, causes them extreme distress; the loss of property or offspring in serious disasters brings untold despair; and the intolerable hardship of having to spend five or ten years in prison causes immeasurable pain and mental suffering. Without belief, all of these calamitous situations turn the world into a terrible prison for those who experience them and life becomes a living hell. But if belief in the Hereafter comes to their aid, they begin to feel relief and, to the degree of their belief, their distress, despair, anxiety and desire for vengeance diminish and, sometimes, even disappear completely.

I can even go so far as to say that if belief in the Hereafter had not come to the aid of myself and some of my brothers in the fearsome calamity that is this wrongful imprisonment, we would not have been able to bear a single day of incarceration: it would have been as unbearable as death and might even have driven us to say goodbye to life altogether. But boundless thanks be to God, for despite suffering the distress of my brothers, whom I love as much as my own life; despite the loss and the weeping over thousands of copies of the *Risale-i Nur* and my precious, gilded books, which I love as much as my eyes; and despite the fact I could not bear the slightest insult or stand to be dominated by others, I swear that the light and strength of belief in the Hereafter gave me the patience, endurance, solace, and steadfastness to cope. Indeed, this has given me enthusiasm to gain a greater reward through bearing the painful exertions of my ordeal, for as I said at the outset of this treatise, I considered myself to be a student in a place of instruction worthy of being called the School of Joseph. Were it not for the occasional pains and illnesses of old age, I would have learned my lessons more diligently and with greater ease of mind. However, we have digressed, and for this I hope I will be forgiven.

Also, everyone's home is a small world for them, perhaps even a small paradise. If belief in the Hereafter does not underpin the happiness of that home, the members of that family will suffer anguish and anxiety in proportion to the compassion, love, and attachment they feel for their family. Their paradise will turn into Hell and they will have no option but to numb their minds with temporary amusements and distractions. Like an ostrich that sticks its heads into the sand thinking it cannot be seen by the hunter, these poor people plunge their heads into heedlessness in the hope that death, decline, and separation may not find them. They seek a way out of their terrifying predicament by temporarily anesthetizing themselves. The mother, for example, trembles constantly at seeing her children, for whom she would sacrifice her soul, exposed to danger. Children, for their part, feel constant sorrow and fear at being unable to save their father or siblings from calamities that visit families too often. Thus, in this tumultuous worldly life, the supposedly contented life of the family loses its happiness in many respects, and the kinship and close connections forged in this brief earthly existence do not result in true loyalty, heartfelt sincerity, disinterested service, or real love. Good character declines proportionately and is often lost completely. However, if belief in the Hereafter enters that home, it illuminates it completely: its members develop respect, love, and compassion for each other, not merely for the sake of relationships in this brief worldly life, but for the sake of their continuance in the eternal realm of happiness that is the Hereafter. They respect, love, and show compassion to each other sincerely; they are loyal to one another and ignore each other's faults and their good character increases accordingly. As a result, the happiness of true humanity begins to develop in the home. Since this too is elucidated in the *Risale-i Nur*, we cut the discussion short here.

Also, a town is like a large home for those who live there. If the members of that large family do not have belief in the Hereafter, rather than sincerity, cordiality, virtue, mutual love and assistance, self-sacrifice, and the seeking of Divine pleasure and otherworldly reward—all of which form the basis of good conduct—vices such as self-interest, pretentiousness, hypocrisy, artificiality, bribery, and deception will dominate. Anarchy and savagery will hold sway beneath the façade of superficial order and a nominal humanity, poisoning the life of the town. The children will become idle troublemakers, the youth will plunge themselves into drunkenness, the powerful will embark on oppression, and the elderly will be left to weep.

By analogy, a country is also a home—the home of a national family. If belief in the Hereafter rules in such a home, sincere respect, earnest compassion, selfless love, mutual assistance, honest service, good social relations, unostentatious charity, and many other excellences and virtues will begin to flourish.

Belief in the Hereafter says to the children: "Stop messing around, for there is Paradise to be won!" and teaches them self-control through instruction from the Qur'an.

It says to the youth: "Hell truly exists: give up your heedlessness!" thus bringing them to their senses.

It says to the oppressor: "Severe torment will be your lot if you continue on this path!" and makes them bow to justice.

It says to the elderly: "In the world to come there exists not only perpetual happiness far greater than anything you could experience in this world, but also eternal youth. Try to win them for yourselves!" thus turning their tears into smiles.

Belief in the Hereafter shows its favorable effects in every group, particular or universal, and illuminates them. Let the sociologists and moral philosophers, who are concerned with the social life of humankind, take note of this. If the rest of the thousands of benefits to be had from belief in the Hereafter are compared with the five or six we have indicated briefly, we can understand that it is only belief that is the means of happiness in this world and the next.

* * *

In The Twenty-Eighth Word and other treatises of the *Risale-i Nur*, powerful replies were given in order to silence the insubstantial doubts which exist concerning bodily Resurrection. Readers who desire a more detailed discussion may refer to these writings; here we will content ourselves with the following brief indication:

Just as the most comprehensive mirror of the Divine Names is to be found in corporeality, so the richest and most active center of the Divine purposes for the creation of the universe is also in corporeality. Likewise, the greatest variety of the multifarious bounties of the Lord lies in corporeality, together with the greatest multiplicity of the seeds of the prayers and thanks offered by many to their Creator through the language of their needs. And the greatest diversity of the seeds of the metaphysical and spirit worlds also lies in corporeality.

Since hundreds of universal truths are centered in corporeality, in order to multiply it and favor it with manifestations of the above truths on the earth, the All-Wise Creator clothes successive caravans of beings in corporeal existence and sends them with awesome speed and activity to that glorious exhibition. Then He dismisses them and sends others in their place, constantly making the factory of the universe operate. Weaving corporeal products, He makes the earth into a seed-bed of the Hereafter and Paradise. In fact, in order to gratify the appetite of the stomach, He listens intently to the supplication for permanence which it makes in the form of hunger and accepts it. In order to respond to this prayer, He prepares innumerable sorts of ingenious foods and precious bounties, all of which produce different pleasures. This demonstrates, beyond a shadow of a doubt, that in the Hereafter the most numerous and diverse pleasures of Paradise will be corporeal, as will the bounties of that eternal abode of happiness to which all human beings aspire.

The All-Powerful and Compassionate, the All-Knowing and Munificent One, accepts the invocation offered by the stomach in the form of hunger and answers it with care and deliberation by providing it with an almost infinite variety of foods. The human is the most important result of the universe and has been appointed as the ruler of the earth: we are the Creator's choice being and adorer. Is it at all possible, then, that the All-Powerful and Compassionate, the All-Knowing and Munificent One, Who accepts the prayer of a stomach and answers it, would not accept the numerous, universal supplications offered by the stomach of all humanity for universal, elevated corporeal pleasures in the eternal realm, which are innately desired and aspired to by humankind? Is it at all possible that He should not answer it with bodily Resurrection, thus gratifying humankind eternally? Would He listen to the buzz of the fly, but not the roar of thunder? Would He be attentive to the needs of a common soldier, but ignore the needs of a whole army? To do so would be infinitely impossible and absurd.

Indeed, as is stated explicitly in the verse: *There will be therein all that souls desire, and eyes delight in* (43:71), the people of Paradise will experience, in a form befitting their state, the corporeal pleasures with which they are most familiar, samples of which they have tasted during their earthly existence. The rewards for the sincere thanks and particular worship offered by each of their members—the tongue, the eye, the ear, and so on—will be given in the form of corporeal pleasures particular to those members. The miraculous Qur'an describes the corporeal pleasures so explicitly that it is impossible not to accept their literal meanings: there is no need to look for metaphorical interpretations.

Thus, the fruits and results of belief in the Hereafter show that just as the existence, nature, and needs of the stomach are decisive proof of the existence of food, the innate need and desire of humankind for eternity, together with the excellences and potentials they possess which demand the consequences and benefits of belief in the Hereafter, provide indubitable proof for the existence of the world to come and of Paradise and its eternal corporeal pleasures. Also, the perfections and meaningful signs which fill the universe, and the existential realities of humanity which are related to these signs, testify absolutely to the certain existence of the realm of the Hereafter, the Resurrection, and the opening up of Paradise and Hell. This fundamental truth has been explained convincingly in several treatises of the *Risale-i Nur*, including in particular The Tenth, Twenty-eighth and Twenty-ninth Words, and The Third and Ninth Rays. For a more detailed discussion, readers are referred to these writings.

The Qur'anic descriptions of Hell are so clear and explicit that they leave no need for further description. Detailed discussions of the subject can be found in the *Risale-i Nur*; here we will clarify in brief just two or three points in order to dispel one or two insignificant doubts.

THE FIRST POINT: The thought of Hell does not diminish the pleasures of the above fruits of belief with the fear it provokes. For infinite Divine Mercy says to the fearful person:

"Come to me! Enter through the door of repentance, so that the existence of Hell will, rather than frighten you, make known in full the pleasures of Paradise and enable you and all creatures whose rights have been violated to avenge, as well as giving you enjoyment. If you have drowned in misguidance, from which you cannot emerge, the existence of Hell is still immeasurably better than eternal annihilation; it is also a kind of compassion for the unbelievers. For humans, and even animals with young, derive pleasure from the pleasure and happiness of their relatives, offspring and friends, and in one respect become happy themselves.

"And so to the disbelieving materialists I would say this: because of your misguidance, you will either fall into eternal non-existence or you will enter Hell. As for non-existence, it is absolute evil, and since it also means the eternal annihilation of you yourself and all those relatives, ancestors and descendants of yours, whom you love and whose happiness also makes you happy, the thought of eternal non-existence pains your heart and spirit more grievously than a thousand Hells. For if there were no Hell, there would be no Paradise. Through your unbelief, everything falls into non-existence. But if you go to Hell and remain within the sphere of existence, your loved ones and relatives will either be happy in Paradise or be favored with compassion in one respect within the sphere of existence. This means that you should defend the notion that Hell exists, for to oppose it is to support non-existence, which in turn is to support the obliteration of the happiness of innumerable relatives and loved ones."

Hell is an awesome, majestic realm which performs the wise and just function of being the place of imprisonment belonging to the Sovereign of Majesty in the sphere of existence, which is pure good. In addition to performing the function of being a prison, Hell has numerous other duties, serving many wise purposes and carrying out many tasks related to the everlasting realm. It is also the awe-inspiring dwelling of many living beings, such as the Angels of Hell.

THE SECOND POINT: The existence and terrible torments of Hell are not contrary to the infinite Mercy, true Justice and balanced Wisdom of God. Rather, Mercy, Justice, and Wisdom demand its existence. For to punish an oppressor who tramples on the rights of a thousand innocents or to kill a savage animal who tears to pieces a hundred cowering animals is not only just, it is a great mercy for the oppressed. To pardon the oppressor and to leave the savage beast free shows a gross lack of pity for hundreds of innocent wretches in return for a single act of misplaced mercy.

Among those who will enter Hell are the absolute unbelievers. They will enter that place on account of the fact that they have transgressed the rights of the Divine Names by denying them, and they have transgressed the rights of all creatures who testify to those Names by denying their testimony and the elevated duties of glorification they perform in the face of the manifestation of the Names in creation. Also, by denying the fact that all creatures are mirrors for the manifestation of Divine Lordship and respond to this Lordship with worship, which is the *raison d'être* of the creation and continued existence of the universe, they transgress the rights of all other creatures even further. Unbelief is therefore such a tremendous crime that it cannot be forgiven; it truly deserves the threat enshrined in the verse: *Assuredly, God does not forgive that partners be associated with Him*

(4:48, 116). Not to cast that unbeliever into Hell would be a misplaced act of compassion, and would serve to withhold justice and mercy from those innumerable claimants whose rights have been transgressed. In the same way that these claimants demand the existence of Hell, the Divine dignity of Majesty and the grandeur of His Perfection most certainly demand it.

If a rebellious outlaw who assaults the people affronts the dignity and authority of a town's governor by saying: "You can't put me in prison!", even if there is no prison in the town, the governor will have one built just to imprison that ill-mannered wretch. Similarly, through their unbelief, the absolute unbelievers commit a serious assault on the dignity and authority of God's Majesty; through their denial they affront the grandeur of His Power and through their aggression offends the perfection of His Lordship. However many functions Hell may or may not have, and however many reasons or instances of wisdom there are which necessitate its existence, it is the Dignity and Majesty of God more than anything else which demand the creation of Hell for unbelievers such as those described above.

Moreover, even the essence of unbelief suggests Hell. For example, if the essence of belief were to be embodied, it would, with its pleasures, assume the form of a private paradise and, in so doing, provide a taste of the Paradise yet to come. Similarly, as has been discussed previously and in other parts of the *Risale-i Nur*, the spiritual pains and torments of unbelief, hypocrisy, and apostasy are such that, if they were to be embodied, they would take on the form of a private hell for those fettered by unbelief and would give them a taste of the Hell yet to come. Also, bearing in mind that the little truths in the field of this world will grow into elaborate trees in the Hereafter, this poisonous seed that is unbelief foreshadows the emergence of the tree of *Zaqqum*, saying: "I am its origin. For the wretched who bear me in their hearts my fruit is a private sample of that bitter tree of Zaqqum."

Since unbelief is a violation of so many rights, it is certainly an infinitely evil crime that will deserve infinite punishment. Human justice considers a sentence of fifteen years imprisonment—approximately eight million minutes—to be appropriate for a murder that has been committed in a minute or less; human justice regards such a sentence to be in conformity with the public interest and the good of society as a whole. Therefore, since one instance of absolute unbelief is the equivalent of a thousand murders, to suffer torments for nearly eight billion minutes for one minute's absolute unbelief is in conformity with that law of justice. A person who passes a year of their life in unbelief deserves punishment lasting countless billions of minutes, thus manifesting the meaning of the verse: *They will abide therein for ever* (4:169; 33:65).

The miraculous descriptions of Paradise and Hell in the wise Qur'an and the proofs of their existence contained in the *Risale-i Nur*, which issues from and interprets it, leave no need for further explanations.

Numerous Qur'anic verses such as:

> They (the people of discernment) reflect on the creation of the heavens and the earth (and they pray): "Our Lord, You have not created this (the universe) without meaning and purpose. All-Glorified are You, so save us from the punishment of the Fire!" (3:191)

> "Our Lord! Ward off from us the punishment of Hell; its punishment is surely constant anguish: how evil indeed it is as a final station and permanent abode!" (25:65–66).

and the prayers of Prophet Muhammad, upon him be peace and blessings, and all other Prophets and people of truth in order to be saved from the punishment of Hell, saying "Preserve us from Hell-fire! Deliver us from Hell-fire! Save us from Hell-fire!"—it becomes clear from all these that the most important issue for humankind is how they are to be saved from eternal perdition in Hell. Hell is an extremely significant, tremendous and awesome reality—one which some of the people endowed with inner vision and the capacity for spiritual unveiling have been able to gaze upon, or see its manifestations and shadows. And such vision has led all of them to cry out in terror, "Save us from it!"

The confrontation, co-existence, and intermingling of good and evil, pleasure and pain, light and darkness, heat and cold, beauty and ugliness, and guidance and misguidance in the universe are there for an extremely important purpose and are full of wisdom. If there were no evil, the existence of good would be indiscernible. If there were no pain, pleasure would have no meaning. Light without darkness would have no importance and the different degrees of heat are realized only through the existence of cold. Through ugliness, a single truth of beauty becomes a thousand truths, and thousands of varying degrees of beauty come into existence. If there were no Hell, many of the pleasures of Paradise would remain hidden.

Extrapolating from these examples we see that in one respect everything becomes known through its opposite; a single truth contained in any one thing produces numerous shoots and becomes numerous truths. Since these intermingled beings flow from this transient abode into the abode of eternal permanence, certainly, just as things such as good, pleasure, light, beauty, and belief flow into Paradise, so harmful matters such as evil, pain, darkness, ugliness, and unbelief pour into Hell. The floods of this continuously agitated universe are emptied into these two lakes. We curtail this discussion here, referring readers to the subtle and meaningful Points and Matters at the end of The Twenty-Ninth Word.

To my fellow students here in this School of Joseph, I would say this: If we take advantage of our worldly imprisonment for the good and, as we are saved from the many sins which are not possible to commit here, repent our former sins and perform our obligatory religious duties, we will be able to make every hour of our prison life into the equivalent of a whole day's worship. If we can do this, our imprisonment will be the best opportunity we have to be saved from that terrible eternal imprisonment; it will be our key to the door of that light-filled Paradise. But if we miss this opportunity, our afterlife will be filled with misery, just as this world is filled with misery, and we will receive the chastisement indicated in the verse: *He (thereby) incurs loss of both this world and the Hereafter* (22:11).

THE CONNECTION OF "GOD IS THE ALL-GREAT" WITH THE RESURRECTION

It was during the Feast of the Sacrifice that this part was being written. On these blessed days of Sacrifice, three hundred million (now over a billion) people declare in one voice: "*God is the All-Great! God is the All-Great! God is the All-Great!*" It is as if the earth would have its fellow planets in the skies hear the sacred words *God is the All-Great!* Also, on the hill of 'Arafat, tens of thousands (now millions) of pilgrims declare in unison *God is the All-Great!* This is the same declaration made by God's Messenger and his Companions fourteen hundred years ago, and is a response in the form of extensive, universal worship to the universal manifestation of Divine Lordship through God's sublime titles *the Lord of the earth* and *the Lord of the heavens*. I was able to imagine all of this and become convinced of it.

Then I wondered whether this sacred phrase has any connection with the question of the Resurrection we have been discussing. It suddenly occurred to me that together with this sacred phrase, similar other phrases and symbols of the Islamic faith such as *There is no deity but God; All praise and gratitude are for God!* and *All-Glorified is God!*, which are referred to as "enduring good works," recall this in both a particular and universal fashion and imply its realization.

For example, the phrase *God is the All-Great!* means in one respect that God's Power and Knowledge are greater than everything: nothing at all can escape His Knowledge or the control and authority of His Power. They are infinitely greater than the things we fear most. This means that they have the absolute ability to accomplish things that are much greater than bringing about the Resurrection, saving us from non-existence, and granting eternal happiness. They are able to do things that we may see as strange, unbelievable, or even unimaginable. For this reason, as is stated explicitly in the verse: *Your creation and your resurrection are but as (the creation and resurrection) of a single soul* (31:28), the resurrection of humankind and their being gathered together in the Place of Resurrection are as easy for that Power as the creation of a single soul. It is in connection with this truth that, when faced by serious disasters or attempting important undertakings, all Muslims say: "*God is the All-Great! God is the All-Great!*" making it a source of consolation, power, and support for themselves.

As was explained in The Ninth Word, the phrases *God is the All-Great!*, *All-Glorified is God!* and *All praise and gratitude are for God!* form the seeds and summaries of the canonical Prayers—the zenith of all worship—and in order to emphasize the meaning of these Prayers and compensate for any defects in them, they are included in recitations both during and after the Prayers. They also point to three supreme truths and provide powerful answers to the questions which arise in our mind from the amazement, pleasure, and awe we feel at the strange, exquisite, and extraordinary things that we see in the universe—things that fill us with wonder and lead us to offer thanks on account of their awe and grandeur. Furthermore, as mentioned at the end of The Sixteenth Word, a private soldier may enter the king's presence in the company of a field marshal at a festival and come to know him directly; at other times, however, he knows him only through the person of his immediate commander. Similarly, like the saints to a certain extent, a person performing the *Hajj* begins to know God through His titles *the Lord of the earth* and *the Lord of all worlds*. As the levels of the manifestations of Divine Grandeur unfold in a person's heart, by repeating the phrase *God is the All-Great!* they answer all of the astounding questions that overwhelm the spirit. Moreover, as was explained at the end of The Thirteenth Gleam, the phrase *God is the All-Great!* provides the most effective replies to the most cunning intrigues of Satan, cutting them off at the root; similarly it also gives a most succinct but powerful answer to the question we posed concerning the Hereafter.

The phrase *All praise and gratitude are for God* also suggests and demands the Resurrection. It says to us: "Without the Hereafter, I would be virtually meaningless. For what I mean with this phrase is this: to God are due all the praise and thanks offered from pre-eternity to post-eternity, regardless of who has offered them and to whom they have been offered. It is only the promise of eternal happiness—the supreme bounty—that actually makes bounties bountiful and saves all conscious creatures from the permanent calamity of non-existence. It is only in eternal happiness that my existence can find true meaning."

Every believer's recitation of *All praise and gratitude are for God!*, uttered at least a hundred and fifty times a day after the canonical Prayers, is not only an act of worship in itself, but it is also the expression of praise and thanks that extends from pre-eternity to post-eternity: this can only be the advance price and immediate fee for Paradise and eternal felicity. The praise and thanks offered through them cannot be restricted to the fleeting bounties of this world, which is marred by the pains of transience; people see these quite rightly as means to the attainment of eternal bounties.

As for the sacred phrase, *All-Glorified is God!*, which declares that God is exalted above having partners, faults, defects, injustice, impotence, mercilessness, need, or deception—indeed, any negative attributes that are opposed to His absolute Perfection, Grace, Beauty, and Majesty—it also points to the eternal happiness of the Hereafter and its Paradise, which are the means to the splendor and glory of His Grace, Beauty, and Majesty, and the perfection of His Sovereignty. For, as has been explained previously, if there were no eternal happiness, His Sovereignty and His Perfection, His Majesty, Grace, Beauty, and Mercy would be sullied by fault and defect.

Like these three sacred phrases, *In the Name of God*; *There is no deity but God* and other similar utterances are all seeds of the pillars of faith: they are extracts of both the pillars of belief and the truths of the Qur'an. In addition to their being the seeds of the five daily Prayers, the three phrases mentioned above are also the seeds of the Qur'an, sparkling like brilliant gems at the beginning of a number of radiant *suras*. They are also the true sources and foundations of the *Risale-i Nur*, many parts of which began to form in my mind while reciting these phrases after the canonical Prayers; they are the seeds of its truths. Also, from the perspective of the worship of Prophet Muhammad, upon him be peace and blessings, and of the sainthood included in his Messengership, these phrases are the regular recitations of the "Muhammadan Way." As such, they are repeated by hundreds of millions of believers after each of the five daily Prayers, as though they were forming a vast circle of remembrance. Their prayer beads in their hands, they declare *All-Glorified is God!* thirty-three times, *All praise and gratitude are for God!* thirty-three times, and *God is the All-Great!* thirty-three times.

Now you must surely understood how worthy and full of reward such recitations are, and how, as explained above, they are the extracts and seeds of the Qur'an, of belief, and of the canonical Prayers.

Just as the first matter discussed at the beginning of this treatise provided an agreeable lesson regarding the five daily canonical Prayers, this last matter has also turned out to be an important lesson regarding the regular recitations following the Prayers.

All praise be to God for His favors!

All-Glorified are You! We have no knowledge save what You have taught us; surely You are the All-Knowing, the All-Wise.

The Ninth Matter

In the Name of God, the All-Merciful, the All-Compassionate.

The Messenger believes in what has been sent down to him from his Lord, and so do the believers; each one believes in God, and His angels, and His Books, and His Messengers: "We make no distinction between any of His Messengers (in believing in them)." (....To the end of the verse) (2:285)

An awesome question and a state of mind that arises from the unfolding of a vast Divine favor have led me to explain a lengthy, universal point concerning this comprehensive, elevated, and sublime verse.

IT WAS ASKED: While belief in God and the Hereafter must, like the sun, remove all darkness of unbelief, why is it that if one denies one of the truths of belief, they are deemed to be an unbeliever? Why, if they do not accept that particular truth, are they considered not to be a Muslim? Moreover, why is it that a person who denies one of the pillars and truths of belief is deemed an apostate, one who has fallen into absolute unbelief and who has left the community of Islam? Surely their belief in the other pillars must save them from absolute unbelief?

THE ANSWER: Belief is a single, united truth composed of six pillars: it cannot be divided up. It is something universal that cannot be separated into parts: it is an indivisible whole. For each of the pillars of belief proves and establishes the other pillars with the proofs that prove and establish it. They are all supremely powerful proofs of one another. Since this is so, one invalid notion that cannot shake all of the pillars together with all their proofs cannot in reality invalidate a single one of those pillars or even a single truth; it cannot deny them. One can only shut their eyes purposefully under the veil of only non-acceptance—not utter rejection—and commit a kind of unbelief that stems from sheer obstinacy. However, they would fall into absolute unbelief by degrees: as a result, their humanity would be destroyed and both their body and spirit would be dispatched to Hell. So in this context, with God's grace, we will explain this supreme matter in certain Points in the form of brief summaries and conclusions.

THE FIRST POINT: Belief in God establishes, with its own proofs, all of the other pillars and belief in the Hereafter, as has been clearly shown in The Seventh Matter of Fruits of Belief. We clearly see that a pre-eternal and everlasting sovereignty of Lordship, an eternal Divine rule, governs the boundless universe and all it contains as though it were a palace, a city, or a country. This Sovereignty makes the globe of the earth revolve in a balanced and orderly fashion, changing it with innumerable instances of wisdom, and equips and directs atoms, planets, flies, and stars all together as though each were a well-disciplined, well-organized army; It continuously drills them and impels them to act, travel, and carry out various duties by His Command and Will as though they were engaged in sublime maneuvers or a worshipful parade. Is it then possible at all that this eternal, perpetual, enduring Sovereignty would not have an eternal locus or everlasting place of manifestation, namely the Hereafter? God forbid! This means the Sovereignty of God Almighty's Lordship and—as described in The Seventh Matter—most of His Names and the proofs of His absolutely necessary Existence all require the Hereafter and testify to it. So see and understand what a powerful support this pillar of belief has and believe in it as though you could see it!

Also, just as belief in God is not possible without belief in the Hereafter, it is neither possible without belief in His Messengers and Books. For in order to manifest His Divinity and to show that He has the exclusive right to be worshipped, God, the All-Worshipped One, has created the universe as an embodied book which demonstrates that its Creator is the Eternally Besought One. Every page of this book is in itself a smaller book full of meanings, and every line a page filled with wisdom. This book is like such an embodied Qur'an that it is filled with endless creational "verses" and words, with points and letters, each of which is a miracle. It is like a magnificent mosque of Mercy, the interior of which is decorated with innumerable inscriptions and adornments, and in every corner of which are species of beings each preoccupied with the worship dictated by its nature and the Divine purposes of its existence. Is it then at all possible that God, the All-Worshipped One, should create the universe in this way and not send masters to teach the meanings of this vast book? Is it at all likely that He should fail to task commentators with the interpretation of the verses of that vast "Qur'an," which shows that it is the work of the Eternally Besought One? Is it at all possible that He should not appoint imams to lead all those who are worshipping in numerous ways in this huge mosque, or that He should not give Decrees—the Divine Scriptures or Books—to those masters, commentators, and leaders of worship? God forbid, a hundred thousand times!

Also, in order to display to conscious beings the beauty of His Mercy, the excellence of His Compassion and the perfection of His Lordship so that He may encourage them to praise and thank Him, the All-Compassionate and All-Munificent Maker has created the universe as a banqueting hall, an exhibition center, and a place of excursion, in which are arranged infinite varieties of delicious bounties and priceless, wonderful arts. So, is it at all possible that He would not speak to these conscious beings at the banquet or fail to inform them through His Messengers of their duties of thanks for the favors He has given them, and their duties of worship in response to the manifestations of His Mercy and His making Himself loved? God forbid, a thousand times over!

Also, the Maker loves His Art and wants it to be loved. As is indicated, for example, by His taking into account the thousand pleasures to be had by the human mouth, He wants His Artistry to be met with appreciation and approval. And so He has adorned the universe with priceless arts and displayed throughout the universe the traces of His transcendent Beauty in such a way that it becomes clear that He wills to make Himself both known and loved. Is it possible, then, that such a Maker would not speak to humanity, the commander of living beings in the universe, through some of the most eminent people whom He has sent as Messengers? Is it at all likely that His fine arts should remain unappreciated and the extraordinary beauty of His Names unvalued? Is it all likely that there should be no response to those Acts of His Which are designed to make Him known and loved? God forbid, a hundred thousand times!

Also, through His infinite bounties and gifts, which indicate purpose, choice, and will, the All-Knowing Speaker answers clearly and at exactly the right time all of the supplications made by living beings for their natural needs, together with all the requests they make through the tongues of their innate disposition. Is it possible, then, that He should speak to the most insignificant living creature and address their most trivial needs, yet fail or refuse to speak to the spiritual leaders of humankind, the choicest of His creations, the one who has stewardship over creation and enjoys the position given to them of commander over most creatures on earth? Given that He speaks to all other living beings, should He not speak to humans and send them His Decrees— the Divine Scriptures or Books? God forbid that this should be so!

Thus, with its certainty and its innumerable proofs, belief in God proves and establishes belief in the Prophets and the sacred Books or Scriptures.

In response to the One Who makes Himself known and loved through all His artifacts, and Who wills and orders that He be thanked, Prophet Muhammad, upon him be peace and blessings, knew Him and made Him known, loved Him and made Him loved, thanked Him and inspired others to thank Him too; he did all of these in the most perfect way through the truth of the Qur'an, which causes the universe to resonate. Also, with his declarations of "All-Glorified is God!" "All praise and gratitude are for God!" and "God is the All-Great!" Prophet Muhammad caused the earth to ring out, echoing through the heavens and bringing the land and sea to heights of ecstasy. Furthermore, for fourteen centuries Prophet Muhammad has led half of the globe or a fourth of humankind, responding to all the manifestations of the Creator's Lordship with extensive, universal worship, and to His Divine purposes by announcing and teaching the messages of the Qur'an to the universe and through the centuries. Thus Prophet Muhammad, upon him be peace and blessings, demonstrated the honor, value, and duties of humankind and was himself confirmed by the Creator through his countless miracles. Is it at all then possible that Prophet Muhammad, who is so worthy in God's sight, should not have been the choicest of God's creatures, the most excellent of envoys, and the greatest Messenger? God forbid! A hundred thousand times, God forbid!

Thus with all its proofs, the truth of "I bear witness that there is no deity but God" proves and establishes the truth of "I bear witness that Muhammad is the Messenger of God."

Also, is it at all possible that the Maker of the universe should cause creatures to speak to one another in myriad tongues, that He should understand and hear their speech, but that He Himself should remain silent? God forbid!

Also, is it at all reasonable that He should not proclaim His purposes and instances of wisdom in the universe through some kind of decree? Is it at all possible that He would not send a book like the Qur'an, which solves the riddle of the universe and provides true answers to the three awesome questions asked by all souls, namely: "Where do creatures come from?", "Where are they going?", and "Why do they follow on, convoy after convoy, stopping for a while and then pass on?" God forbid!

The miraculous Qur'an has illuminated fourteen centuries of human history. It circulates every hour through hundreds of millions of respectful tongues and is inscribed with its sacredness in the hearts of the millions of those who commit it to memory. Through its laws it governs a considerable part of humankind, educating, purifying, and instructing their souls, spirits, hearts, and minds. As demonstrated in certain parts of the *Risale-i Nur*, the Qur'an has forty aspects of miraculousness. It is explained in The Nineteenth Letter that through each of these aspects the Qur'an addresses a different class or level of humankind. Moreover, Prophet Muhammad, upon him be peace and blessings, who is himself a miracle of the miraculous Qur'an, proves decisively through his numerous miracles that the Qur'an is the Word of God. Is it then at all possible that this miraculous Qur'an should not be the Word and Decree of the Eternal Speaker and the All-Permanent Maker? God forbid! A hundred thousand times, God forbid!

That is to say, with all its proofs, belief in God proves and establishes that the Qur'an is the Word of God.

Also, is it all possible that the All-Majestic Ruler, Who continuously fills and empties the earth with living beings and populates this world of ours with conscious creatures in order to make Himself known, worshipped, and glorified—it is possible that He should leave the heavens and stars empty and vacant, without creating inhabitants appropriate to them and settling them in these lofty palaces; is it possible that in His most extensive lands He should leave the sovereignty of His Lordship without servants, majesty, officials, envoys, lieutenants, supervisors, spectators, worshippers, or subjects? God forbid! To the numbers of the angels, God forbid!

Also, the All-Wise Ruler, the All-Knowing, and the All-Compassionate One, has written the universe in the form of a book; He inscribes the entire life-stories of trees and the life-duties of grasses and plants in their seeds. He has the lives of conscious beings recorded precisely in their memories, which are as tiny as mustard seeds; He preserves with innumerable photographs all the actions and events which occur in all His dominions and in all the spheres of His Sovereignty. He creates mighty Paradise and Hell, the Supreme Bridge, and the Supreme Scales of Justice in order to allow for the manifestation and realization of absolute justice, wisdom, and mercy, which are among the most significant foundations of His Lordship. Is it at all possible that the One Who does all this should not have all the acts of humankind relating to the universe recorded? Is it possible that He would not have their deeds recorded so that they may be rewarded or punished, nor write their good and bad deeds on the tablets of Divine Destiny? God forbid! To the number of letters inscribed on the Supreme Tablet of Divine Determining or Destiny, God forbid!

Thus the truth of belief in God proves and establishes the truth of both belief in the angels and belief in Divine Determining or Destiny. The pillars of belief prove and establish each other as clearly as the sun shows the daylight and daylight shows the sun.

THE SECOND POINT: All the claims made by the Divinely-revealed Books and the Prophets—the Qur'an and Prophet Muhammad, upon him be peace and blessings, in particular—are established on five or six basic points, which they have continuously striven to teach and prove. All the proofs and evidences which testify to their Prophethood and veracity are concerned with these fundamentals and corroborate their truthfulness. These fundamentals are belief in God, belief in the Hereafter, and belief in the other pillars of faith.

That is to say, it is not possible to separate the six pillars of belief. Each one proves the rest and they all require and necessitate each other. The six form a whole that it is absolutely indivisible. Consider a mighty tree—like the *Touba* tree of Paradise—whose roots are in the heavens. Each branch, fruit, and leaf of that mighty tree relies on its universal, inexhaustible life. A person unable to deny that powerful life, which is as clear as the sun, cannot deny the life of a single one of the leaves that are attached to it. If one does deny it, the tree will refute them to the number of its branches, fruits, and leaves, and that person will be silenced. Belief, with its six pillars, is similar to this.

At the beginning of this Matter, I intended to expound the six pillars of belief in thirty-six points, each pillar in a point with six sub-sections. I also intended to give a detailed reply to the awesome question at the beginning, but certain unforeseen circumstances have intervened. However, I think that the first point provides a sufficient basis, leaving no need for further explanation, particularly for those of keen intellect.

It must by now be fully understood that if a Muslim denies one of the pillars of belief, they will fall into absolute unbelief. Unlike other religions, Islam elucidates its pillars of belief with incomparable comprehensiveness, and the pillars of belief are inextricably bound together. A Muslim who does not recognize Prophet Muhammad, upon him be peace and blessings, and does not confirm him will also fail to recognize God with His Attributes and will not know the Hereafter. A Muslim's belief is based on powerful and unshakeable proofs which are so innumerable that there is no excuse for denial: these proofs quite simply compel human reason to accept them.

THE THIRD POINT: I once said "All praise and gratitude are for God!," and searched for a Divine gift that would be equal to its infinitely broad meaning. Suddenly the following sentence occurred to me:

"All thanks be to God for the gift of belief in God, for His necessary Existence, His Unity, and for His Attributes and Names, to the number of the manifestations of His Names from pre-eternity to post-eternity."

I looked and saw that it was completely appropriate.

The Tenth Matter: The Flower of Emirdağ[3] Apparent Repetitions in the Qur'an

The following is a persuasive response to objections that have been raised about the apparent repetitions in the Qur'an.

My dear, faithful brothers (and sisters)!

Confused and ill-expressed though it may be on account of my distressing situation, the following is a reflection on one aspect of the Qur'an's miraculousness. While I find it difficult to articulate, since it concerns the Qur'an, it will be instructive and lead to reflection. It may be likened to the wrapper on a bright, invaluable gem. So consider the gem being offered, rather than its shabby covering. I wrote this with some speed and concision during a few days in Ramadan while I was malnourished and ill, so please forgive any shortcomings it may have.

My dear, faithful brothers (and sisters)!

The Qur'an issues, first of all, from the greatest and most comprehensive rank of the Eternal Speaker's universal Lordship. It is addressed, first of all, to the comprehensive rank of the one who received it in the name of humankind, indeed of the entire universe. Its purpose is to guide humanity from the time of its revelation until the end of time. It therefore contains entirely meaningful and comprehensive explanations concerning the Lordship of the Creator of the universe, Who is the Lord of this world and the Hereafter, the earth and the heavens and eternity, and clarifications of the Divine laws which pertain to the administration of all creatures. It is because of these and similar other attributes of the Qur'an that this Divine discourse is so comprehensive and elevated, and therefore so inclusive and miraculous—so much so that even its most apparent, literal meanings which target the simple minds of ordinary people, who make up the largest group of the addressees of the Qur'an, is enough to satisfy those among the

---

[3] A district of Afyon province (western Turkey) where Said Nursi lived for some time. (Tr.)

people who have attained the highest and most sophisticated levels of understanding. Even its narratives are not a collection of historical stories that were revealed to teach only the people of a certain age, but it address-es and is revealed to every age and all levels of understanding and learning as a collection of universal principles. For example, while describing the punishments meted out to the people of Pharaoh or of 'Ad and Thamud for their sins, and with its severe threats against wrongdoers, it warns all tyrants and criminals, including those of our own time, of the consequences of their tyranny and wrongdoing. By mentioning the final triumphs of Prophets such as Abraham and Moses, upon them be peace, it consoles wronged believers of all eras.

The Qur'an of miraculous expression revives the past, which, for those mired in heedlessness and misguidance, is a lonely and frightful realm, a dark and ruined cemetery. It transforms the past centuries and epochs into living pages of instruction, into a wondrous, animated realm under the direct control of the Lord—a realm that has significant connections with us. By transporting us back to those times or displaying them to us like the scenes on a cinema screen, the Qur'an teaches us, in its own inimitable and most elevated and miraculous style. In the same manner, it shows the true nature of the universe. The misguided see it as an unending, lifeless, lone-ly, and frightening place, replete with decay and separation, while the Qur'an shows it to be a book of the Eternally Besought One, a city of the All-Merciful and a place where the Lord's works of Art are exhibited. In it, lifeless objects become animate beings performing their particular duties and helping one another within a perfect system of communication.

This most glorious Qur'an, which enlightens and instructs angels, jinn, and humanity in Divine Wisdom in the most pleasing manner, has sacred distinctions which are such that a single letter of it sometimes brings ten merits, sometimes a hundred and sometimes a thousand or, indeed, thou-sands. If all the jinn and human beings pooled their talents, they would not be able to produce anything to rival or equal the Qur'an in any way. It speaks to all people and the whole universe in the most appropriate way; it is inscribed continuously and with great facility on the minds of millions of people; however frequently it is recited, it never bores or tires its listeners; despite its similar sentences and phrases which may confuse some, children are able to commit it to memory with ease; it gives pleasure and tranquility to the sick and the dying, for whom listening to even a few human words causes great discomfort. The Qur'an causes its students to attain felicity in both this world and the next.

Observing the unlettered nature of the one who conveyed it, and without any hint of pretentiousness or ostentation, the Qur'an preserves its stylistic fluency and purity while never ignoring the level of understanding of the common masses. At the same time it instructs people in the extraordinary miracles of Divine Power and meaningful instances of Divine Wisdom which underpin all events that occur in the heavens and the earth, thereby displaying a fine aspect of miraculousness within the grace of its status as a book of guidance.

The Qur'an demonstrates that it is a book of prayer and invocation, a call to eternal salvation, and a declaration of God's Unity, all of which require reiteration. Consequently it repeats this or that sentence or story, giving numerous meanings to many different groups or categories of addressees, and informs its readers that its Author treats with compassion even the slightest and apparently most insignificant things and events, including them in the sphere of His Will and Control. By paying attention to even the most particular or apparently trivial events involving the Companions of the Prophet in the establishment of Islam and the legislation of its laws, it presents universal principles and suggests that those events function as though they were seeds, destined to produce numerous important fruits in the establishment of Islam with its Law. In this way, it demonstrates another aspect of its miraculousness.

When needs are expressed repeatedly, answers must accordingly be repeated. Therefore, the Qur'an answers many questions which were asked repeatedly during the twenty-three years of its revelation and seeks to satisfy all levels of understanding and learning. To prove that all things, from minute particles to vast stars, are controlled by a Single One and that He will destroy the universe in order to bestow on it a new form on Doomsday, replacing it with the extraordinary realm of the Hereafter; to establish a mighty and all-comprehensive revolution in minds that will, for the sake of the purposes and results of the creation of the universe, demonstrate the Divine rage and wrath in the face of the human injustice and wrongdoing which fill the universe, the earth and the heavens with rage, the Qur'an repeats certain verses and phrases that are the conclusions of innumerable proofs and which are as weighty as thousands of conclusions. In such cases, repetition is an extremely powerful aspect of

Qur'anic miraculousness, an extremely elevated example of its eloquence and the beauty of its language that is in conformity with the requirements of the subject matter.

For example, as is explained in The Fourteenth Gleam and The First Word of the *Risale-i Nur*, the phrase *In the Name of God, the All-Merciful, the All-Compassionate*, which appears a total of 114 times in the Qur'an—at the beginning of every *sura* apart from *at-Tawba* and once in the middle of the *sura* entitled *an-Naml*—is a truth that links the earth to God's Supreme Throne as well as to all the spheres of the universe, thus illuminating the universe. As everybody is in constant need of this, it is worth repeating millions of times. We need it not only every day, in the same way that we need bread, but at every moment, in the same way that we need oxygen and light.

Another example is *Your Lord is He Who is the All-Glorious and All-Mighty, the All-Compassionate*, which has the strength of thousands of truths and is repeated eight times in *Suratu'sh-Shu'ara*. It tells of the Prophets' final triumph and salvation and the ruin of their rebellious peoples. If, for the sake of the purposes or results of the universe's creation, in the name of God's universal Lordship, and to teach people that the Lord's Glory and Dignity require the wrongdoers' ruin and His Compassion demands the Prophets' triumph and salvation, this sentence were to be repeated thousands of times, there would still be a need for it. Thus it is a concise and miraculous aspect of the Qur'an's eloquence.

Also, the verses: *Which of the favors of your Lord will you two deny?* (55:13) and *Woe on that day to the deniers* (77:15), which are repeated several times in their respective *suras*, are threats repeated in front of jinn and humanity throughout the ages, and across the heavens and the earth, concerning the ingratitude, unbelief, and wrongdoing of all those whose unrighteousness provokes the fury of the heavens and the earth, ruin the results of the universe's creation, and show contempt and denial in the face of the Divine Sovereign's Majesty. They also denounce the violation of the rights of all creatures. Since they constitute a universal teaching which has the strength of a thousand truths, even if these two verses were repeated thousands of times, it would still not be enough. Therefore this repetition represents a majestic example of conciseness and the miraculousness of eloquence in grace and beauty.

Also, the invocation of the Prophet known as *al-Jawshanu'l-Kabir* (The Great Shield), inspired by the Qur'an, consists of a hundred sections, each of which ends with the words: *All-Glorified are You! There is no deity but You. Mercy! Mercy! Deliver us from the Fire!* These sentences contain affirmation of God's Unity, which is the greatest truth in the universe. This affirmation is the greatest of the mighty duties of all created beings toward their Lord, namely glorification, praise, and declaring Him to be All-Holy and free from all defect, exalted above what polytheists attribute to Him. It is also a supplication for humanity to be saved from eternal punishment, which should be our most immediate concern and is the expected result of our servanthood to God and our helplessness before Him. And so, even if we were to repeat these phrases thousands of times over, it would still not be enough.

Thus, the Qur'an includes reiterations on account of such substantial principles. As required by the occasion and the demands of literary eloquence, and to facilitate understanding, it sometimes expresses the truth of Divine Unity twenty times in one page, be it explicitly or implicitly. Yet, it never bores its listener; rather, it enforces the meaning and gives its reader encouragement.

The *suras* revealed in Makka and Madina differ from one another in eloquence and miraculousness, and in degrees of elaboration and conciseness. The Makkans were mainly Qurayshi polytheists and unlettered tribesmen. Given this, the Qur'an uses forceful, eloquent, and concise language with an elevated style, repeating certain points to better establish its truths. In the Makkan *suras*, the pillars of belief and the categories and degrees of Divine Unity's manifestations are expressed repeatedly in a forceful, emphatic, concise, and most miraculous language. They prove the beginning and end of the world, the Existence of God and the coming of the Hereafter with powerful proofs and are expressed not only on a single page, or in one verse, sentence, or word, but sometimes even in a single letter, through such subtle changes in word order, through the use or non-use of definite articles or the inclusion or omission of certain words, phrases, and sentences that masters of the art of literary eloquence have been amazed. The sublime eloquence and conciseness of the Makkan chapters have been discussed in *Isharatu'l-I'jaz* and The Twenty-Fifth Word, which explain forty aspects of the Qur'an's miraculous inimitability.

The *suras* revealed in Madina, during the second phase of the Prophet's mission, are in the main addressed to believers, Jews, and Christians. As required by the rules of eloquence and the practical need for guidance, rather than the pillars and principles of belief, they focus more on explaining the laws and commands of the Shari'a in a simple, clear, and detailed language. However, in the unique, peerless style that is particular to the Qur'an, the explanations are usually concluded with an elevated, powerful sentence or phrase related to belief, Divine Unity, or the Hereafter, thus securing obedience to them by relating them to belief in God and the Last Day. By doing so, the Qur'an also uses certain particular events as a basis upon which the universality of the Shari'a's laws is established.

For an understanding of the elevated aspect of eloquence and the subtleties to be found in the phrases that come at the end of certain verses, such as *God has full power over everything; God has full knowledge of all things; He is the All-Glorious and All-Mighty, the All-Wise; He is the All-Glorious and All-Mighty, the All-Compassionate,* the reader may refer to The Second Ray of The Second Light in The Twenty-Fifth Word.

While explaining Islam's secondary principles and social laws, the Qur'an draws its audience's attention suddenly to elevated, universal truths, leading them from the lesson of the Shari'a to the lesson of Divine Unity, and changes from a plain style to an elevated one. In so doing it demonstrates its aim of guidance on every occasion and shows itself to be a book of law and wisdom, a book of creeds, belief, reflection, invocation, prayer, and the call to the Divine Message. Thus, the Qur'an's Madinan chapters display a most miraculous eloquence and purity of language which is different from the styles evident in the Makkan chapters.

For example, by modifying *Lord* with *your* or *my* or *his* or *her* (your, my, his, her Lord) or *the worlds* (the Lord of the worlds), the Qur'an declares, respectively, God's Oneness in His particular relationship with a person as his or her Lord (*Ahadiya*) or His Unity in His universal relationship with the whole of creation (*Wahidiya*). In using *my Lord* or *your Lord*, it introduces God from the perspective of His special attentiveness and compassion, while in using *the Lord of the worlds*, it introduces Him with all His Majesty, expressing the latter (*Wahidiya*) within the former (*Ahadiya*). Sometimes when the Qur'an sees and fixes an atom in the pupil of the eye, it uses the same "hammer" to fix the sun in the sky and make it an eye of the heavens.

For example, in the expressions: *He has created the heavens and the earth* (57:4), and *He makes the night pass into the day and He makes the day pass into the night* (57:6), the Qur'an considers the understanding of common people, including those who are unlettered among them. However, it concludes the verses with: *He has full knowledge of whatever lies in the bosoms* (57:6); this means: "Together with the magnificent creation and administration of the earth and the heavens, He also has full knowledge of whatever occurs in people's hearts." Thus, the simple style of speech that is aimed at ordinary people is manifested here as an elevated and appealing address for the guidance of all.

QUESTION: Sometimes an important truth may remain hidden to superficial views. Also, the reason for ending the narration of an ordinary event with a universal principle or an aspect of Divine Unity cannot always be readily discerned. Some may consider this Qur'anic style defective. For example, after narrating how Prophet Joseph, upon him be peace, managed to detain his brother (12:69–76), the Qur'an mentions an exalted principle: *Above every owner of knowledge there is (always) one more knowledgeable.* From the perspective of the rules of eloquence, this seems unrelated to the actual context. What is the reason for this?

THE ANSWER: The Qur'an is a book of belief, reflection, and invocation, as well as a book of law, wisdom, and guidance; it therefore contains numerous "books." For this reason, in many pages and passages of long and medium-length *suras*, each of which is a small Qur'an, many teachings and aims are pursued. For example, in order to express the all-comprehensive and magnificent manifestations of Divine Lordship, since it is a kind of copy or reflection of the great book of the universe, the Qur'an gives instructions on every occasion that concerns knowledge of God, aspects of Divine Unity, and the truths of belief. Whenever a suitable occasion arises, no matter how insignificant it seems, the Qur'an expounds different teachings, thus using that occasion to present new instructions or to reveal certain universal rules or principles. This corresponds perfectly to the discussion and adds to the Qur'an's eloquence.

QUESTION: Be it implicitly or explicitly, the Qur'an dwells much on Divine Unity, the Hereafter, and God's judgment of humanity. Why is this so?

THE ANSWER: The Qur'an was revealed to teach humanity about the Existence of God, Divine Unity, and the absolute control that He exercises over the universe and the changes, upheavals, and revolutions which take place in it; it was revealed to dispel all doubts concerning these truths and to break the obstinacy of those who continue to desist from confirming them. It was also revealed to instruct humanity, who has accepted to bear the Supreme Trust as vicegerent of the earth, which they are to rule and develop in accordance with Divine laws, in the mightiest and most important aspects of humanity's duties concerning eternal happiness or perdition. In order to have humanity confirm the instructions of the Qur'an and assent to the most essential matters concerning them, even if the Qur'an were to focus attention on these matters a million times, this would not be a waste of time or words; they would be read and studied over and over again without causing the least boredom.

For example, we read in *Suratu'l-Buruj*:

> Those who believe and do good, righteous deeds, for them there are Gardens through which rivers flow. That is the great triumph. (85:11)

This verse teaches us that death, which stands ever present before us, is something that saves us, our world, and our loved ones from eternal annihilation, for it leads us to a magnificent, everlasting life. Even if this verse were repeated billions of times, and if as much importance were attached to it as is attached to the whole of existence, it would still not be excessive enough to devalue or detract from its meaning. In teaching countless, invaluable matters of this sort and in trying to prove and make people aware of the awesome revolutions that continuously change and renew the universe, the Qur'an draws attention to these matters repeatedly, either in an explicit manner or through allusions. Since they are bounties like light, air, food, and medicine—things which we always need and which require constant renewal and refreshment—the fact that they are repeated so often in the Qur'an is an instance of Divine grace.

Also, consider the following:

The Qur'an reiterates severely, angrily, and emphatically such threatening verses as:

> For the wrongdoers there is a painful punishment (14:22); and

> As for those who disbelieve, for them is the fire of Hell (35:36).

As discussed in detail in the *Risale-i Nur*, humanity's unbelief is such a heinous violation of the rights of the universe and most of its creatures that it angers the earth and infuriates the elements. It is for this reason that they smite unbelievers with floods and similar disasters.

As is stated explicitly in

> When they are cast into it, they will hear its raucous breath (by which they are sucked in) as it boils up, almost bursting with fury... (67:7–8)

Hell is so furious with the unbelievers that it is described as if it were nearly bursting with rage. If, not from the perspective of the physical insignificance of humanity but of the enormity of the unbeliever's wrongdoing and the awesomeness of unbelief as a heinous crime and boundless aggression, and in order to show the importance of His subjects' rights as well as the ugliness in the unbelief and iniquity of unbelievers, the Sovereign of the universe were to describe and denounce such crimes a billion times, it would still not count as a defect. Countless people have read these words every day for fourteen centuries with the utmost eagerness and without the slightest feeling of boredom or weariness.

Every day, for each person a world disappears and the door of a new world is opened. Thus by repeating *There is no deity but God* a thousand times out of need and with the desire to illuminate each of our transient worlds, we make each repetition a lamp for every changing scene. In the same way, one of the reasons the Qur'an repeats the Eternal Sovereign's threats and punishments so often is to seek to break humanity's obduracy and free them from their rebellious carnal soul. It thus seeks to prevent them from darkening the changing scenes and the freshly-recruited worlds, from disfiguring their images which are reflected in the mirror of their lives, and from turning against them those fleeting scenes that will testify for them in the Hereafter. For this reason, even Satan does not consider the severe and forceful repetition of threats in the Qur'an as being out of place. These threats demonstrate that the torments of Hell are pure justice for those who do not heed them.

Another example is the repetition of the stories of the Prophets, particularly that of Moses, upon him be peace.

Such stories contain many instances of wisdom and benefit. The Qur'an shows the Prophethood of all previous Prophets as an evidence of

Muhammad's Messengership, upon him be peace and blessings. This means that from the point of view of truth, no-one can deny Muhammad's Messengership unless one denies all the other Prophets. Also, since not everyone can recite the entire Qur'an every time they open it, it includes these stories, together with the essentials of belief, in almost all the long and medium-length *suras*, thus making each *sura* like a miniature Qur'an. This is done because it is demanded by the principles of literary eloquence and also because the Qur'an wishes to show that Prophet Muhammad, upon him be peace and blessings, is the most important of people and the noblest phenomenon in the universe.

The ritual declaration of belief in Islam—the *Kalimatu't-Tawhid*—is *There is no deity but God and Muhammad is God's Messenger*. The Qur'an accords the highest status to the person of Muhammad and since part of this declaration—*Muhammad is God's Messenger*—points to four of the six pillars of belief, it is often considered equal to the first part, namely *There is no deity but God*. Muhammad's Messengership is the universe's greatest truth, as an individual he is the most noble of God's creatures, and his collective personality and sacred rank, known as *the Muhammadan Truth*, is the brightest sun of both this world and the next. Among many of the proofs in the *Risale-i Nur* which show how worthy he is of occupying such an extraordinary position, the following are but a few:

According to the rule "The cause is like the doer," an amount of reward equal to the number of the good deeds that his community has ever done or will do in the future is added to Prophet Muhammad's account. Since he illuminated the universe with the light he brought, not only jinn, humanity, and angels, but also the heavens and the earth are indebted to him. We see clearly that the supplications of the plants and animals that they offer through the tongue of potentiality and need are accepted. This shows that the prayers of millions of righteous ones among Muhammad's community must be acceptable. They have been praying to God many times a day for centuries to bestow peace and blessings on him and give him the same reward as they have earned. Furthermore, his record of good deeds also contains countless lights from his followers' recitation of the Qur'an, each letter of which brings as many as ten, a hundred or a thousand rewards.

Knowing beforehand that his collective personality—*the Muhammadan Truth*—would be like a blessed, elaborate tree of Paradise in the future, and considering him as a person to be the seed of that majestic tree, the All-Knower of the Unseen attached the greatest importance to him in His Qur'an. In His Decree He has emphasized the need for others to obey him and to gain the honor of his intercession by following his *sunna* or path and has confirmed it as the most important and serious matter of humanity.

Thus, since the truths repeated in the Qur'an have such a great value, anyone with a sound, uncorrupted nature will testify that in its repetitions can be found a powerful and extensive miracle, unless one is afflicted with some sickness of the heart or malady of the conscience due to the plague of materialism, and is therefore included under the following rule:

> A person denies the light of the sun because of their diseased eyes,
> A mouth denies the taste of sweet water on account of sickness.

Two Concluding Notes

THE FIRST: Twelve years ago, I heard that a most dangerous and obstinate enemy of Islam had instigated a conspiracy against the Qur'an and ordered it to be translated so that "people could see its repetitiousness and understand just what it really is." He also intended to substitute a translation for the original Arabic in the canonical Prayers. However, as the *Risale-i Nur* shows decisively, an exact translation of the Qur'an is impossible. No other language can preserve the fine virtues and subtleties of the Arabic language, given how strict and precise it is in grammar and syntax. No translation can replace the Qur'an's miraculously inimitable words and phrases, which are extremely comprehensive in meaning, and each letter of which yields from ten to a thousand merits.

The *Risale-i Nur* also stymied the plan to have only translations of the Qur'an recited in mosques. But since hypocrites taught by that heretic continue to seek a way to extinguish the sun of the Qur'an in the name of Satan, I felt compelled to write the *Flower of Emirdağ*. However, since I have not met with people for a long time, I have no knowledge of the latest developments.

THE SECOND: After our release from Denizli Prison, I was sitting on the top floor of the well-known Hotel Şehir. The graceful dancing of the leaves, branches, and trunks of the poplar trees in the fine gardens opposite me, each with a rapturous motion like a circle of dervishes touched by the breeze, pained my heart, which was already grieving at being parted from my brothers and finding myself alone. Suddenly I thought of fall and winter, and a kind of heedlessness overcame me. I pitied those graceful, swaying poplars and joyful living creatures so much that my eyes began to brim with tears. Since they reminded me of the deaths and separations which lie beneath the ornamented veil of the cosmic façade, the grief at a world full of death and separation took me in its grip and began to squeeze me. But then the light of the *Muhammadan Truth* came and changed that grief to joy. Indeed, I felt eternally grateful to the person of Muhammad, upon him be peace and blessings, for the help and consolation that came to me at that time, for only a single instance of the boundless grace of that light for me, as for all believers and everyone. It was as follows:

The heedlessness that had overcome me had shown me that these blessed and delicate creatures only appear in the season of summer in a purposeless and fruitless life. Their movements were not due to joy; rather they were trembling at the thought of death, separation, and the journey to non-existence. This view was deeply injurious to my passionate desire for permanence, to my love of beauty and my compassion for all creatures and living things. This way of thinking transformed the world into a kind of Hell and my intellect into an instrument of torture. But just at that point, the light that Prophet Muhammad, upon him be peace and blessings, brought as a gift for humanity lifted the veil and showed that rather than extinction, non-existence, nothingness, futility, or separation, the existence of these poplar trees had as many meanings and purposes as the number of their leaves. Moreover, it revealed that they had several duties and that their lives yielded many results, as follows:

One kind relates to the All-Majestic Maker's Names. For example, everyone applauds and congratulates an engineer who makes an extraordinary machine. By carrying out its functions properly, the machine in turn can be said to congratulate and applaud its engineer. Every created being in the universe is such a machine and congratulates and applauds its Maker.

Another instance of wisdom in things such as poplar trees is that each of them resembles a text which, when studied, reveals knowledge of God to conscious living beings. Having left their meanings in the minds of beings such as these, and having left their forms in these beings' memories, as well as on the tablets of the World of representations or "ideal forms" and the records of the World of the Unseen, they leave the material world for the World of the Unseen. In other words, they are stripped of apparent existence and gain many existences that pertain to meanings, the Knowledge that lies behind them and the knowledge of conscious beings, and the unseen realm.

Since God exists and His Knowledge encompasses all things, certainly there can be no such thing in reality, or in the world of a believer, as non-existence, eternal annihilation, or nothingness. An unbeliever's world, however, is filled with notions such as non-existence, separation, and extinction. As the famous proverb has it: "Everything exists for the one for whom God exists; nothing exists for the one for whom God does not exist."

In short, then, just as belief saves us from eternal punishment when we die, it saves everyone's particular world from the darkness of eternal extinction and nothingness. Unbelief, especially the denial of God, destroys both the individual themselves and their particular world with the fear of death, casting them into dark, hellish pits and changing their life's pleasures into pain. Those who prefer this world over the Hereafter should pay heed to this. They should either find a solution for this intractable problem or they should accept belief, thus saving themselves from a most fearful eternal loss.

> All-Glorified are You! We have no knowledge save what You have taught us. Surely You are the All-Knowing, the All-Wise.

> Your brother who is in dire need of your prayers and misses you greatly,

> *Said Nursi*

The Eleventh Matter

> Hundreds of the innumerable fruits, both particular and universal, of the sacred tree of belief, one of which is Paradise, another, eternal happiness, and the other the vision of God, have been explained in certain other parts of the *Risale-i Nur*. Referring interested readers to these parts, we will set out here just a few examples of its most minor and particular fruits rather than those of its universal pillars.

One day while praying, "O my Lord! In veneration of Gabriel, Michael, Israfil and Azra'il, and through their intercession, preserve me from the evil of humans and jinn!" I felt particularly exhilarated and consoled when I mentioned Azra'il—the name of the Archangel of death and one who usually causes people to tremble with fear. "All praise and gratitude be to God!" I uttered, and began to feel earnest love for him. I will point out extremely briefly only a few of the fruits of belief in the angels, together with certain particular fruits of belief in other pillars. They are as follows:

ONE FRUIT: Everyone's most precious possession which they try their utmost to preserve is their spirit. I felt great joy at having submitted it to a powerful and trustworthy hand—Azra'il, thereby saving it from aimlessness and preventing it from being lost or annihilated. Then the angels who record human actions came to mind, and I saw that their existence yields numerous sweet fruits such as this one.

ANOTHER FRUIT: Everyone tries eagerly to preserve worthwhile sayings or deeds of theirs through prose, poetry, or film-making, thus immortalizing what they have said or done. And if their deeds are to produce everlasting fruits in Paradise, they are even more anxious to preserve them. The fact that the recording angels perch on people's shoulders to record those deeds which will gain them perpetual rewards and which people will watch as everlasting scenes in the everlasting realm, seemed so lovely and agreeable to me that I cannot describe it.

THIRD FRUIT: Then, when the worldly authorities had isolated me from everything connected with social life, keeping me away from all my books, friends, assistants and things that console me, and when I was being crushed by exile and the empty world was tumbling down all around me, one of the many fruits of belief in the angels came to my aid. It cheered up my world and lightened my life, filling it with angels and spirit beings, and making everything around me smile with joy. It showed too that the worlds of the people of misguidance weep in desolation, emptiness, and darkness.

FOURTH FRUIT: While enjoying the pleasures of this fruit, my imagination received and tasted one of the numerous fruits of belief, namely belief in the Prophets. Suddenly, my belief in all of the past Prophets so powerful as if I had actually lived among them lit up the past, expanding my belief and giving it universality. It also served to endorse the teachings of the Seal of the Prophets, upon him be peace and blessings, concerning belief to the number of the past Messengers, thus silencing the satanic ones.

Then a question occurred to me, which is also discussed in The Thirteenth Gleam, concerning the wisdom which lies in seeking refuge in God from Satan. It was as follows:

QUESTION: Although the people of guidance are supported and strengthened by innumerable sweet fruits and benefits such as these, by the fine results of good deeds and the compassionate help of the Most Merciful of the Merciful, why is it that the people of misguidance are frequently able to defeat them? Why, at times, are twenty unbelievers able to crush a hundred believers?

THE ANSWER: While thinking about this, I recalled the emphatic warnings of the Qur'an concerning feeble intrigues of Satan, and how it reminds us frequently that God Almighty is with the believers and sends angels to assist them. This matter has been explained in detail elsewhere in the Risale-i Nur and so we will allude to it here only briefly.

It may be that when a single arsonist tries to set fire to a palace, the palace can remain standing only through the efforts of a hundred men protecting it, a hundred men who have recourse to the full force of the law. For like its existence, the subsistence of the palace is possible only through the continued existence of all its parts, together with the presence of all the conditions and causes necessary for its subsistence. Its destruction and non-existence, however, may occur through the non-existence of a single condition. Just as the palace can be razed to the ground by a vandal with a single match, vast destruction and mayhem may be wrought by satanic ones among jinn and humanity with comparative ease. The basis and origin of all evil and sin is non-existence and destruction. Their apparent existence veils actual non-existence and destruction— that is, although evil and sin appear to actually exist, in truth they are the absence of good and therefore pure non-existence. Thus the satanic ones from among jinn and humanity are able to resist a great force with what is in actual fact an extremely weak one, thus compelling the people of truth to seek refuge continuously at the Court of the Divine. For this reason, the Qur'an attaches extreme importance to the protection of the good. It offers as a source of their support ninety-nine Divine Names and orders them sternly to withstand these enemies.

This answer unveiled a great truth and the basis of an awesome matter. Paradise displays the crops of all the worlds of existence and causes the seeds sown in the world to sprout and grow into eternal plants or trees. Similarly, in order to display the grievous consequences of the innumerable terrible worlds of non-existence and nothingness, Hell burns up the products of these worlds and cleanses the universe of the filth from the world of non-existence. But this is a matter which we will discuss elsewhere.

FIFTH FRUIT: Another example of the fruits of belief in the angels concerns the "questioning angels," known as *Munkar* and *Nakir*:

I once imagined entering the grave, as one day, like everyone else, I will. As I lay there, terrified by the desolation and despair of that dark, cold, narrow pit, two blessed friends from among the species of angels called *Munkar* and *Nakir* appeared and began to converse with me. At once both the grave and my heart were broadened, illuminated, and warmed as windows were opened, one after the other, onto the world of spirits. I was filled with joy at this imaginary situation, knowing that I would experience such a thing in the future and I offered heartfelt thanks.

It was narrated that a *medrese* student who was studying Arabic died. In response to the question of *Munkar* and *Nakir*, who asked him "Who is your Lord?" he imagined for a moment that he was back in *medrese* and answered: "The word 'who' is the subject and 'your Lord' is its predicate; now ask me something difficult!" His answer made both the angels and the other spirit beings and a saintly person who was observing this incident from the world laugh, and brought a smile to the metaphorical face of Divine Mercy. God willing, the student was delivered from torment. I hope that like the late Hafiz Ali, a martyred student of the *Risale-i Nur* who died in prison while studying and enthusiastically copying the treatise known as *Fruits of Belief*, and answered the questions of *Munkar* and *Nakir* with the truths set forth in this treatise, we as students of the *Risale-i Nur* may also be graced with the ability to answer the questions to be posed by *Munkar* and *Nakir* with the powerful proofs explained in the *Risale-i Nur*.

SIXTH FRUIT: Another small benefit to be had from belief in angels concerns worldly happiness. An innocent child who had learnt his lesson of belief from a manual concerning Islamic daily life once said to another child who was weeping at the death of his little brother: "Don't cry! Be thankful, for your brother has gone to Paradise and is now with the angels. He is enjoying himself there and having a better time than we are. He is flying around like the angels and taking a look at everything." With these words he turned his friend's mournful tears into happy smiles.

Exactly like that weeping child, during this sorrowful winter I received painful news of two deaths. One was the death of my nephew, Fuad, one of the most successful high school students in the country and someone who had published the truths studied and taught by the *Risale-i Nur*. The second was the death of my sister, Alima Hanim, who died while circumambulating the Ka'ba during *Hajj*. While the deaths of my two relatives were making me weep, as did that of Abdurrahman, which is described in *Treatise for the Elderly* (that is, The Twenty-Sixth Gleam), I saw in my heart through the light of belief that the innocent Fuad and that righteous woman had as their companions the angels and *houris* of Paradise, and had been saved from the perils and sins of this world. Feeling overwhelming joy instead of that dreadful sorrow, I congratulated both of them and Fuad's father, Abdülmecid, along with myself, and offered thanks to the Most Merciful of the Merciful. This has been mentioned here as a supplication for mercy for the two deceased.

All the comparisons and descriptions in the *Risale-i Nur* describe the fruits of belief that are the means of happiness in this world and the next. Compared with the happiness and pleasures of life they engender in this world, these universal and extensive fruits suggest that their belief will gain every believer everlasting happiness; indeed, it is bound to produce shoots and develop in that way. Five of these numerous universal fruits were described at the end of The Thirty-first Word as fruits of the Ascension, while five are included as examples in The Fifth Branch of The Twenty-fourth Word.

We said at the beginning that each of the pillars of belief has innumerable different fruits, and that one of the fruits of the totality of these pillars is the vast Paradise, while another is eternal happiness, and yet another, perhaps the sweetest, is the vision of God. Also some of the fruits of belief that are the means for happiness in both worlds have been described in the comparison which comes at the end of The Thirty-second Word.

SEVENTH FRUIT: Belief in Divine Decree and Destiny also yields precious fruits in this world. Evidence of this can be seen in the well-known saying "Whoever believes in Divine Destiny is secure against grief." A universal fruit of belief in Divine Destiny is explained in the fine example which is given at the end of *Treatise on Divine Decree and Destiny*, which is about two men who enter the lovely garden of a palace. I have had innumerable personal experiences which have convinced me that a lack of belief in Divine Destiny destroys the happiness of this worldly life. Whenever I consider grievous misfortunes from the perspective of Divine Destiny, I see that the misfortune is greatly lightened. I often wonder how those who do not believe in it can continue to live at all!

EIGHTH FRUIT: One of the universal fruits of the pillar of belief in the angels is mentioned in The Second Station of The Twenty-second Word as follows: the Archangel Azra'il, upon him be peace and blessings, said to God: "Your servants will be annoyed with me and complain about me when I carry out my duty of seizing the spirits of the dying."

God replied: "I will make illnesses and calamities a veil to cover your duties, so that my servants' complaints will be directed at these phenomena and not at you."

Like these veils, the duty of Archangel Azra'il, upon him be peace, is also a veil, so that unjustified complaints are not directed toward God Almighty. For not everyone can fathom the wisdom, mercy, beauty, and benefits of death: people see only its outward face and start to object and complain. It is in order that unjustified complaints are not directed to the Absolutely Compassionate One that the function of Azra'il has been veiled. In exactly the same way, the tasks of all the angels, indeed of all apparent causes, are veils that cover the hand of Power, so that the dignity and holiness of Divine Power and the all-embracing nature of Divine Mercy are preserved with regard to things whose essential beauty is not apparent and whose wisdom is not understood; they are preserved so that they do not become the target of objections, and so that those who view things superficially do not see Divine Power as something which is occupied with things that are base, trivial or cruel. For as was discussed convincingly in the *Risale-i Nur*, no cause or agent can play any essential role in the creation or control of things, and everything most evidently bears the stamp of Divine Unity. Invention and creation are particular to God exclusively; causes are merely a veil. Conscious beings like angels can do nothing but carry out certain duties with their partial, limited will-power and in accordance with the Divine purpose for their existence. This is called "acquisition."[4] What they do is a kind of worship that they offer in the form of their vital duties.

> The Dignity and Grandeur of God demand that in the view of the mind causes are veils to cover the hand of Power;
>
> While Divine Unity and Oneness demand that causes have no creative part in creation.

Just as the angels and the apparent causes employed in creational tasks are all means of preserving Divine Power from the attribution to It of defects and apparent evil that some see in things or events, the essential beauties and instances of wisdom of which are invisible or unknown; they are means of sanctifying God, of believing in and declaring His absolute freedom from any shortcoming or wrong, so too, harmful elements and satanic individuals from among human beings and jinn are employed in evil deeds and actions that pertain to non-existence so that they may assist in the preservation of Divine Power from the attribution of injustice or unjustified objections and complaints. They also help to pave the way for the glorification of God Almighty as being absolutely free of all the defects and faults in the universe. For defects and faults arise from non-existence or a lack of sufficient ability, from destruction or the failure to perform certain duties, all of which lead to non-existence and arise from acts which bring about destruction or non-existence. The defects and faults are ascribed to these satanic and evil veils; objections and complaints are directed at them, and thus they function as the means by which God Almighty is declared absolutely free from all defects.

In fact, evil and destructive works pertaining to non-existence do not need any notable power or strength: some trivial act, some insignificant power, or even the non-performance of a duty may cause great destruction and extensive non-existence. Despite this, it is often supposed that the doers of evil have real power and ability, even though they play no role other than to cause non-existence and no power other than minor "acquisition." But since the evils arise from non-existence, the doers of evil are their

---

4 "Acquisition" denotes the volitional acts of responsible beings like humanity and jinn which yield certain results and for which they are responsible. (Tr.)

agents. If they are intelligent beings, they deservedly suffer the consequences. That is to say, the perpetrators of evil deeds are their agents or doers. However, since good deeds and acts pertain to and are means of existence, those who do them are not their true doers: rather, they are the means through which Divine favor manifests itself; the wise Qur'an states that their reward too is purely a Divine favor: *Whatever good happens to you, it is from God; and whatever evil befalls you, it is from yourself* (4:79).

In short: The worlds of existence and the innumerable worlds of non-existence clash, producing fruits like Paradise and Hell. All the worlds of existence declare, "All praise and gratitude are for God!" thus declaring Him to possess all attributes of perfection to an absolute degree, while all the worlds of non-existence announce, "All-Glorified is God!" thus declaring God to be absolutely free of all defect and injustice. Angels and demons, together with instances of good and instances of evil, including the beneficent inspirations and satanic whisperings which enter the heart, all struggle against each other. And as these clashes occur, one fruit of belief in the angels is suddenly manifested, illuminating the universe. Showing us one of the lights of the verse: *God is the Light of the heavens and the earth* (24:35), it causes us to taste how sweet this fruit is.

NINTH FRUIT: Another universal fruit of belief in the angels is to be found in The Twenty-fourth and Twenty-ninth Words.

In every corner of the universe, in every realm of being and in everything, whether particular or universal, is the compassionate majesty of Lordship, which makes itself known and loved. And most certainly it is necessary to respond to that majesty, that compassion and that will to make itself known and loved with thanks and comprehensive, conscious worship, declaring them to be free of all defects. It is only the countless angels that can perform this duty on behalf of unconscious inanimate creatures and the universal elements; they are the only creatures who can represent the wise, majestic activity of the sovereignty of that Lordship everywhere on the earth, from its very core to the Pleiades and beyond.

For example, the lifeless, soulless laws of philosophy show the creation of the earth and its "natural" duties to be dark and desolate. However, Ibn 'Abbas narrates in reference to earlier Prophets of the Children of Israel that the earth sits on the shoulders of two angels called *Thawr* (the Ox) and *Hut* (the Fish). According to this narration, these angels supervise the earth. Furthermore, a substance called *sakhra*, belonging to the other world, is said to be the foundation stone of the earth and will be used in the transformation of a certain part of the earth into Paradise. This provides a perspective from which one may understand the real meaning of the narration, namely that the earth rests on the shoulders of these beings known as *Thawr* and *Hut*. Unfortunately, this figurative description came to be taken literally over the course of time, taking on a completely irrational complexion, whereas the fruit of belief in the angels illuminates the earth, its creation and duties. Since the angels travel through earth and rock and the center of the globe in the same way that they travel through the air, neither they nor the earth have need of physical rocks, or a fish or an ox to support them!

Also, since the earth offers Divine glorifications with as many heads as there are species of beings, with tongues to the number of the members of those species, and to the number of the parts, leaves, and fruits of those members, then surely in order to consciously represent this magnificent, unconscious "natural" worship and offer it to the Divine Court, there will be an appointed angel with forty thousand heads, glorifying God with each of its forty thousand tongues, and with each tongue uttering forty thousand Divine glorifications. The Trustworthy Reporter, upon him be peace and blessings, informed us of this as a truth. This shows that the existence and extraordinary nature of angels, such as Gabriel, upon him be peace, who communicates and manifests God's relationship with humanity, the most significant result of the creation of the universe; Israfil and Azra'il, upon them be peace, who represent and watch with adoration the awesome activity of the Creator in the world of living beings, such as giving life, restoring to life, and discharging from duties through death; Michael, upon him be peace, who, in addition to watching the All-Merciful's providing for His creatures, which is the most extensive and pleasurable act of Mercy in the sphere of life, consciously represents unconscious thanks. The existence and extraordinary nature of angels like these and the immortality of their spirits are necessitated by the sovereignty and magnificence of Divine Lordship. Their existence and that of the species to which each belongs is as certain as the existence of the sovereignty and magnificence that can be observed in the universe as clearly as the sun. Other matters concerning the angels may be approached from this perspective.

The All-Powerful One of Grace and Majesty has created hundreds of thousands of species of living beings on the earth; He has created beings with spirits in great abundance, even out of base and rotten substances, filling the cosmos with them. With regard to the miracles of His Art He causes them to declare: "What wonders God has willed! How blessed is God and how great are His blessings! All-Glorified is God!", and with regard to the gifts of His Mercy: "All praise and gratitude are for God! All thanks be to God! God is the All-Great!" Most certainly, therefore, He has created inhabitants and spirit beings appropriate for the vast heavens, beings who never rebel and perform constant worship. Not leaving the heavens empty, He has created countless different kinds of angels, far greater in number than the animal species. Some of them ride on the raindrops and snowflakes and applaud the Divine Art and Mercy in their own languages. Others ride on the moving stars and, on their journeys through space, proclaim to the world their worship in the form of the exaltation of God and the declaration of His Unity with regard to the grandeur, dignity and magnificence of Lordship.

The agreement of all the revealed Scriptures and religions since the time of Adam concerning the existence and worship of the angels, and the numerous unanimous reports in all ages of the conversations and meetings that human beings have had with angels, prove that their existence is as certain as the existence of the people of America, whom we have never seen; it is also clear that the angels are concerned with us.

Now come and experience, through the light of belief, this universal fruit: see how it fills the universe from end to end, beautifying it and transforming it into a vast mosque or place of worship. While scientific materialism and atheistic philosophy show the cosmos to be cold, lifeless, dark and desolate, belief reveals that it is full of life and light. It shows that it is conscious, familiar, and most agreeable, allowing the people of belief to experience a manifestation of the pleasures of eternal life, each according to the degree of their belief while still in this world.

In conclusion: On account of the unity in the universe which arises from God's Oneness, the same Power, the same Names, the same Wisdom, and the same Art prevail in every part of the universe, and all creatures, individually or as a species, proclaim the Creator's Unity, His absolute Control and Authority, His Creativity, Lordship, and Holiness through their tongues of disposition. In the same way, He has created the angels and populated the heavens with them, causing them to represent and offer through their worshipful tongues the glorifications which all unconscious creatures

The
Second Chapter

The Second Chapter

God's Final, Conclusive Argument

This treatise consists of eleven proofs for belief.

The First Proof: The Supreme Sign

This consists of the observations (in nineteen steps) of a traveler who questions the universe concerning their Creator.

In the Name of God, the All-Merciful, the All-Compassionate.

The seven heavens and the earth, and whoever is therein, glorify Him. There is nothing but it glorifies Him with His praise (proclaiming that He alone is God, without peer or partner, and all praise belongs to Him exclusively), but you cannot comprehend their glorification. Surely He is All-Clement, All-Forgiving. (17:44)

The First Step

NDEED, EVERY GUEST WHO COMES TO THE GUESTHOUSE OR THE ABODE of this world opens their eyes and sees that this exquisite guesthouse is a place of the most generous of banquets, an extremely artistically-built exhibition, a most magnificent military camp and training ground, a most amazing, inspiring, and enthusing place of recreation and observation, and a most meaningful and wise place of instruction. Such a person asks themselves who is the owner of this exquisite guesthouse, the author of this supreme book, the sovereign of this splendid realm. The first thing that they catch sight of is the beautiful face of the heavens, inscribed as they are with the gilt lettering of light. It calls out to this person, saying, "Look at me, and I will guide you to whom you seek."

They then look and see the manifestation of a supreme lordship—mastership and administration—which holds aloft, without any supporting pillars, hundreds of thousands of heavenly bodies, some of which are a thousand times heavier than the earth and which move many times faster than a cannon-ball. It causes these bodies to move together in harmony and at an extraordinarily great speed without colliding. It also causes innumerable lamps to give constant light without the use of any oil; it controls and manages these great masses without any disturbance or disorder; it makes huge bodies like the sun and the moon work at their respective tasks without allowing any rebellion; it operates within infinite space—the measure of which cannot be calculated or expressed with figures—all at the same time, with the same strength, in the same established fashion and manner, without the least fault. It makes all those bodies with their massive, aggressive powers obey its law unconditionally and absolutely, without allowing any aggression; it keeps the face of the heavens constantly clean and shining without allowing any refuse to remain behind to sully it; it causes those bodies to maneuver like a disciplined army, and by making the earth revolve, it shows to the audience of creation many other real or imagined forms of that magnificent maneuver, every night and every year, like the scenes on a movie screen. This supreme mastership and administration manifests subjugation, management, direction, ordering, cleansing, and employment. This is a sublime and comprehensive truth, and with this sublimity and comprehensiveness this truth bears witness to the absolutely necessary Existence and Unity of the Creator of the heavens and testifies openly to the fact that His Existence is clearer than the existence of the heavens. Hence, in the first step, it is proclaimed as follows:

> There is no deity but God, the Necessarily Existent One, Whose necessary Existence in His Unity is demonstrated clearly by the heavens with whatever there is in them. This is testified to by the sublimely comprehensive, vast and perfect reality of subjugation, management, direction, ordering, cleansing, and employment, all of which are clearly observable.

The Second Step

Then the atmosphere, which is a place of wonders, begins to proclaim thunderously to that traveler who has arrived in the world as a guest, "Look at me! You can discover and know through me the One Whom you are seeking, the One Who has sent you to the world!" The traveler looks at the apparently sour, but compassionate face of the atmosphere, and listens to its roaring messages, awesome, yet laden with glad tidings. The traveler comes to observe the following:

The clouds, suspended between the sky and the earth, water the garden of the world in a most wise and merciful fashion, bringing the water of life to the inhabitants of the earth, modifying the natural heat of life, and running to provide aid wherever it is needed. Having fulfilled these and other duties, like a well-organized army that reveals or conceals itself instantaneously according to the commands given to it, the vast clouds, filling the atmosphere, suddenly hide themselves, retiring to rest with their constituent parts so that no trace can be seen. Then, when they receive the command: "March forth to pour down rain!" the clouds come together in an hour, or in a few minutes, filling the atmosphere and standing as though in readiness for further orders from their commander.

Next the traveler looks at the winds and sees that the air is employed wisely and generously in so many tasks that it is as if each of the unconscious atoms of the inanimate air were able to hear and understand the orders coming from the Sovereign of the universe. Without neglecting a single one of them, it carries out its Master's orders in a perfectly methodical fashion, through the Power of the Sovereign. That is, it gives breath to all beings on the earth, conveys to all living creatures the heat, light, and electricity they need, and transmits sound, as well as aiding in the pollination of plants. It is employed by an unseen Hand in these universal tasks in an extremely conscious, knowledgeable, and life-sustaining manner.

The traveler then looks at the rain and sees that in these delicate, shining, and sweet drops that have been sent from a hidden treasury of Mercy there are so many merciful gifts and tasks that it is as if mercy itself were embodied in rain and flowing forth from the Divine treasury in the form of drops. It is for this reason that rain is called "mercy."

Then the traveler looks at the lightning and listens to the thunder and sees that both of these, too, are employed in the most amazing and wonderful tasks.

Taking their eyes off these, the traveler then turns to their reason and says to themselves: "This inanimate, lifeless cloud that resembles carded cotton certainly has no knowledge of us, and it does not come to our aid on its own because it has no consciousness so that it may take pity on us. Nor can it appear and disappear without an external command. Rather, it must act in accordance with the commands of a most Powerful and Compassionate Commander. It disappears without leaving a trace and then suddenly emerges again to embark on its task. By the Decree and Power of a most active and transcendent, a most magnificent and self-manifesting Sovereign, from time to time it fills and empties the atmosphere. It turns the sky into a tablet upon which things are written and erased, inscribing with wisdom and effacing by halting for a while, thus displaying an example of the Resurrection. By the order of a most generous and bountiful, a most munificent and attentive Ruler and Director, it mounts the wind and is laden with the treasuries of rain as heavy as mountains, hastening to the aid of places in need. It is as if it were weeping with pity over those places, spraying gardens with water, causing them to smile with flowers, cooling the heat of the sun and cleansing the face of the earth."

The curious traveler then tells their reason: "These hundreds of thousands of wise, merciful, and ingenious tasks, and these acts of generosity and helpfulness which seem to occur by means of this lifeless, unconscious, unstable, stormy, unsettled, and inconstant air, which cannot possess a conscious aim, prove beyond all doubt that the wind, this assiduous servant, never acts of its own volition; rather, it merely carries out the command of a most powerful and knowing, a most wise and munificent Commander. It is as though each of its atoms were aware of every task and, like a soldier who understands and heeds every order of his commander, were able to hear and obey every Divine command that courses through the air. It serves the breathing and survival of all animals, facilitates the pollination and growth of all plants, and provides all of the substances vital for their existence. It also serves the movement and direction of the clouds, the driving forward of sailing ships and the transmittance of sounds uttered or sent particularly by means of wireless, telephone, telegraph, and radio. In addition to serving in these and other universal functions, and despite being a composition of two simple materials—nitrogen and oxygen—and resembling one another, the particles of air are employed in hundreds of thousands of different tasks with a perfect order by a Hand of wisdom.

> Surely in the creation of the heavens and the earth, and the alternation of night and day (with their periods shortening and lengthening), and the vessels that sail the sea for profit to people, and the water that God sends down from the sky, therewith reviving the earth after its death and dispersing therein all kinds of living creatures, and His disposal of the winds, and the subservient clouds, resting between the sky and the earth—surely there are signs (demonstrating that He is the One God deserving worship, and the sole Refuge and Helper) for a people who reason and understand (2:164).

As stated in the above verse, the traveler concludes that the one who disposes of the winds and employs them in innumerable tasks of sustaining, maintaining, and nurturing; who subjugates the clouds so that they may be used in uncountable errands of mercy and who generates and employs the air in the fashion mentioned above—that such a being can be none other than the All-Majestic and All-Munificent Lord, One Who is Necessarily Existent, Who is All-Knowing and in possession of absolute Power over all things.

The traveler then looks at the rain and sees that it has as many merciful uses, benefits, and instances of wisdom as the number of drops contained in it. Moreover, these lovely, delicate, and blessed drops, as well as the drops of hail and snowflakes, are created so beautifully and with such order and are dispatched with such balance and regularity that not even those stormy winds which cause large objects to collide can destroy this order: the drops do not collide with one another or combine in such a way as to form harmful masses of water. This simple substance, water, which is composed of two simple, inanimate and unconscious elements—hydrogen and oxygen—is employed in hundreds of thousands of wise, purposeful tasks and arts, particularly in animate beings. This means that rain, which is the very embodiment of mercy, can be manufactured only in the unseen treasury of mercy of the One Who is All-Merciful. And through its descent it expounds in physical terms the verse: *He it is Who sends down the rain, useful in all ways, to rescue (them) after they have lost all hope, and spreads out His mercy far and wide (to every being). He it is Who is the Guardian, and the All-Praiseworthy* (42:28).

The traveler then listens to the thunder attentively and looks again at the lightning. He perceives that in addition to interpreting in physical terms the verses: *The thunder glorifies Him with His praise* (13:13), and *The flash of the lightning almost takes away the sight* (24:43), these two awe-inspiring atmospheric events also announce the coming of rain, thus giving glad tidings to those in need of it. And in causing the atmosphere to speak suddenly with an extraordinary uproar, in filling the dark atmosphere with the marvelous light and fire of lightning, and in setting alight the clouds that resemble mountains of cotton or spouts from which hail or snow or rain pours, these and other wondrous and wise phenomena strike blows on the heads of the negligent people who "look down and cannot see them." They warn, saying: "Lift up your heads and look at the wonderful acts of an Ever-Active and Powerful Being Who wills to make Himself known. Just as you are not left to your own devices, so too these phenomena are not random events left to chance. Each of them is employed in many wise tasks; each is employed by an All-Wise Director."

Thus, the curious traveler hears the loud and manifest testimony of a truth which is composed of the subjugation of the clouds, the disposal of the winds, the descent of the rain and the direction of atmospheric events, and says: "I believe in God." That which is pronounced in this second step expresses the above-mentioned observations of the traveler concerning the atmosphere:

> There is no deity but God, the Necessarily Existent One, Whose Necessary Existence is demonstrated clearly by the atmosphere with whatever there is in it. This is testified to by the sublimely comprehensive, vast and perfect reality of subjugation, disposal, and causing to descend, and management or direction, all of which are clearly observable.

The Third Step

And then the earth addresses that reflective traveler, who has now been accustomed to their journey of reflection, in the tongue of its disposition: "Why are you wandering through space, through the heavens? Come, I will make known to you the One Whom you are seeking. Look at the tasks I carry out and read my pages!"

The traveler looks and sees that, like an ecstatic Mevlevi dervish, the earth, having two movements that are the means for the occurrence of days, seasons, and years, is drawing a circle around the Place of Supreme Gathering. They see that it is a magnificent, subjugated vessel which holds within itself hundreds of thousands of species of living creatures together with all the food and equipment needed by them, a vessel that is traveling around the sun in the ocean of space with perfect balance and order.

The traveler then looks at the pages or sheets of the earth and sees that each page of every chapter proclaims the existence of the Lord of the earth in thousands of its "verses." Having no time to read the entire work, they look at the page which describes the creation and administration of living creatures in spring, and observe the following:

The forms of the numberless members of hundreds of thousands of species are opened up from a simple material with the most extraordinary orderliness and precision; they are then nurtured and raised in a most merciful fashion. Subsequently, the seeds of some of these members are, in a most miraculous fashion, given wings and caused to fly, thus allowing them to be scattered over the earth. All these numberless members of hundreds of thousands of species are directed with the utmost efficiency and fed and nurtured with the greatest affection. Their countless, diverse, and delicious nourishment is provided and made to reach them in the most compassionate manner from nothing more than dry clay, drops of water, and seeds and roots that resemble bones, differing little one from the other. In the same way that cargo is loaded onto a goods wagon, hundreds of thousands of different kinds of food and equipment are loaded on every spring from an unseen treasury and are dispatched with perfect orderliness to living creatures. In particular, the sending of canned milk in these food packages, brought to the mouths of infants in the form of the sweet milk that springs forth from the affectionate breasts of their mothers, demonstrates such affection, compassion, and wisdom that it can clearly be seen to be the gift and most affectionate and attentive manifestation of the Mercy of an All-Merciful One.

In short: By displaying hundreds of thousands of examples of the Resurrection and Supreme Gathering, this living page of spring interprets in brilliant fashion the verse, *Look, then, at the imprints of God's Mercy—how He revives the dead earth after its death: certainly then it is He Who will revive the dead (in a similar way). He has full power over everything* (30:50). Similarly, this verse expresses in a miraculous fashion the meanings of that page. The traveler thus understands that with all its pages the earth proclaims

"There is no deity but He," in a fashion and with a strength that is proportionate to its size.

Through the brief testimony of one of the twenty aspects of a single page out of more than the twenty big pages of the earth, the observations the traveler made in the other pages of the earth is expressed in this third step as follows:

> There is no deity but God, the Necessarily Existent One, Whose Necessary Existence in His Unity is demonstrated clearly by the earth with whatever there is in and upon it. This is testified to by the sublimely comprehensive, vast and perfect reality of subjugation, management, raising, opening up, the distribution of seeds, preservation, administration, and the provision of all living creatures, and the all-encompassing and all-inclusive mercifulness and compassion, all of which are clearly observable.

The Fourth Step

Then, as that reflective traveler reads each page of the earth, their belief, which is the key to true happiness, begins to gain strength; their knowledge of God, the key to spiritual progress, increases, and the truth of belief in God, the source and foundation of all perfection, develops in them one degree more, bestowing upon them many spiritual pleasures and further arousing their curiosity and eagerness. Having listened to the perfect and convincing lessons taught to them by the heavens, the atmosphere, and the earth, the traveler asks: "Is there more?" At which point they hear the loud, rapturous invocations of God made by the seas and the great rivers which flow into them; they listen awhile to these mournful and pleasant sounds. Both verbally and with mute eloquence they are saying: "Look at us and read us too!" And so the traveler looks, and this is what they see:

Although the seas, which are constantly surging with life, and which have an innate tendency toward pouring forth and flooding the land, and are made to move together with the earth, which revolves around the sun so speedily that it in one year it covers a distance that a person could walk in twenty-five thousand years, they neither disperse nor overflow, never encroaching on the land at whose edge their waters lap. This means that they are made to move and are held in place by the command and power of a most powerful and sublime being.

Looking into the depths of the sea, the traveler sees that in addition to the extremely beautiful, well-adorned, and proportioned jewels, thousands of kinds of animals are provided for, maintained, brought to life and caused to die in a perfectly balanced and orderly fashion. They also see that these creatures are provided for from nothing more than mere sand and water, but in such a perfect way that beyond doubt they establish the Existence of an All-Powerful One of Majesty, an All-Compassionate One of Grace.

The traveler then looks at the rivers and sees that the benefits they supply, the tasks they carry out, and the waters which both flow in and out of them display such wisdom and mercy that they prove quite clearly that all rivers, springs and streams flow forth from the treasury of mercy of an All-Merciful One of Majesty and Munificence. They are fed, preserved and dispensed in such an extraordinary fashion that it has been reported from the Prophet, upon him be peace and blessings: "Four rivers originate from Paradise." That is, since the reality of their flowing transcends apparent causes, they issue forth from the treasury of an immaterial heavenly source, from the superabundance of an unseen and inexhaustible wellspring.

The blessed Nile, for example, (the longest river of the world,) that turns the sandy land of Egypt into a paradise, originates from the Mountains of the Moon (or some highlands or hills or lakes) in central Africa and flows without exhaustion, as though it were a small sea. If the water it carries in six months were gathered together in the form of an iceberg, it would be larger than the mountains (or highlands or lakes) that act as its source. Yet the source of the river in those mountains does not equal even a sixth of their mass. As for the water which feeds the river, and the rain that enters its reservoir, they amount to very little in such a hot region and are quickly swallowed up by the thirsty soil; as a result they are incapable of maintaining the balance between the amount of the water being added to and flowing away from the river. Thus the Prophetic Tradition which says that the blessed Nile originates, in an extraordinary fashion, from an unseen heavenly source is extremely meaningful and expresses a beautiful reality.

Thus, the traveler sees a thousandth part of the ocean-like truths and testimonies contained in the oceans and rivers. All of these truths pronounce unanimously and with a power that is proportionate to the size of

the seas, "*There is no deity but He,*" while the seas produce as many witnesses for this testimony as all the creatures that inhabit them. This much the
traveler perceives.

Intending and expressing the testimony of the seas and the rivers, it is
declared in this fourth step:

> There is no deity but God, the Necessarily Existent One, Whose
> Necessary Existence in His Unity is demonstrated clearly by all the
> seas and rivers with whatever there is in them. This is testified to by
> the sublimely comprehensive, vast and perfect reality of subjugation,
> preservation, storing, and management, all of which are clearly ob-
> servable.

The Fifth Step

Then the mountains and the plains summon that traveler on their journey
of reflection, saying: "Read our pages too!" Looking, the traveler sees:

The universal tasks carried out by the mountains, along with the purposes they serve, are so great and full of wisdom that they astonish the mind.
For instance, the mountains burst forth from the earth's crust by the command of their Lord and thereby calm down the unrest, anger and fury that
arise from commotions within the bowels of the earth. Yet while the earth
is delivered from the harmful tremors and upheavals within it and is allowed
to breath through the bursting forth of these mountains, it does not disturb
the rest or comfort of its inhabitants as it carries out its duty of rotation. Just
as masts are placed on ships to protect them against turbulence and maintain their balance, according to the Qur'an of miraculous exposition, the
mountains are like masts that have been planted on the deck of the vessel
that is the earth:

> And the mountains as masts, (78:7)

> And the earth—We have spread it out, and set therein firm moun-
> tains, (15:19; 50:7)

> And the mountains He has set firm. (79:32)

Furthermore, prepared and stored up in the mountains are countless
things that are needed by living beings, such as springs, waters, minerals
and medicinal substances; these are stored up and preserved there in such
a wise, skilful, generous and careful fashion that they can only be the

storehouses and servants of one of infinite power and wisdom. This much the traveler deduces, and comparing with these two the other duties and instances of wisdom that are inherent in the mountains and plains, they can see the testimony they give and the Divine Unity they pronounce, saying, "*There is no deity but He,*" through the general instances of wisdom hidden in them and, in particular, in regard to the things providentially stored up in them. And seeing that their pronouncement is as powerful and firm as the mountains and as vast and expansive as the plains themselves, the traveler too declares: "I believe in God."

As an expression of this meaning, it is proclaimed in this fifth step:

> There is no deity but God, the Necessarily Existent One, Whose Necessary Existence is demonstrated clearly by all the mountains and plains, with whatever there is in or on them. This is testified to by sublimely comprehensive, vast and perfect reality of storing up and management, by the dissemination of seeds, the preservation and precautionary measures that are particular to Divine Lordship, all of which are clearly observable.

The Sixth Step

Then as that traveler is journeying in their mind through the mountains and plains, the gateway to the world of trees and plants is opened to them. They are invited to enter with the words: "Come, travel through our world and read our inscriptions." Entering there, the traveler sees that they have formed a magnificent and well-adorned assembly that proclaims God's Unity and a circle that mentions Him by His Names and offers thanks to Him. The traveler can understand from the very appearance of all the trees and plants that, with all their species they unanimously proclaim: "*There is no deity but God.*" For they notice three great, universal realities which indicate and prove the fact that in the tongue of their well-proportioned and eloquent leaves, with the phrases of their richly-adorned and fluent flowers, and the words of their well-ordered and articulate fruits, all fruit-bearing trees and plants glorify God and testify to His Unity, saying "*There is no deity but He.*"

THE FIRST REALITY: Each of the plants and trees gives the clear impression that they have been provided with a deliberate purpose and are intentionally maintained. This fact is also observed in the totality of the trees and plants with the brilliance of sunlight.

THE SECOND REALITY: In the countless varieties and species a wise and purposeful distinguishing and differentiation, and a willful and compassionate fashioning, equipping and adorning, none of which is in any way attributable to chance, can be seen as clearly as daylight: they reveal quite clearly the fact that they are the works and embroideries of an All-Wise Maker.

THE THIRD REALITY: Each of the members of these hundreds of thousands of species of plants and trees is given a separate, distinct form with the most perfect order, balance, proportion and beauty, with vitality and wise purposefulness, and without the least error, from simple and solid seeds and grains that are identical or nearly identical to one another. This is a reality more brilliant than the sun and there are as many witnesses that prove this truth as there are flowers, fruits and leaves that appear in spring. The traveler perceives this and says: "All praise be to God for the blessing of belief."

As an expression of these realities and the testimonies given to them it is said in the sixth step:

> There is no deity but God, the Necessarily Existent One, Whose Necessary Existence in His Unity is demonstrated clearly by all species of trees and plants, which glorify God and speak with the words of their well-proportioned, eloquent leaves, their fluent, richly-adorned flowers and their well-ordered, articulate fruits. This is testified to by the sublimely comprehensive, vast and perfect reality of purposeful and compassionate provision, bestowal and favoring, and of willful and wise distinguishing, adorning and fashioning, all of which are clearly observable. It is also clearly indicated by the fact that each of these trees and plants is given a well-proportioned, decorated, distinctive, separate form from similar or near-identical seeds and grains, all of which are finite and limited.

The Seventh Step

Then, as that curious traveler, whose journey of reflection becomes more pleasurable with every step, returns from the garden of spring with a bouquet of knowledge of God and belief, itself like a spring, the gateway to the realm of earth's animals and birds open before their truth-perceiving mind and intellect, which has by this time acquired knowledge of God to a certain degree. With hundreds of thousands of different voices and various tongues, they summon the traveler inside.

Entering, they see that all the species, groups and nations of the animals and birds of the earth are pronouncing: *"There is no deity but He,"* both verbally and in the language of mute eloquence of their disposition, turning the earth into a vast assembly for the proclamation of God's Unity and the mentioning of Him by His Names. The traveler sees that they are describing their Maker and praising Him as if each is an ode dedicated to Him as the Lord, a word which glorifies Him or a letter that indicates His mercy. It is as if the senses, powers, members and instruments of these animals and birds are graceful, rhythmical, well-proportioned words, or perfect and orderly expressions. The traveler observes three great and comprehensive realities which indicate decisively that they offer thanks to their Creator and Provider and testify to His Unity.

THE FIRST REALITY: Animals and birds are brought into existence from nothing with wisdom, they are created and fashioned with complete artistry and perfect knowledge and given life in a way that displays in twenty aspects the manifestation of knowledge, wisdom and will—all of this, which occurs in such a way that it cannot be attributed to chance, testifies to the Necessary Existence, the Seven Essential Attributes, and the Unity of the All-Living, Self-Subsistent One—a testimony that is based on as many proofs as there are living beings.

THE SECOND REALITY: In the distinction of facial features which exists among these infinite beings, in their adorned forms, and in their perfectly calculated numbers and well-ordered fashioning, there appears a truth so magnificent and powerful that it is absolutely impossible and inconceivable for anyone other than the One Who has absolute Power and Knowledge to be able to achieve such a comprehensive act, an act that displays thousands of wonders and instances of wisdom in every respect.

THE THIRD REALITY: Each of the hundreds of thousands of species of these innumerable animals and birds is given in the most orderly and proportionate fashion and without the least error, a distinctive face and form— a miracle of wisdom—that emerges from eggs and drops of fluid called sperm, which are identical to or closely resemble one another. This is so brilliant a reality that it is illuminated by as many different proofs as there are animals and birds in existence.

Through the consensus of these three realities, all the species of animals testify together that *"There is no deity but He."* It is as if the whole earth, like a vast human being, were saying *"There is no deity but He,"* in a manner commensurate with its vastness, and conveying its testimony to the inhabitants of the heavens. The traveler sees this and understands it perfectly. As an expression of these realities, it is declared in the seventh step:

> There is no deity but God, the Necessarily Existent One, Whose Necessary Existence in His Unity is demonstrated clearly by all the species of the earth's animals and birds, which praise God and bear witness to Him with the measured, well-proportioned and fluent words of their senses, powers, and faculties, and with the perfect and eloquent words of their members, limbs, and organs. This is testified to by the sublimely comprehensive, vast and perfect reality of purposeful inventing, making, and originating, by the reality of purposeful distinguishing and adorning, and by the reality of wise determining, identifying, and fashioning, all of which are clearly observable. It is also decisively indicated by the fact that each of these animals and birds is given a well-ordered, different, and distinctive form that emerges from similar or seemingly-identical eggs and drops of fluid, all of which are finite and limited.

The Eighth Step

Afterwards, the reflective traveler wishes to enter the world of humanity in order to advance further in the infinite ranks and unlimited degrees of pleasure and the lights of knowledge of God. And thus, humankind, headed by the Prophets, invites the traveler inside. Entering there, and looking first into the vast mansion that is the past, the traveler sees that all of the Prophets, upon them be peace, who are the most luminous and perfect of all people, proclaim in unison: *"There is no deity but He."* With the power of their innumerable brilliant and confirmed miracles, they are affirming and pronouncing God's Unity, and in order to raise humanity from the rank of animals to that of angels, they are instructing people in belief in God and summoning them to it. Kneeling down in that school of light, the traveler also pays heed to the lesson and observes the following:

All of these teachers, the most exalted and renowned of all celebrated human beings, have in their hands numerous miracles that have been bestowed on them by the Creator of the universe as a sign that confirms their mission. In addition, a large group of people, a whole community, has confirmed their claims and reached belief through their instruction. The traveler sees how powerful, decisive, and definitive a truth it is that was agreed on unanimously and confirmed by these more than one hundred thousand serious and veracious individuals. The traveler also understands that by denying a truth attested to and affirmed by so many absolutely truthful instructors, the people of misguidance are committing a most grievous error—nay, a crime—and are thus deserving of a most painful everlasting punishment. The traveler perceives, in contrast, how truly righteous are those who confirm the message of the Prophets and come to belief, and thus a further degree of the sanctity of belief becomes apparent to the traveler.

Apart from the innumerable miracles worked by the Prophets, upon them be peace, as a sign of God's actual confirmation of them and their mission; apart from the heavenly blows dealt to their opponents, which demonstrate the truthfulness of the Prophets; apart from their individual perfections and veracious teachings, which indicate their truthfulness and righteousness; apart from the strength of their faith, their supreme seriousness, and self-sacrifices, which demonstrate their honesty; apart from the sacred Books and Scrolls they hold in their hands, and apart from their countless pupils who have attained truth, perfection, and light by following them, thus proving the truthfulness of their paths—apart from all of these realities, the unanimous agreement of the Prophets, who are the most earnest conveyors of God's Messages, and their followers on all true, positive matters, and their concord, mutual support, and affinity in establishing and proving the same all constitute a proof so powerful that no power in the world is able to confront it, and no doubt or hesitation can be cast. The traveler comes to understand that belief in all the Prophets, upon them be peace, as one of the pillars of belief, is another source of power, and they derive great benefit of belief from the lessons that they taught.

In expression of the lessons learned by this traveler, in the eighth step it is declared:

> There is no deity but God, Whose Necessary Existence in His Unity is demonstrated clearly by the consensus of all the Prophets with the power of the manifest miracles which confirm (their missions and Messages) and are confirmed (by innumerable people and unanimously accepted reports).

The Ninth Step

While the questing traveler, who has derived an elevated taste of truth from the power of belief, is coming from the assembly of the Prophets, upon them be peace, they are invited to step into the schoolroom of the profound, veracious and purified scholars who confirm the claims of the Prophets, upon them be peace, with the most decisive and powerful proofs which reach the degree of certainty based on knowledge. Entering here, the traveler sees that with their profound studies and investigations, thousands of geniuses and hundreds of thousands of veracious and exalted scholars are first and foremost proving the necessity of God's Existence and His Unity, together with all other articles of belief, which are absolutely true. And they are doing this in a manner which leaves absolutely no room for doubt. Indeed, the fact that they unanimously agree on the principles and pillars of belief, despite the fact that they differ in their capacities and outlook, each of them leaning on their own firm and certain proof, constitutes in itself evidence so strong that it cannot be doubted. Or, rather, we can see that it can be doubted only if the doubter possesses more intelligence and perspicacity than all of these scholars combined, and only if they are able to counter their arguments with a single proof that is more compelling than all those of the scholars put together. Otherwise, the deniers can oppose them only in order to display their ignorance— their utter ignorance—and their obstinacy and biased inattention with respect to negative matters that admit neither denial nor affirmation. One with a biased inattention or who closes their eyes turns day into night only for themselves.

The traveler realizes that the lights which these respected and profound scholars disseminate from this magnificent and vast school have been illuminating half of the world for more than a thousand years. The traveler finds in these lights such moral and spiritual power that if all the people of denial were to come together against them, they would neither be able to confuse or shake the traveler.

In a brief reference to the lesson the traveler has learned in this school, in the ninth step it is said:

> There is no deity but God, Whose Necessary Existence in His Unity is demonstrated clearly by the agreement of all the pure, saintly and veracious scholars with the power of their brilliant, certain and unanimous proofs.

The Tenth Step

As the reflective traveler, who eagerly desires to see the lights and pleasures in the strengthening and development of belief and in the progression from the degree of certainty that arises from knowledge to certainty that comes from vision or observation, is leaving the school of religious sciences, they receive another invitation. This time, it comes from the thousands, indeed, millions of spiritual guides who are working for the truth and have attained the rank of certainty of vision or observation along the highway of Muhammad and in the shade of his Ascension, upon him be peace and blessings. They invite the traveler into a vast, light-diffusing school of spiritual training, a place of the remembrance of God, which has been formed from the merging of countless small schools of spiritual illumination.

Entering here, the traveler sees that these spiritual guides, who are the masters of extraordinary deeds and adept at unveiling the Divine truths and spiritual mysteries, are proclaiming in unison *"There is no deity but He"* on the basis of their unveilings, visions, and wonder-working, and to the entire universe they announce the necessary Existence and Unity of the Lord. The traveler sees here how clear and self-evident this truth is, a truth upon which all of these sacred genius and luminous savants have achieved total consensus, even though they follow numerous different spiritual paths. The traveler sees how, in the same way that the sun radiates seven colors in its light and is known through them, these luminous individuals are, in their knowledge of God, holding fast to an array of colors emitted by the Sun of Eternity, as great in number as the All-Beautiful Names of God Himself. The traveler sees that the supreme consensus formed through the unanimity of the Prophets, the agreement of the purified and veracious scholars and the accord of the saints is more brilliant than the daylight which makes known the existence of the sun.

In a brief reference to the rays of light received by the traveler from the school of spiritual training, in the tenth step it is proclaimed:

> There is no deity but God, Whose Necessary Existence in His Unity is demonstrated clearly by the agreement of the saints with their manifest, verified, and confirmed spiritual discoveries and extraordinary deeds or achievements.

The Eleventh Step

The traveler is now aware that the greatest and most important of all human perfections, indeed the very origin and foundation of all such perfections, is the love of God that arises from belief in God and knowledge of Him. With this in mind, the traveler wishes with all their strength and faculties to advance still further in strengthening their belief and in the development of their knowledge. And thus the traveler raises their head and, gazing at the heavens, addresses their own reasoning mind as follows:

> Because the most valuable thing in the universe is life and all things in the universe are subservient to life, and because the most valuable beings among all living beings are those which are endowed with spirit, and because the most valuable among beings endowed with spirit are those who are conscious, and because each century and each year the earth is emptied and refilled in order to increase without cessation the number of living beings due to their value— because of all this, one must undoubtedly conclude that these splendid and ornate heavens must also have living, conscious inhabitants that are peculiar to them. Experiences relating to seeing and speaking with the angels—such as the appearance of Archangel Gabriel, upon him be peace, in the form of a human being in the presence of Prophet Muhammad, upon him be peace and blessings, in full view of the Companions—have been transmitted and related from the most ancient times through reliable channels of transmission. Given that this is so, if only I could talk to the inhabitants of the heavens and learn their views on this matter. For their words concerning the Creator of the universe are of utmost importance.

As the traveler is thinking thus, he suddenly hears a heavenly voice: "If you wish to meet us and hear our words, then know that we before all others have believed in the truths of belief that we conveyed to the Prophets, and first and foremost to Prophet Muhammad, upon him be peace and blessings, who brought the Qur'an of miraculous exposition.

"Furthermore, all of the pure spirits from among us who have appeared before human beings have, unanimously and without exception, borne witness to the necessary Existence and sacred Attributes of the Creator of the universe, and proclaimed this with one accord. The concord and mutual correspondence of these uncountable proclamations is a guide for you that is as bright as the sun." As a result, the traveler's light of belief grows more radiant and ascends from the earth to the heavens.

In a brief reference to the lesson the traveler has learned from the angels, it is said in the eleventh step:

> There is no deity but God, Whose Necessary Existence in His Unity is demonstrated clearly by the agreement of the angels who appear to human beings in human form and who speak to the spiritually distinguished ones among humankind with their mutually corresponding and conforming messages.

The Twelfth and Thirteenth Steps

Then the extremely inquisitive and ardent traveler, who has already learned from the tongues and dispositions of various species and nations that belong to the visible realm, expresses the desire to travel through the realm of the Unseen and the Intermediate Realm in further pursuit of the truth. And so there opens before them a door that leads to the world of upright and enlightened intellects and of sound and illuminated hearts, which are like the seeds of humankind, the fruit of the universe, and which can expand to embrace virtually the whole of the universe, despite their small size. The traveler looks and sees that these intellects and hearts form a link between the Unseen and visible realms, and that the contacts and exchanges between these two realms which relate to humankind occur at this point. Addressing their reason and heart, the traveler says: "Come, the path leading to the truth through the gate of these counterparts of yours is shorter. We should benefit from studying the qualities, natures, and colors that belief has given them, in a manner different from that which we have employed in learning through the tongues which pertain to previous paths."

Beginning this study, the traveler sees that the belief and firm conviction concerning Divine Unity which all upright and enlightened intellects possess and display throughout their lives is, despite their varying capacities and their different and sometimes opposing methods and outlooks, in complete accordance; the traveler sees that their constant and ever-confident certainty and assurance are as one. This means that they are holding fast to a single, unchanging truth: their roots have penetrated deeply into this truth and cannot be pulled out. As a result, their agreement concerning belief and the necessary Existence and Unity of God is like a luminous, unbreakable chain, a brightly lit window that opens onto the truth.

The traveler also sees that the rapturous spiritual discoveries and visions of all these sound and illuminated hearts concerning the pillars of belief are, despite their different spiritual paths, in correspondence with one another, and that they are in absolute agreement on Divine Unity. All of these illuminated hearts, each of which is an embodiment of truth, a small throne of knowledge of God and a comprehensive mirror that is held up to the Eternally Besought One, are like windows that open onto the sun of the truth. Taken together, they are a supreme mirror, like an ocean that reflects the sun. Their agreement and unanimity concerning the necessary Existence and Unity of God is an unfailing and most perfect guide, a most elevated master. For it is in no way possible or conceivable that any false assumption or erroneous belief should be able to delude or deceive so many sharp, truth-seeing eyes at the same time. Not even the foolish sophists, who denied the existence of the universe, could agree with the corrupt and dissipated intellect that deemed such a thing possible. Understanding all of this, our traveler says with their heart and intellect: "I have come to believe in God."

In a brief reference to the knowledge of belief which the traveler has learned from upright intellects and illuminated hearts, in the twelfth and thirteenth steps it is proclaimed:

> There is no deity but God, the Necessarily Existent, Whose Necessary Existence in His Unity is demonstrated clearly by the unanimous agreement of all upright, enlightened intellects, with their congruent creeds, their convictions and corresponding certainties, despite their differences in capacity and outlook. His Necessary Existence in His Unity is also demonstrated by the agreement of all sound, illuminated hearts, with their mutually supporting discoveries and their congruent observations and visions, despite their varying paths and methods.

The Fourteenth and Fifteenth Steps

Then that traveler, who is journeying with their mind and heart, begins to look at the Realm of the Unseen more closely. Knocking inquisitively on the door of that world in order to learn its message, they think to himself: "It is obvious that behind the veil of the Unseen is One Who wills to make Himself known through all these innumerable, finely adorned artifacts in the visible world; He wills to make Himself loved through these countless, sweet, and adorned bounties, and to make His hidden Perfections known through these uncountable, miraculous, and skilful works of Art. It is clear that there is One Who reveals His will to make Himself known and loved, and to make His hidden Perfections known, in a manner more manifest than speech. Given this, just as He reveals His will through acts and deeds, it is clear that He must also make Himself known and loved through speech. Thus, we must know Him from His manifestations with regard to the World of the Unseen." Thinking this, the traveler enters that world with their heart and sees the following with the eye of their intellect:

The truth of the Revelations prevails at all times throughout the World of the Unseen as the most powerful means of manifestation. A testimony to God's Existence and Unity that is much more powerful than that of the universe and its contents proceeds from the One All-Knowing of the Unseen through the truths of Revelation and inspiration. He does not restrict the recognition and affirmation of Himself, His Existence, and Unity to the testimony of His creatures alone. Rather, He speaks with a preeternal Speech which befits His own Being. The Speech of the One Who is Omnipresent everywhere with His Knowledge and Power is also infinite, and just as the meaning of His Speech makes Him known, His discourse also makes Himself known together with His Attributes.

The truth of Revelation has been established and made clear to a self-evident degree through the consensus of more than one hundred thousand Prophets, may peace be upon them, and through the fact that all the instructions and proclamations of these Prophets are based on Divine Revelation; it has also been made clear through the evidence and miracles contained in the sacred Books and heavenly Scrolls, which are the fruits of Revelation and guides for all human beings, the overwhelming majority of whom have confirmed the truths therein. Realizing this, the traveler understands further that the truth of Revelation sets forth the following five sacred realities.

THE FIRST REALITY: Revelation is a form of Divine kindness or condescension and is described as "God's lowering His speech to the level of human capacity so that they can understand it." God enables all of His conscious creatures to speak and understands their speeches, so it is a requirement of His being the Lord of all creation that He participates in them with His own speech.

THE SECOND REALITY: The One Who, in order to make Himself known, has created a universe filled with miraculous, invaluable artifacts that cause countless tongues to speak of His Perfections, will, self-evidently, make Himself known with His own words also.

THE THIRD REALITY: It is a characteristic of His being the Creator that God responds with His speech, as He does with His deeds, to the supplications and thanks that are offered by the most select, the neediest, the most delicate and the most ardent of His beings—those who are truly human.

THE FOURTH REALITY: The attribute of speech, which is an essential requirement of knowledge and life and a luminous manifestation of both, will by necessity be found in a comprehensive and eternal form in the Being Who has comprehensive Knowledge and eternal Life.

THE FIFTH REALITY: It is a consequence of Divinity that the Being Who endows His most loved and lovable, His most anxious and indigent creatures—those who are most in need of a point of reliance and who are most desirous of finding their Owner and Master—with innate impotence and yearning, poverty and need, worries about the future, and love and adoration—it is a consequence of His Divinity that He should communicate His own Existence to them by way of His speech. Thus, the universal, heavenly Revelations, which involve the realities of God's lowering His speech to the level of human understanding, His will as the Lord to make Himself known, and His merciful response, majestic conversation, and self-communication as the Eternally Besought One, bear unanimous witness to the Existence and Unity of the Necessarily Existent One. This testimony is a proof that is more powerful than the testimony of the rays of sunlight to the existence of the sun. This is what the traveler has come to understand.

The traveler then considers the gift of inspiration and sees that true inspiration resembles the Revelation in one respect and is a form of the Lord's discourse. However, Revelation and inspiration differ in two respects:

THE FIRST DIFFERENCE: Revelation, which is much more exalted than inspiration, is generally conveyed by angels, whereas inspiration generally comes directly.

For example, a king has two ways to speak and communicate his orders. The first is that, in the name of the glory of his kingdom and his sovereignty over the whole country, he sends a lieutenant to a governor. Sometimes, in order to demonstrate the magnificence of his sovereignty and the importance of his imperial order, he may hold a meeting with his lieutenant, and then the decree is conveyed to the governor. The second is that he speaks on his private phone, not with the title of monarch or in the name of kingship, but in his own person, to a trusted servant or some ordinary subject with whom he has a special relationship or a particular business.

Similarly, the Pre-Eternal Sovereign may either, with the Name, the Lord of all the worlds and with the Title, the Creator of the universe, speak through Revelation or the comprehensive inspiration that has the function of Revelation, or He may speak in a private fashion, as the Lord and Creator of every and each living being, from behind a veil and in accordance with the capacities of the addressee.

THE SECOND DIFFERENCE: Revelation is clear, pure and reserved for the most elect. Inspiration, however, is not as clear as Revelation; colors may intervene in it and it is more general. There are numerous different kinds of inspiration, such as that which comes to angels, that which occurs to human beings, and that which is vouchsafed to animals; inspiration thus forms a field for the multiplication of God's words to the extent of the drops in the oceans. The traveler understands that the multiplication of God's words is a kind of commentary on the verse: Say: "If all the sea were ink to write my Lord's words, the sea would indeed be exhausted before my Lord's words would be exhausted, even if We were to bring the like of it in addition to it" (18:109).

Then the traveler looks at nature, wisdom, testimony, and the result of inspiration and sees that they comprise the following four lights:

THE FIRST LIGHT: This emerges because God is the All-Loving and the All-Merciful and thus He makes Himself loved through word, presence, and conversation just as He makes Himself loved by His creatures through His deeds.

THE SECOND LIGHT: This is a consequence of God's being the All-Compassionate; in the same way that He answers His servants' prayers in the form of deeds, He also answers them in words, from behind veils.

THE THIRD LIGHT: God's Lordship demands that just as He responds in deed to the pleas and cries for help of those creatures of His who have been afflicted with grievous tribulations and hardships, He also comes to their aid with words of inspiration, which are like a form of His speech.

THE FOURTH LIGHT: Just as God makes His existence, presence, and protection perceptible through His deeds to those among His conscious creatures who are poor, weak, and most in need of finding their Master, Protector, Guardian, and Preserver, it is also a consequence of His being the All-Affectionate Deity and the All-Compassionate Lord that He should also communicate His presence and existence by speech, through the filter of true inspiration—a mode of His discourse as the Lord—to individuals in a manner befitting them and their capacities, through the "telephone" of their hearts. This the traveler has come to understand.

The traveler then looks at the testimony of inspiration and sees that, for example, if the sun possessed consciousness and life, with the seven colors in its light being its seven attributes— like the seven positive or affirmative Attributes of God—then it would also possess a kind of speech through the rays and manifestations of its light. As it has reflections and images in all transparent things, it would speak to all mirrors, shining objects, fragments of glass, bubbles and droplets of water in accordance with the capacity of each. It would respond to the needs of everything in which it is reflected and all of these would testify to the existence of the sun. Furthermore, none of its acts would form obstacles to other acts, and addressing one object would not prevent it from addressing all other objects simultaneously. Similarly, the Speech of the Sun of Eternity, the eternal All-Majestic Sovereign, the All-Glorious, All-Gracious Creator of all things, Which is universal and all-encompassing, like His Knowledge and Power, manifests Itself according to the capacity of each thing or being. Its response to one request does not form an obstacle to Its response to all other requests, nor does any task It performs prevent Its fulfillment of other tasks. No matter how many beings It addresses, It never becomes confused. The traveler comes to understand, to the degree of certainty based on knowledge and vision, that all these manifestations, conversations, and inspirations—separately and together—bear unanimous witness to the Omnipresence and necessary Existence of that Sun of Eternity and to His Unity and Oneness.

In a brief reference to the lesson the inquisitive traveler has received regarding knowledge of God from the World of the Unseen, it is said in the fourteenth and fifteenth steps:

There is no deity but God, the Necessarily Existent One, the Single and the All-Unique, Whose Necessary Existence in His Unity is demonstrated clearly by the consensus of all true Revelations that involve God's lowering His Speech to the level of human understanding, His glorious discourses, His self-communication as the Lord, His responses to the pleas of His servants as the All-Merciful, and His indications of His Existence to His creatures as the Eternally Besought One. His necessary Existence in His Unity is also demonstrated by the unanimous agreement of all veracious inspirations that involve instances of God's making Himself loved, His responses to the prayers of His creatures as the All-Merciful, His responses to the appeals of His servants for help as their Lord, and His intimations of His Existence and Omnipresence to His creatures as the All-Glorified.

The Sixteenth Step

The traveler then addresses their own intellect, saying: "Since I am seeking the Creator and Owner of this universe by means of these creatures, I should first visit the most renowned of His creatures—one who, as confirmed even by his enemies, is the most perfect of them, and the most accomplished commander, the most celebrated ruler, the most exalted orator and possessor of the most brilliant intellect. I should visit the person who has illuminated the past fourteen centuries with his virtues and with the Qur'an: Muhammad the Arabian, upon him be peace and blessings. We should go together to the Age of Happiness in order to ask him about that which I seek." And so the traveler enters that age together with their intellect and sees that, thanks to Muhammad, upon him be peace and blessings, this was an age of true happiness; this man had transformed a most primitive and illiterate people into the masters and teachers of the world and he had done this in a very short time by means of the light he brought.

The traveler says to their intellect: "First of all, we must know as a certainty the value of this extraordinary being, the veracity of his words and the truthfulness of his messages. Then we should ask him about our Creator." And so the traveler begins to investigate. Here we will refer briefly to nine of the countless universal and conclusive proofs that the traveler finds. They are as follows:

THE FIRST: This person, upon him be peace and blessings, possessed all possible laudable virtues and excellent characteristics; this was affirmed even by his enemies. In addition, it has been reported through reliable channels of transmission that hundreds of miracles were performed by his hands, such as the splitting of the moon with a mere gesture, or causing many soldiers to flee by tossing a handful of soil at them—miracles which are referred to in the verses, *And the moon split* (54:1), and *It was not you who threw when you threw, but God threw* (8:17). He also famously quenched an entire army's thirst with water that flowed forth in abundance from his fingers. In fact, more than three hundred of these miracles have been set forth with decisive proofs in The Nineteenth Letter, known as *Miracles of Prophet Muhammad*. Readers wishing to learn about the Prophet's other miracles should refer to that treatise. And so the traveler concludes: "One who in addition to his most noble characteristics and perfections performs such clear miracles must be the most truthful in speech. How could he ever lower himself to lies and trickery, which are the vices of vile people?"

THE SECOND: Prophet Muhammad, upon him be peace and blessings, holds in his hand the Decree of the universe's Owner, namely the mighty, glorious Qur'an, which has been accepted and confirmed in every century by hundreds of millions of people. The fact that the Qur'an is the word of the Creator of the universe and is miraculous in at least forty aspects has been explained with convincing proofs in The Twenty-fifth Word, known as *Miraculousness of the Qur'an*. Readers interested in learning more about those aspects should refer to that treatise. Understanding this, the traveler says: "The translator, expounder and conveyor of such a Decree of pure truth could not lie, for that would violate the Decree and betray its Owner."

THE THIRD: Consider the following:

- Prophet Muhammad, upon him be peace and blessings, appeared with a Sacred Law, a Religion, a code of worship, a mode of prayer, a message and a way of belief the like of which has never existed. And without him, none of these could ever have come to pass. The peerless Law brought by that unlettered Prophet has ruled over one-fifth of humankind for fourteen centuries in a just and precise manner.

- Islam, which originated in and is represented by the Prophet's deeds, sayings, states, and example, is also without peer. Regardless of time or place, it has served hundreds of millions of people as a guide and competent authority in their lives. It has taught and trained their minds, illuminated and purified their hearts, trained and refined their souls, and perfected their spirits.

- Prophet Muhammad, upon him be peace and blessings, is the best example of the mode of worship that is prescribed by Islam; he is the most God-conscious and God-revering person of all. He worshipped with the utmost care and attention, down to even the minutest details, during times of great peril and throughout a life of constant struggle and activity. He imitated no one in his worship, and perfectly combined the alpha and omega of spiritual evolution.

- His prayers and his knowledge of God are similarly unparalleled: with *al-Jawshanu'l-Kabir* alone, which is just one of his thousands of prayers and supplications, he describes his Lord with such a degree of knowledge that no saint or gnostic has ever been able to achieve a similar degree, despite their having been able to build upon the achievements of their predecessors. Even a cursory study of just one of the ninety-nine parts of *al-Jawshanu'l-Kabir* will show that there can never be another one even remotely like it.

- While conveying his message and calling his people to the truth, the Prophet, upon him be peace and blessings, displayed such steadfastness and courage that he never faltered or hesitated. And this was despite the hostilities of the surrounding powers and religions, as well as those of his own people and tribe, including even his uncle. He successfully challenged the whole world, thereby making Islam superior to all other religions and systems. This proves that no other person can equal him in his preaching to humankind or his calling them to the message of truth.

- His belief was so extraordinarily strong and assured, so miraculously developed and ingrained in his heart, and so elevated and world-enlightening that none of the ideas, beliefs, philosophies or spiritual teachings prevalent at the time could engender any doubt within him. Despite the opposition and hostility of his enemies, they were unable to shake him or make him unsure of his cause. Moreover, the saints of all ages, first and foremost his Companions, who have advanced in spirituality and through the various degrees of belief, have always benefited from his faith, which they admit to be of the highest degree. This proves that his belief is also without peer.

The traveler who seeks God thus understands and, with his intellect, concludes that lying and deception can have had no place in the traits of one who brought such a unique law and peerless Religion, who displayed such a wonderful form of worship and extraordinary excellence in prayer, whose preaching was admired the world over, and whose belief was at a degree of miraculous perfection.

THE FOURTH: Just as the consensus of the Prophets forms very strong proof of God's Existence and Oneness, it also represents a sound testimony to that exalted person's truthfulness and Messengership. For history confirms that he possesses to the utmost degree all of the sacred attributes, miracles and duties that indicate a Prophet's mission and veracity. Just as the previous Prophets predicted his coming by giving glad tidings of him in the Torah, the Gospels, the Psalms, and other Scriptures—more than twenty of the clearest of these joyous predictions have been set forth in The Nineteenth Letter—they also confirmed him with their own missions and miracles, attesting to the truthfulness of this person, who is the most perfect in carrying out the mission and tasks of Prophethood, in effect putting their signature to his claims. The traveler perceives that all of the previous Prophets bore witness to this person's truthfulness through the unanimity of their actions, just as they testified to God's Oneness through verbal consensus.

THE FIFTH: Having attained truth, perfection, the rank of working wonders, insight into the reality of things, and spiritual discovery and vision by following that person's deeds and principles, thousands of saints bear witness unanimously to God's Oneness and to the truthfulness and Messengership of that person, who is their master. The fact that through the light of their sainthood the saints witness some of the truths he proclaimed concerning the World of the Unseen, and through the light of belief they believe in and confirm all of these at the degrees of certainty of knowledge or certainty of vision or certainty of experience, demonstrates in a manner more brilliant than the sun the extent of the truthfulness and rectitude of that person, who is their master.

THE SIXTH: Millions of exacting, meticulous, purified, and truthful scholars and sages, all of whom have reached the highest station of learning through the teaching contained in the sacred truths that have been brought by that unlettered person, through the sublime sciences which he introduced, and through the knowledge of God which he discovered—all prove and affirm with unanimity not only God's Oneness, which is the foundation of Prophet Muhammad's mission, but also the truthfulness of that supreme master and the veracity of his words. This is proof of his Messengership and truthfulness that is as clear as daylight.

THE SEVENTH: After the Prophets, the Family and Companions of Prophet Muhammad, upon him be peace and blessings, are the most elevated in insight, discernment, and perfection; they are the most renowned, respected, pious, and keen-sighted members of humankind. Having thoroughly scrutinized all of the Prophet's thoughts and his hidden and apparent states and conditions, they have concluded unanimously that he was the noblest and most truthful and honest person in the world. The traveler understands that such an unshakable affirmation of him from such extraordinary people proves the truth of his cause, just as daylight proves the existence of the sun.

THE EIGHTH: This universe indicates the Maker, Author, Inscriber and Designer Who determined and fashioned it and Who controls and administers it like a palace, a book, and an exhibition of marvels. Given this, there should therefore exist an exalted herald, a truthful revealer, an exacting master, and a veracious teacher who knows and makes known the Divine purpose behind the creation of the universe, who teaches others about the Divine wisdom that underpins the universe's purposeful motions and transformations, who declares its inherent value and the perfections of the creatures in it, and who expounds the meanings of this great cosmic book. The traveler comes to realize that the one carrying out such duties most perfectly is the most truthful in his cause, serving as the most trusted and exalted officer of the Creator of the universe.

THE NINTH: Behind the veil of creation is One Who, through these purposeful and skilled works, wills that His perfect skills and artistry be displayed. Behind that veil there is One who wills to make Himself known and loved through the countless adorned creatures that He brings into being, and to evoke praise and thanksgiving in return for His boundless precious bounties, encouraging worship with gratitude and appreciation for His Lordship by means of His affectionate and protective sustaining of life, as well as by satisfying the most delicate tastes and appetites that His creatures possess. He also wills to demonstrate His Divinity through His wise and awe-inspiring creativity and through the magnificent, majestic, and purposeful activity that is displayed, for example, during the changes of seasons and the alternation of day and night—all of this so that humankind may come to believe in, submit to, and obey Him in His Divinity. Furthermore, He wills the manifestation of His Justice, Rightfulness, and Uprightness by protecting virtue and the virtuous while destroying evil and those who perpetrate it, and by annihilating liars and oppressors with heavenly blows.

Thus, the most beloved creation and the most devoted servant in the sight of that Unseen Being will certainly be the one who serves the above-mentioned Divine purposes to the highest degree. This will be one who discloses the mystery and talisman of the creation of the universe, who always acts in the name of His Creator, and who asks Him alone for help and success, and receives both. This is Prophet Muhammad al-Qurayshi, upon him be peace and blessings.

The traveler addresses their reason or intellect, saying: "Since these nine truths testify to the truthfulness of that person, he must undoubtedly be the source of humanity's honor and the pride of the world. Therefore he is worthy of being called 'the Pride of the World' and 'the Glory of Humankind.' Moreover, the Qur'an, that miraculous Word and Decree of the All-Merciful which this person held in his hand has drawn half of the old world into its magnificent spiritual domain. Together with the Messenger's personal perfections and elevated virtues, it shows that he is the most important being in the world, and accordingly that his words about our Creator are the most important."

Come now and see! Based on the strength of his hundreds of miracles and thousands of sublime, established truths contained in Islam, his sole aim was to prove and bear witness to the Necessarily Existent Being's Existence and Oneness, and to proclaim Him with all His Attributes and Names. He is the "spiritual sun" that enlightens the universe, our Creator's most brilliant proof and the "Beloved of God." Each of the following forms of great, truthful, and unshakable consensus affirms and corroborates the witness that he bears:

THE FIRST: The unanimous confirmation of the illustrious community known and celebrated as Muhammad's Family and descendants, among whom are thousands of spiritual poles and supreme saints who have such keen spiritual insight that they can even penetrate into the Unseen. Imam 'Ali, for instance, said: "Were the veil to be lifted from the Unseen, my certainty would not increase." And then there is 'Abdu'l-Qadr al-Jilani, who observed God's Supreme Throne and the Archangel Israfil's awesome form while still on this earth.

THE SECOND: The unanimous confirmation of the Companions, which was based on a belief so strong that they were prepared to sacrifice their lives and properties, their parents and their tribes for its sake. Although brought up among a primitive people and in a climate of ignorance devoid of any positive notions about social life or administration, devoid of a guiding Scripture and immersed into the darkness of the uncivilized era when there were no Prophets, these people began to follow in Muhammad's footsteps and soon became the masters, guides, and just rulers of the most civilized and socio-politically advanced peoples and states of their time.

THE THIRD: The unanimous confirmation, which is based on certainty of knowledge, of innumerable exacting and profound scholars among his Community. Each century has seen thousands of people like these who have become extraordinarily advanced in every branch of science and art.

Thus, this person's testimony to God's Existence and Unity is so universal and unshakable that even if all beings hostile to it were to unite, they would still be unable to challenge it. Such is the conclusion reached by the traveler. In reference to the lesson which the traveler learned in that school of light while visiting the Age of Happiness in their mind, it is said in this sixteenth step:

> There is no deity but God, the Necessarily Existent One, the Single and Unique, Whose necessary Existence in His Unity is demonstrated clearly by the Pride of the World and the Glory of the children of Adam, through the majesty of the Qur'an's sovereignty, the splendor of Islam's inclusiveness, the multiplicity of his perfections, and the sublimity of his moral qualities, as confirmed even by his enemies. Again, he bears witness through the strength of hundreds of miracles that prove his truthfulness and which have been firmly established, and through the strength of thousands of evident and decisive truths contained in his Religion, as affirmed by the consensus of his illustrious, light-diffusing Family and descendants, the agreement of his Companions with penetrating sight and prudence, and the concord of the scholars of his Community with their enlightening proofs and insight.

The Seventeenth Step

The tireless and insatiable traveler, who realizes the aim and essence of life in this world to be belief, addresses their own heart and says: "Let us have recourse to the book known as the Qur'an of miraculous exposition, which is said to be the Word of the Being Whom we are seeking: let us examine 'the most famous, most brilliant and wisest book' in the world, one which issues a challenge in every age to whoever refuses to submit to it. Let us see what it says. But first, we must establish that this book is from our Creator." Saying this, they begin to investigate.

Since the traveler lives in the present age, they first look at the *Risale-i Nur*, which comprises gleams from the miraculousness of the Qur'an, and they see that its one hundred and thirty parts consist of the subtle meanings, lights and well-founded explanations of certain verses from that Criterion between truth and falsehood—the Qur'an. They understand from its content and forceful diffusion and defense of the Qur'anic truths in this age of obstinacy and unbelief that the Qur'an, its master, source, authority, and sun, is a revealed book. Among the hundreds of proofs for the Divine authorship of the Qur'an in the different parts of the *Risale-i Nur*, The Twenty-fifth Word, which is a single proof of the Qur'an, and the end of The Nineteenth Letter establish forty aspects of the Qur'an's miraculousness in such a way that whoever sees them will not only raise any criticism or objection but will also have to appreciate their arguments highly. Therefore, leaving the establishment of the Qur'an as God's Word and the explanation of its various aspects of miraculousness to the *Risale-i Nur*, the traveler notices a few points that briefly demonstrate the Qur'an's greatness.

THE FIRST POINT: Just as the Qur'an, with all its aspects of miraculousness and truths that show its veracity is a miracle of Prophet Muhammad, upon him be peace and blessings, Prophet Muhammad himself, with all his miracles, proofs of Prophethood and perfections of knowledge is a miracle of the Qur'an and a decisive proof that it is the Word of God.

THE SECOND POINT: As well as bringing about a substantial, happy, and enlightening transformation in human social life, the Qur'an has brought about a revolution in the souls, hearts, spirits, and intellects of people, and in their individual, social, and political lives. Furthermore, it has perpetuated this revolution in such a way that at every moment over the past fourteen centuries it has been read with the utmost respect by more than a hundred million people, training and refining their souls and purifying their hearts. For spirits it has been a means of development and advancement; for intellects, a guidance and light; and for life, it has been life itself and felicity. Such a book is without doubt unparalleled in every respect: it is a wonder, a marvel and a miracle.

THE THIRD POINT: From the age of its revelation down to the present day, the Qur'an has demonstrated such eloquence that it caused the value attached to the "Seven Hanging Poems"—poems which were recognized as the best, written in gold and hung on the walls of the Ka'ba during the Age of Ignorance—to decrease to such a low level that when taking down her father's ode from the Ka'ba, the daughter of (the famous poet) Labid said: "Compared with the verses of the Qur'an, this no longer has any worth."

A Bedouin poet once heard the recitation of the verse which means: *Proclaim what you are commanded to convey openly and in an emphatic manner* (15:94) and immediately prostrated. When they asked him: "Have you become a Muslim?" he replied: "No! I was merely prostrating before the eloquence of this verse!"

Also, thousands of scholars, authors and geniuses of the science of eloquence and rhetoric, such as 'Abdu'l-Qahir al-Jurjani, Sakkaki and Zamakhshari, have unanimously concluded that the eloquence of the Qur'an is beyond human capacity and cannot be replicated by any created being.

Moreover, from the outset, the Qur'an has also challenged all arrogant and egoistic poets and rhetoricians by saying, in a manner that will bring down their arrogance: "(If you do not believe that I am the Word of God, then) either produce a single *sura* like mine or accept perdition and humiliation in this world and the Hereafter." Despite this challenge, the obstinate rhetoricians of that age abandoned the shorter route of attempting to produce a single *sura* like the Qur'an and instead chose the longer route of (fighting against it and) casting their persons and property into danger. This proves that the shorter route cannot be taken.

Millions of Arabic books are in circulation, written since that time either by friends of the Qur'an in order to imitate it or by its enemies in order to confront and criticize it; such books have been improved over time with developments in science and thought. However, to this day not one of them has been able to attain the level of the Qur'an. Should even a common human being listen to them, he would be sure to say: "The Qur'an does not resemble these other books and is in a different class entirely. It must be either below them or above them." And since no-one in the world—not

even an unbeliever or a fool—can say that it is below them, one must therefore conclude that in eloquence it is higher than all of them.

A man once read the verse which means, *Whatever is in the heavens
and on the earth glorifies God* (57:1). He said: "I cannot see any miraculous
eloquence in this verse." He was told: "Go back to that age in your mind
and listen to the verse as it was recited there." Imagining himself to be
there, he saw that all the beings in the world were perceived as lifeless and
without either consciousness or purpose, living in an unstable, transient
world, surrounded by empty, infinite and unbounded space, and flounder-
ing in confusion and darkness. Suddenly he heard the above verse proclaimed by the voice of the Qur'an. At once the verse removed the veil
from the face of the universe and illuminated it. This pre-eternal Speech,
this eternal Decree, gave instruction to all conscious beings, drawn up in
the ranks of succeeding centuries, in such a fashion that the universe
became like a vast mosque. The whole of creation, and in particular the
heavens and the earth, were engaged in vital remembrance of God and
proclamation of His Glory, fulfilling this function with joy and contentment. All of this the traveler has observed. Thus, by tasting one degree of
the eloquence of the Qur'an and comparing the other verses to it, the traveler can understand one of the many thousands of wise reasons why the eloquence of the Qur'an has conquered half of the earth and a fifth of humanity; they see how it has increased its majestic dominion, without let or hin-
drance, and with utmost respect throughout the fourteen centuries since its
advent.

THE FOURTH POINT: While repetition of even the most pleasant thing
eventually leads to disgust, the sweetness of the Qur'an is such that however
many times it is recited, it causes neither tiredness nor repulsion. Indeed, it
has become axiomatic that for those whose hearts are not corrupted and
whose taste has not been spoilt, repeated recitation of the Qur'an leads not to
weariness but, rather, to an increase in its sweetness and appeal. Also, the
Qur'an demonstrates such freshness, youth, and originality that even though
it has lived for fourteen centuries and been available to everyone, its vitality
is such that one would think it has only just been revealed. Every century has
seen the Qur'an enjoy a new youth, as though it were addressing that century in particular. Similarly, even though scholars in every branch of learning
keep the Qur'an at their side constantly in order to benefit from it and follow

its method of exposition, they see that the Qur'an continues to maintain the originality of its style and manner of explanation.

THE FIFTH POINT: One wing of the Qur'an is in the past and one is in the future. Its root and one wing are the unanimously confirmed truths of the former Prophets, who affirm it with the tongue of unanimity and whom it in turn affirms and corroborates. Similarly, all saints and purified scholars—the other wing—those fruits of the Qur'an who have received life from it, have shown through their vital spiritual progress that their blessed "Tree" is the living and most radiant means to truth, and beneficial in every respect. All the true spiritual paths or ways of sainthood and Islamic sciences, which have all grown under the protection of the Qur'an's second wing, unanimously testify that the Qur'an is truth itself and a collection of truths that is unequaled in comprehensiveness.

THE SIXTH POINT: The Qur'an is luminous in each of its following six aspects or sides, all of which indicate its truthfulness and veracity:

- Beneath it lie the pillars of argument and proof;
- above it shine the gleams of the stamp of miraculousness or inimitability;
- before it stand the gifts of happiness in both worlds as its goal;
- behind it are the truths of the heavenly Revelation as its point of support;
- to its right is the well-documented and substantiated confirmation of innumerable sound and upright minds;
- and to its left one can see the true satisfaction, sincere attraction, and submission of sound hearts and pure consciences.

These six, taken together, prove that the Qur'an is an extraordinary, firm, and unassailable heavenly citadel that stands on the earth. From these six aspects it is clear that the Qur'an is pure truth, that it is not human words, and that it contains no errors at all.

Also:

- The Controller and Director of the universe, Who has made it His practice to always exhibit beauty in the universe, to protect goodness and truth, and to eliminate imposters and liars, has confirmed and set His seal on the Qur'an by giving it the most acceptable, highest, and most dominant place of respect and success in the world.

- The person who represented and communicated Islam and inter-
  preted and explained the Qur'an throughout his life, upon him be
  peace and blessings, believed in it much more powerfully than
  anybody else and held it in greater respect.
- He assumed a different state when it was revealed.
- His own words (hadiths) did not resemble the Qur'an and could
  never be on the same level.
- Despite being illiterate, with the Qur'an as his basis, he was able to
  describe with complete confidence many past and future events and
  numerous cosmic phenomena from behind the veil of the Unseen.
- As the supreme translator of the Qur'an, in whose behavior no
  trickery or shortcoming had ever been witnessed, even by the
  sharpest eyes, he believed in and affirmed every pronouncement
  of the Qur'an with all his might, allowing nothing to shake him
  in his conviction.

All of these six facts serve to confirm beyond doubt that the Qur'an is
the Divinely-revealed Word of his All-Compassionate Creator.

Furthermore:

- More than a fifth of humanity has devoted themselves to the
  Qur'an with piety and rapture, paying heed to it eagerly in their
  desire to know the truth. According to the testimony provided by
  many indications, events, and spiritual unveilings, the jinn, the
  angels, and the spirit beings gather around it in truth-adoring
  fashion, like moths, whenever it is recited. This too serves to confirm that the Qur'an enjoys universal acceptance and occupies
  the highest position.
- In addition, each of the different classes of humankind, from the
  simplest and lowly to the cleverest and learned, is able to take its
  full share of the Qur'an's instruction and understand its most profound truths (each according to their capacity).
- Moreover, all of the celebrated scholars in all branches of the religious sciences, in particular the great interpreters of the Supreme
  Shari'a, together with the brilliant and exacting scholars of theology and the basic principles of the Religion are able to exact all the
  answers needed for their various disciplines from the Qur'an. All of

these facts confirm that the Qur'an is a source of truth and a mine of reality.

- Also, although the disbelieving ones among the Arab authors and poets, the most advanced in literature and eloquence, felt the greatest need to dispute the Qur'an, they were never able to match it in eloquence by producing the like of even a single *sura*, despite the fact that eloquence is only one of the seven most prominent aspects of the Qur'an's miraculousness. Up until today, not even renowned rhetoricians or linguistic experts who have contested the Qur'an in order to make a name for themselves have been able to oppose even a single aspect of its miraculousness, and as a result have been forced to remain in impotent silence. This is further confirmation that the Qur'an is a miracle and completely beyond human capacity.

- The value, superiority, and eloquence of speech are based on the answers given to the questions posed with regard to it: "Who does it come from, for who is it intended, and what is its purpose?" In respect to these points, the Qur'an has no like, and none can approach it. For the Qur'an is a speech and address by the Lord and Creator of all the worlds; it is His conversation with us that is in no way derivative or artificial. It is addressed to the one who was sent in the name of all humanity, indeed of all beings, the most famous and renowned of humankind; it is addressed to the one whose belief had such a strength and breadth that it gave impetus to mighty Islam and raised its owner to the station of "The nearness (with God) of the distance between two bow strings, or even nearer," returning him as the addressee of the Eternally Besought One. It describes and explains matters concerning happiness in this world and the next, the results of the creation of the universe, and the purposes of the Lord within it. It expounds also the belief of its first and primary addressee—Prophet Muhammad—which is the highest and most extensive belief, encompassing all the truths of Islam. It reveals and shows every facet of the enormous universe like a map, a clock, or a house, describing it in a manner which befits the Craftsman Who made it. To produce the like of this Qur'an of miraculous exposition is therefore not possible, nor can its degree of miraculousness be attained.

- Also, thousands of meticulous, learned scholars of high intelligence have written commentaries that expound upon the Qur'an, some of which consist of as many as seventy volumes, proving with clear evidence and argument its innumerable qualities, characteristics, mysteries, subtleties, and elevated meanings, showing numerous indications concerning every sort of hidden or unseen matter. The one hundred and thirty parts of the *Risale-i Nur*, in particular, each proves with decisive arguments one quality or subtle point of the Qur'an. Each part of it—such as The Twenty-fifth Word on the miraculousness of the Qur'an; The Second Station of The Twentieth Word, which deduces many things from the Qur'an concerning the wonders of civilization such as the railway and the airplane; The First Ray, called *Signs of the Qur'an*, which explain some verses' allusions to electricity; the eight short treatises known as *The Eight Signs*, which show how well-ordered, full of meaning, and mysterious the words of the Qur'an actually are; the small treatise ("The Seventh Gleam" in *The Gleams*) which proves five aspects of the miraculousness of the verses at the end of *Suratu'l-Fath* (*sura* 48) from the perspective of their giving news of the Unseen—in short, each part of the *Risale-i Nur* shows one truth or one light of the Qur'an. All of this serves to confirm the fact that the Qur'an has no like: it is a miracle and a wonder; it is the tongue of the World of the Unseen in this visible earthly realm, and it is the Word of One Who is the All-Knowing of the Unseen.

It is on account of these qualities and characteristics of the Qur'an that we have indicated above, in eighteen points contained in the successive three groups, that its sublime, luminous sovereignty and its sacred, mighty rule have been able to continue with perfect splendor, illuminating the faces of the centuries and the visage of the earth for (more than) thirteen centuries. It is also on account of these qualities of the Qur'an that each of its letters has the sacred distinction of yielding at least ten rewards, ten merits, and ten eternal fruits; indeed, the letters of certain verses and *suras* yield a hundred or a thousand fruits, or even more, while at certain blessed times the light, reward, and value of each letter multiplies a hundredfold. Our traveler, journeying through the world, understands this and says in their heart: "The Qur'an, which is thus miraculous in every respect, through the consensus of its *suras*, the agreement of its verses, the accord of its lights and mysteries, and the concurrence of its fruits and works, testifies with its proofs to the Existence, Unity, Attributes, and Names of a Single Necessarily Existent One, and its testimony has caused to issue forth the permanent testimony of all believers."

Thus, in a brief reference to the instruction in belief and Divine Unity that the traveler received from the Qur'an, it is said in the seventeenth step:

> There is no deity but God, the Necessarily Existent, the One and Unique, Whose necessary Existence in His Unity is demonstrated clearly by the Qur'an of miraculous exposition, the Book accepted and desired by all species of angels, humanity and jinn; the verses of which are read each minute of the year, with the utmost reverence, by hundreds of millions of people and whose sacred sovereignty is permanent over all regions of the earth and the universe and the face of time; its spiritual and luminous authority has run over half the earth and a fifth of humanity for fourteen centuries with the utmost splendor. This is also testified to and evidenced by the unanimity of its sacred and heavenly *suras*, the agreement of its luminous Divine verses, the congruence of its mysteries and lights, and the correspondence of its fruits and effects, by witnessing and clear vision.

The Eighteenth Step

The traveler who is journeying through life now knows that belief is the most precious capital a human being can have, for it bestows on indigent humanity not some transient field or dwelling, but a huge universe, an eternal property that is as vast as the world. Belief also bestows ephemeral humankind with all that they need for eternal life; it delivers from eternal annihilation a wretched one who is waiting as though on a gallows for the arrival of fate, opening to humanity an eternal treasury of everlasting happiness. The traveler then says to themselves: "Onward! In order to gain a further degree from among the infinite degrees of belief, let us consider the totality of the universe and listen to what it says. We should perfect and illuminate the lessons we have received from its components and parts."

Looking through the broad and comprehensive telescope they have taken from the Qur'an, the traveler sees that the universe is so meaningful and well-ordered that it appears as an embodied book, a created Qur'an, of the All-Glorified Lord, a finely adorned palace of the Eternally Besought One and an orderly city of the All-Merciful. Through their constant, meaningful effacement and reaffirmation, and through their wise changes, alterations, and transformations, all of the *suras*, verses and words of that book of the universe—even its very letters, lines, pages, chapters, and divisions—describe the Existence and Presence of One Who has absolute power over and knowledge of all things as the Author of the book—a Perfect and All-Majestic Inscriber Who sees all things in all things and knows the relationship of all things with all things.

Similarly, with all its numerous divisions, species, and particles, with all its inhabitants and contents, with all that enters it and leaves it, and with all the providential changes, transformations, and wise processes of renewal and refreshment that occur in it, the universe also proclaims the Existence and Unity of an All-Exalted Craftsman, a peerless Maker Who acts with limitless power and infinite wisdom. The testimony of the following two mighty realities, as immense as the universe itself, affirms this supreme witness of the universe.

THE FIRST REALITY: This is the reality of "coming into existence within time and space" and "contingency," which has been established with countless proofs by gifted scholars of the principles of the Religion and the science of theology, as well as the sages of Islam. According to these people, since change and alteration are observed in the world and in all things, the world must be ephemeral and created within time: it cannot be uncreated and pre-eternal. If it has been created, then there must be a Maker Who has created it. And if it is equally possible for something to come into existence or not and if there is no necessary or imperative cause for it to come into existence or not—a cause which essentially originates in itself, then that thing cannot be necessary or imperative and eternal in the past. It has also been proven with decisive arguments that it is not possible for things to create each other one after the other until eternity in the past; in other words, things cannot go back to eternity in cycles with the former having created the latter. Hence, the existence of a Necessary Existent One becomes necessary—One Whose like cannot exist, Whose similitude is impossible, and all other than Whom is contingent and created by Him.

The reality of "bringing or coming into existence within time and space" has permeated the whole of the universe. Many instances of this are visible to the eye, while the rest can be seen by the intellect. For in front of our eyes a whole world dies every fall; together with it perish hundreds of thousands of different kinds of plants and small animals, each member of each species being like a small universe in itself. It is, however, so orderly a death that all things leave behind in their places seeds and eggs—tiny miracles of Mercy and Wisdom, of Power and Knowledge—so that in spring they will be the means of a new resurrection and rebirth. They hand to the seeds and eggs the books of their deeds and the plans and records of the duties they have carried out, entrusting them to the Wisdom and Protection of the All-Majestic Preserver, and only then do they die.

In spring, the dead trees, roots, and some among the animals come to life again exactly as they were, thus providing hundreds of thousands of examples, specimens, and proofs of the supreme Resurrection. In the place of some others, plants and animals that closely resemble them are brought into being and life, thus publishing the pages of the beings of the preceding spring, together with their deeds and functions, just like an advertisement. Thus, they demonstrate one meaning of the verse, *And when the scrolls (of the deeds of every person) are laid open* (81:10). And then, each fall, a whole world dies, and each spring a fresh world comes into being. This death and rebirth proceeds in such an orderly fashion, and the death and rebirth of so many species occur within them in such a methodical and regular fashion, that it is as if the world were a guesthouse where animate beings reside for a time, where traveling worlds and migrant realms come, fulfill their duties, and then go on their way. And so, apparent to all intellects, with the clarity of the sun, is the necessary Existence, the boundless Power and the infinite Wisdom of an All-Majestic Being Who creates and brings into existence in this world numerous animate realms and dutiful universes with perfect wisdom, knowledge, harmony, balance, order, and regularity, and Who then employs them for purposes of training, sustaining, raising, and maintaining—all for the sake of Divine aims and Merciful goals, with absolute power and compassion. We leave to the *Risale-i Nur* and books of theology the further discussion of matters related to the bringing and coming into existence within time and space.

As for contingency, it too prevails over and surrounds the entire universe. For we see that all things—be they universal or particular, large or small, from the highest firmament down to the ground, from the atom to the planet—have been brought into existence with a particular essence, a specific form, a distinct identity, particular attributes, wise qualities, and beneficial components. Now,

- to bestow on that particular essence and nature its characteristics from amongst infinite possibilities;
- to clothe it in its specific, distinctive, and appropriate form from among possibilities and probabilities as numerous as the forms that may be conceived;
- to distinguish that being with the identity suited to it from among the possibilities as numerous as the members of the species;
- to give it unique, suitable, and beneficial attributes while it is formless and hesitant amidst possibilities and probabilities that are as numerous as the varieties of the attributes and their degrees;
- and to bestow wise qualities and beneficial organs upon that formless creature, perplexed and aimless as it is amidst innumerable possibilities and probabilities resulting from the infinite number of conceivable paths and modalities—all of these are indications and proofs of the necessary Existence, the infinite Power, and the unlimited Wisdom of the Necessarily Existent Being: they confirm that it is He Who assigns, chooses, specifies, distinguishes, and creates the specific concrete forms and shapes, attributes and situations of all these contingent beings, whether they be universals or particulars. They indicate, too, that no object or matter is hidden from Him, that nothing is difficult for Him, and that the greatest task is as easy for Him as the smallest; they show that He can create a spring as easily as a tree and a tree as easily as a seed. All this, then, pertains to the reality of contingency, and forms one wing of the supreme witnessing borne by the universe.

Since this testimony of the universe, with its two wings and two realities under discussion has been established and explained in various parts of the *Risale-i Nur*, in particular in The Twenty-second and Thirty-second Words, as well as in The Twentieth and Thirty-third Letters, we refer our readers to these treatises and cut short here what has been an extremely long exposition.

THE SECOND REALITY: This reality proceeds from the entire scheme of the universe, which is also the second wing of its great and universal testimony. It is as follows:

There is a reality of cooperation or mutual assistance that can be observed among beings who are trying to maintain their existence—and, if they are animate, their life—and to fulfill their duties in the midst of the constant agitation stirred up by various revolutions and transformations, an endeavor that lies far beyond their capacities.

We see that the elements hasten to aid living being: clouds, in particular, come to the aid of the plant kingdom, while the plant kingdom hastens to help the animal kingdom, and the animal kingdom rushes to help the world of humans. Milk gushes forth from breasts, like the fountain of Paradise, to provide for the young; living beings are given their sustenance and other necessities of life from unexpected places in a manner that is completely beyond their capacity; particles of food hasten to sustain and repair the cells of the body, and so on. These and many other similar examples of the reality of cooperation under the absolute control, direction, and employment of the All-Merciful Lord demonstrate the universal and compassionate Lordship of the Master of all worlds, Who runs the universe like a palace.

Indeed, objects which are solid, inanimate, and unfeeling, but which nonetheless help one another in a tender and conscious fashion, are undoubtedly caused to rush to each other's assistance by the Power, Mercy, and Command of an infinitely Compassionate and Wise Lord of Majesty.

The universal cooperation prevalent throughout the universe; the all-inclusive balance and all-embracing preservation which prevail with the utmost order in all things, from the planets to the members, limbs and bodily particles of animate beings; the adornment whose pen glides over the entire universe, from the gilded face of the heavens and the ornate face of the earth to the delicate faces of flowers; the ordering and organizing that prevail over all things, from the Milky Way to the vegetables and fruits, such as corn and pomegranates; and the assigning of duties to all things, from the sun, the moon, the elements and the clouds, right down to honey-bees—all of these vast realities offer a testimony in proportion to their vastness, and their testimony forms the second wing of the testimony offered by the universe. Since the *Risale-i Nur* has explained this elsewhere, we will be content here with this brief indication.

In a brief reference to the lesson of faith which the traveler through the world learned from the universe, it is said in the eighteenth step:

There is no deity but God, the Necessarily Existent, the like of Whom can in no way exist, and all other than Whom are contingent; the Single, the Unique, Whose necessary Existence in His Unity is demonstrated clearly by the universe—that huge book clothed in a corporeal form, the supreme Qur'an incarnate, the ornate and orderly palace, the magnificent and well-arranged city—with all of its *suras*, verses, words, letters, chapters, parts, pages and lines, and with the agreement of its basic divisions, species, parts and particles, its inhabitants and contents, and what enters it and what leaves it. This is testified to by the sublimely comprehensive, vast and perfect reality of bringing or coming into existence within time and space, by change and contingency, and by the agreement of all scholars in the science of theology. It is a testimony which also comprises the reality of the changing of its form and contents with wisdom and regularity and the renewal of its letters and words with order and harmony. It is also a testimony offered by the greatness and all-inclusiveness of the reality of cooperation, mutual response, solidarity, interconnectedness, measure, balance, and preservation—all of which are clearly observable in all of the beings which exist within it.

The Nineteenth Step

The inquisitive and yearning traveler, who has by this stage reached the throne of truth by having advanced through the above-mentioned eighteen ranks, and who has risen from the rank of knowing the Creator of the world indirectly to the station of addressing Him directly, addresses their own spirit as follows: "At the beginning of the *Fatiha* (the Opening Chapter of the Qur'an) we praise God indirectly, (saying: "All praise and gratitude are for God."). However, when we reach the word *iyyaka* ("You alone"), we enter His Presence and address Him directly. Taking our cue from this, we should abandon this indirect search and address the One Whom we are seeking, questioning Him directly about Himself. After all, if one wishes to know about the sun, which shows all things, one should ask the sun itself."

That which shows all things shows itself even more clearly. Just as we perceive the sun through its rays, we can also try to know our Creator through His All-Beautiful Names and Sacred Attributes, in accordance with the extent of our capacities. We will set forth here, with brevity and concision, two of the countless paths which lead to this goal; we will explain two of the innumerable stages of these two paths and two of the numerous realities of these two stages.

THE FIRST REALITY: We are able to observe quite clearly the comprehensive, constant, orderly, and awesome reality of an all-prevailing activity which directs, changes, and renews all things and beings in the heavens and on the earth. Within the reality of that comprehensively wise activity one is able to perceive immediately the truth of the manifestation of Lordship. In turn, within the truth of that comprehensively merciful manifestation of Lordship, one is able to recognize the truth of the demonstration of Divinity.

From behind the veil of this constant, imperious, and wise activity, the Acts of an All-Powerful and All-Knowing Doer can be discerned so clearly that it is as though one is witnessing them directly. And from behind the veil of these nurturing, directing and administering acts of Lordship, the Divine Names Which are manifested in all things can be perceived most clearly. Then from behind the veil of the All-Beautiful Names, Which manifest themselves with majesty and grace, the existence and operation of the seven sacred Attributes can be deduced at the degree of certainty of knowledge, or rather, the degree of certainty of vision or observation, or even certainty of experience. And as is evidenced by the whole of creation, through the endless manifestations of these seven Attributes, that is, Life, Knowledge, Power, Will, Hearing, Seeing, and Speech, the Existence of the Necessarily Existent One described by these Attributes, that Single One of Unity known by these Names, that All-Independent, Eternally Besought One, becomes known self-evidently, necessarily, with the eye of faith in the heart, as though He were being seen more clearly and brilliantly than the sun.

For a beautiful and meaningful book and a well-built house presuppose the acts of writing and building respectively; the acts of writing beautifully and building well self-evidently presuppose the titles of writer and builder; the titles of writer and builder obviously imply the arts and attributes of writing and building; and these arts and attributes necessitate clearly one who is qualified by these names and attributes, and who is an artist, a craftsman and an agent. For, just as it is impossible for there to be a deed without a doer, or a name without one designated by the name, it is also impossible for there to be an attribute without one qualified by the attribute, or for there to be a craft without a craftsman.

On the basis, then, of this reality and principle, the universe and all that it contains resembles a collection of countless meaningful books and letters written by the Pen of Divine Destiny and countless buildings and palaces constructed with the tools of Divine Power. All of these, individually in thousands of ways and together in innumerable ways, provide infinite testimonies to the limitless deeds of Lordship and Mercifulness. Together with these deeds, one thousand and one All-Beautiful Names, Which are the origins of these deeds, and the seven Attributes of Majesty, Which are the source of the Names, testify, through their endless manifestations, and in endless and infinite ways, to the necessary Existence and Unity of an All-Majestic Being Who is the source of these seven sacred, all-embracing Attributes and is qualified by them. And so too, all the instances of beauty, grace, value, and perfection that are found in those beings testify as one to the sacred beauties and perfections of the acts of Lordship; they testify to the Divine Names and Attributes of the Eternally Besought and the Essential Characteristics of the All-Glorified, which are fitting and worthy of them. And together with all these Names, Attributes, and Characteristics, they bear witness to the sacred Beauty and Perfection of the All-Pure and Sacred Divine Essence.

Thus, the truth of Lordship that manifests itself within the reality of all activity reveals itself in qualities and acts such as creating, inventing, making, and originating with knowledge and wisdom; it shows itself in determining, fashioning, directing, and administering with order and balance; it manifests itself in transforming, changing, causing to descend, and perfecting with purpose and will; it makes itself known through feeding, nurturing, and the bestowal of bounties and gifts with tenderness and mercy. And the reality of the self-demonstration of Divinity found and perceived within the reality of the manifestation of Lordship makes itself known and recognized through the compassionate and munificent manifestations of the All-Beautiful Names and through the Majestic and Graceful manifestations of the seven established, positive or affirmative Attributes: Life, Knowledge, Power, Will, Hearing, Seeing or Sight, and Speech.

Just as the Attribute of Speech makes the All-Sacred Divine Essence known through Revelation and inspiration, the Attribute of Power makes Him known through Its skilled works and effects, which are Its embodied words. Presenting the entire universe in the form of a book of embodied criteria that distinguish truth from falsehood, the Power describes and makes known an All-Powerful One of Majesty.

As for the Attribute of Knowledge, through all of the innumerable wise, well-ordered, and balanced artifacts, and through all of the countless beings that are administered, directed, adorned, and made distinct through knowledge, It makes known a single, All-Knowing and All-Sacred Divine Essence.

As for the Attribute of Life, It is established both by Its own proofs and by all the works that proclaim God's Power; It is made known by all the well-ordered, wise, balanced and adorned forms and states that indicate God's Knowledge, as well as by all proofs provided by the other Attributes. Thus Life, which together with all Its proofs shows as witnesses all living beings, which act as Its mirrors, makes known an All-Living and Self-Subsistent Being. Life also makes the universe into a supreme mirror which is composed of countless smaller ones—a mirror that is continuously changed and renewed in order to display an ever-changing array of fresh and varied manifestations and designs. Similarly, each of the Attributes of Sight and Hearing and Will and Speech reveals and makes known the All-Sacred Divine Essence in the same way that the universe does.

Moreover, just as the Attributes demonstrate the Existence of the All-Majestic Divine Essence, they also indicate in evident fashion the existence and reality of Life and the fact that the Divine Essence is eternally living. For knowing is a sign of life; hearing is an indication of being alive; seeing belongs only to the living; and willing is possible only through life. Purposeful power is found only in living beings, while speech is a faculty of those who are endowed with life and knowledge. It follows from all these realities that the Divine Attribute of Life has proofs seven times as great as the universe, and proofs that proclaim both Its own existence and the existence of the One Whom It qualifies. It is because of this that Life is the foundation and source of all other Attributes: it is the origin and axis of God's Greatest Name. Since the *Risale-i Nur* has established this primary truth with powerful proofs and, to a certain extent, clarified it, we will content ourselves now with a drop from this ocean.

The Second Reality: This is the Divine discourse which stems from the Divine Attribute of Speech.

As stated in the verse: *If all the sea were ink to write my Lord's words, the sea would indeed be exhausted before my Lord's words would be exhausted, even if We were to bring the like of it in addition to it* (18:109), Divine Speech is infinite. The most manifest sign demonstrating the existence of a being is its speech. Thus, this reality constitutes an infinite testimony to the Existence and Unity of the Eternal Speaker. As has been expounded in the Fourteenth and Fifteenth Steps of this treatise, Revelation and inspiration are two powerful proofs of this reality; the divinely-revealed Books are, as mentioned in The Tenth Step, an expansive proof, and as indicated in The Seventeenth Step, the Qur'an of miraculous exposition is a most brilliant and comprehensive proof. So, referring the explanation of this reality to those Steps, and being content with the lights and mysteries of the mighty verse: *God (Himself) testifies that there surely is no deity but He, and so do the angels and those endowed with knowledge, being firm in upholding truth and uprightness: (these all testify that) There is no deity but He, the All-Glorious with irresistible might, the All-Wise* (3:18), which proclaims this reality in a miraculous fashion and adds its own testimony to all of the preceding ones, our traveler goes no further.

In reference to the brief meaning of the lesson that the traveler has learned at this sacred station, it is proclaimed in the nineteenth step:

> There is no deity but God, the Necessarily Existent One, the Single, the Unique, Who possesses the All-Beautiful Names and the all-exalted Attributes, and to Whom applies the most sublime description. His necessary Existence in His Unity is demonstrated clearly by all His sacred and all-encompassing Attributes and all of His All-Beautiful Names, Which manifest themselves constantly, and the manifestations of Which are demonstrated by the concurrence of His Essential Characteristics and operative Acts. This is testified to by the sublime reality of the self-revelation of Divinity in the manifestation of Lordship, Which reveals Itself in constant, all-permeating activity through the acts of inventing, creating, making, and originating through Will and Power, through the acts of determining, fashioning, administering and directing through Choice and Wisdom, and through the acts of expending, ordering, preserving, managing and providing through Determining and Mercy—all with complete order, harmony, and balance. It is also testified to by the sublime and all-inclusive truth of the mysteries of the verse: *God (Himself) testifies that there surely is no deity but He, and so do the angels and those who possess knowledge, being firm in upholding truth and uprightness: (these all testify that) There is no deity but He, the All-Glorious with irresistible might, the All-Wise* (3:18).

The Second Proof: Creation Rejects
Associating Partners with God

In the Name of God, the All-Merciful, the All-Compassionate.

Had there been in the heavens and the earth deities other than God, both (of those realms) would certainly have fallen into ruin. (21:22)

There is no deity but God, He alone; having no partner; His is the Dominion and to Him belongs all praise; He alone gives life and causes to die; He is All-living and dies not; in His hand is all good. He has full power over everything, and to Him is the homecoming.

One night during Ramadan I mentioned that each of those eleven statements of affirmation of Divine Unity contained an aspect of Unity and a particular good tiding (for believers). I explained only the meaning of having no partner in the form of an allegorical conversation or parable. Now, at the request of brothers at the mosque and friends attending me, I am committing this conversation to writing.

Imagine someone who, on behalf of all kinds of associating partners with God and varieties of unbelief and other ways of misguidance—such as attributing everything to nature or material causes or idol-worship—presumes to be Lord or exercise Lordship over some part of creation. That is, this being alleges that he or she owns or rules, controls or disposes, of that part. Coming upon an atom first, he or she informs it in the language or according to the presumptions of materialistic science or natural philosophy that he or she is its true master and owner. The atom answers in the language of truth and revealed wisdom:

I perform innumerable tasks; I work within, alongside, or upon an infinite variety of created entities. Do you have the knowledge and power to direct me in these tasks? I work and move in a measured relationship with innumerable other atoms of a like constitution.[5] Can

---

5 Each object that moves, from minute particles to planets, displays the Eternally Besought's stamp and Unity. Also, by virtue of its motion, each takes possession of the places in which it enters in Unity's name, thus adding them to the property of its true Owner. Each immobile entity, from plants to fixed stars, is like a seal of Unity that shows its location as missives of their Maker. Each plant and fruit is a stamp and seal of Unity that demonstrates, in Unity's name, that its habitat and native place is the missive of its Maker. In short, by moving in Unity's name, each entity takes possession of all entities, which means that one who cannot master all stars cannot master a single particle.

you command and employ all of these? If you own, arrange, or manage the infinite complexity of entities of, for example, red blood corpuscles, of whose atoms I am but one, and do so with perfect knowledge and discipline, then presume to be my Lord, and only then presume me to be attributable to any other than God.

But you cannot do so, so be silent! You do not own me and cannot interfere in my operation, for all of my movements and activities are so purposeful and arranged that only one with infinite wisdom and all-encompassing knowledge can run them. If any other had a hand in it, there would be confusion. How can anyone who, like you, cannot even give himself life, whose seeing and feeling are blind to truth, who sees himself as subject to chance and accidents of nature, even presume to interfere in my functioning?

The pretender responds as all materialists do: "Be your own master then! Why do you claim to be in the service of some other power?" The atom replies:

If I had a mind with knowledge as all-encompassing as the sun's light and with power as intense as its heat; if I had powers of feeling as all-embracing as the seven colors in its light; if I had faces and eyes turned to every being and every place with which my being and my place are connected; and if I had authority in and over all these connections— then perhaps, perhaps, I might have claimed to be my own master. Yet even then, had I done so, I only would have been as foolish as yourself. Now get away from me, for I can have no business with you!

The pretender, despairing of the atom, hopes to pursue the matter with a red blood corpuscle. Coming upon one, he or she speaks to it in the name of material causality and the language of natural philosophy: "I am your Lord and Master." The red blood corpuscle answers in the language of truth and Divine Wisdom:

I am not alone. If you also possess all my fellows in the blood army with whom I share the same formation pointing to our Maker, as well as the same duties and functions, and if you have the full and detailed knowledge, the awesome and subtle power, as well as the perfect wisdom to direct all the body cells through which we move and in which we operate, there might be some sense to your pretensions. But as you depend on blind and deaf nature or natural forces, you can have no influence over us, let alone mastery over me. Our order is so perfect and intricate that only one who sees, hears, and knows all things could be our true sovereign and master. So, be silent! I have so important duties and we work in such discipline that I have no time to answer your nonsensical pretensions!

Unable to deceive the red blood corpuscle, the pretender moves on and comes across a larger entity they call "cell." Addressing it in the familiar language of natural philosophy, he or she says: "True, the atom and the red blood corpuscle did not listen to me. I hope you can understand me. As I can see, you are composed of several smaller elements, like things arranged in a room. I can have a hand in this arrangement, and arrange and rearrange it. You can be my creature, and I can have power over you." The body cell answers with wisdom and in the language of truth:

> Although I am small, I perform vital tasks. I have the subtlest and yet strongest connections with all my neighboring cells, and with the whole organism of which I am a part. I perform vital functions with, for example, arteries and veins, sensory and motor nerves, electrical forces of attraction and repulsion, and the principles or elements determining my size, shape, and reproduction. If you have the knowledge and power to form an entire organism, to order and regulate the arteries and veins and nerves, and to put to work all the diverse forces and principles managing our form and function; if you can direct, with irresistible power and all-comprehending wisdom, the innumerable body cells similar to me in artistry and quality, then show your ability. Then perhaps, perhaps, you might claim to master or make me.
>
> But as you cannot, leave me—there are even now red blood cells carrying nourishment for me, white blood cells confronting diseases that might threaten me—I am busy, so do not waste my time any further with your vanity. No one as empty as you are of true understanding, of true hearing and seeing, could ever meddle in our being. Our order is so precise, delicate, and perfect that only one with absolute wisdom, knowledge, and power could control us.[6] If it were otherwise, our cohesion and order would not exist or would quickly fall into chaos.

---

6 The All-Wise Maker has created the human body like a well-ordered city. Some nerves function as telephones and telegraphs, while some of the blood vessels function as pipes carrying blood (the water of life). Blood contains two types of corpuscles: red ones convey nutrients to the body's cells, their sustenance, according to a Divine law (analogous to merchants and officers distributing food); white ones, fewer in number, defend (analogous to soldiers) against such invaders as disease. When actively engaged in defense, they perform two revolutions like Mevlevi dervishes and display a striking and rapid fluidity.

Blood repairs damage to the cells and cleans the body by collecting waste matter from the cells. As for arteries and veins, one forms channels to transport purified blood while the other forms channels for the unclean blood that gathers waste. The All-Wise Maker created

Disappointed, the pretender comes across a human body, reiterates the argument in the language of unenlightened nature and erring philosophy: "I can say that you are mine, that I have a share in owning and managing you." The human body answers in the language of wisdom and truth and in the tongue of its order:

> Do you have the knowledge and power to control and direct all human bodies similar to me that manifest the same signs of supreme power and creation? Do you have dominion over the treasuries of light, air, and water, as well as of all plants and animals, which are the ground and store of my provision and sustenance? Do you have the boundless wisdom and infinite power by which such invaluable, immaterial entities as the mind, intellect, and soul are so securely disposed in a narrow, bodily envelope, such as me, and made to "worship" by performing extremely important tasks? If you have such power, knowledge, and wisdom, demonstrate it—only then claim to own and manage me.
>
> But as you cannot, be silent! My Maker is All-Powerful, All-Knowing, All-Seeing, and All-Hearing—this is testified to by the perfection with which I am organized and by the sign of Oneness in my face. A being as ignorant and incompetent as you could never have the least hand in His Art.

The pretender, nonplussed that all points in the human body reject his or her claim to have a say, moves on and surveys humanity as a species, thinking: They live in diverse and complex societies. I see that Satan finds ways to interfere in their affairs of will and their social life. Therefore I can find a way to enter into the creation, constitution, and operation of their

---

two elements in the air: nitrogen and oxygen. When oxygen encounters blood during respiration, it draws the impure carbon element polluting the blood to itself, just like amber. Combining with carbon, it transforms both substances into carbonic acid gas. Oxygen also helps to maintain body temperature and purifies the blood. The All-Wise Creator has given oxygen and carbon a mutual ardor, a sort of chemical affection, so that, according to Divine law, they approach each other and then combine. Science has explained how this combining, being a form of combustion, generates heat as follows:

Oxygen and carbon atoms have distinct motions that, when combined, become one motion, each pair of atoms now having the motion of one atom. Thus one of the original two motions is "lost." This "lost" motion is transformed into heat by a law of the All-Wise Creator. "Motion produces heat" is an established principle. This chemical combination removes carbon from the blood and maintain bodily temperature while, at the same time, purifying the blood. While inhaling, oxygen cleanses the body's water of life and kindles its fire for life. While exhaling, oxygen enables words (miracles of Divine Power) to form in the mouth. *All-Glorified is He at Whose works minds are amazed.*

bodies? If I can find a point of control in their bodies, I will be able to control the body and its cells that turned me down.

With this intention, he or she addresses the species in the familiar language of blind nature and erring philosophy: "You appear very diverse and at great odds. I am your master and owner or, at the very least, I have a share in your making and life." To this, humanity responds in the language of truth and reality, and in the tongue of wisdom and order:

> Do you have the power, knowledge, and wisdom to create the rich texture covering the earth's face, woven with perfect wisdom from varied fabrics, thousands of mineral and plant and animal species? Can you, with a like wisdom, renew this texture and do so continuously? Do you possess the all-extensive power and all-comprehending science that manages the earth, of which we are a fruit, and the universe, of which we are the seed? Can you send us, from across the universe and in measured amounts, the provisions we need for our sustenance? Can you generate all individuals of my kind, past and future, whose faces bear the same sign of supreme majesty and power as mine? If so, you might then, perhaps, claim Lordship over me.
>
> But as you cannot, be silent! Do not dare to say that you have a hand in me just from remarking the diversity in my kind, for that diversity is part of our ordering's perfection. Diversity and multiplicity are copies made with a perfect order from the Book of Destiny [containing the origins of beings in a perfect order] by Power. Our diversity of appearance is a sort of reproducing of our forms [dictated by Destiny]—as the perfect diversity and order of plants and animals (which are inferior to us, under our vigilance, and which we study) also testifies.
>
> Is it at all plausible that the One Who weaves the diverse fabrics spread over and through this world's texture with great skill is other than its Maker, that the Creator of a fruit is other than the Creator of the tree from which it grows, and that the Creator of a seed is other than the Creator of the plant or tree into which it grows? You are blind, for you do not see the miracles of Power in my face and the wonders of His Creation in my constitution. If you had seen, you would have understood that nothing escapes my Maker's observation or tasks Him capriciously. He makes the stars as easily as He makes an atom. He creates springtime as smoothly as He creates a flower. He has placed the vast universe's index in my constitution with perfect correspondence. Could anyone who is, as you are, corporeal, incompetent, blind, and deaf have had a hand in such a Being's artistry? So be silent, and be gone!

The pretender then turns to the widespread texture overlaying the earth's face like an embellished cloak and speaks to it in the name of causality and in the language of natural philosophy: "I can manage you. I own you, or at least have a share in you." The texture[7] answers in the name of truth and in the language of wisdom:

> If you have the skill and power to create and weave all the textures in which the earth is closed anew every year and every century, and which have been hung on the line of past time, laid, unlaid, and relaid seamlessly throughout all time, and that will be hung on the line of future time, according to programs and patterns predesigned with the greatest precision and in accordance with Destiny's framework, each elegant, purposeful, and uniquely adorned; if you possess immaterial hands that can reach out from the earth's creation to its destruction, or rather, from the eternity of no-beginning to the eternity of no end; if you have the power and science to create all individuals within this texture, restoring and renewing them in exact order and wisdom; if you can create and possess the earth itself which is, as it were, a model for me and puts me on like a veil—only if you can, only then claim Lordship over me—if not, leave! You have no business here!
>
> In my rich and harmonious diversity are demonstrated clear signs of Oneness, and the clear stamp of His Uniqueness. Only He Who controls the whole cosmos, Who can do innumerable tasks simultaneously, Who can see all beings and their actions, whether inner or outer, at the same instant, Who is present and vigilant everywhere while being unbounded by time, space, or dimension, and Who has infinite wisdom, science, and power—only such a Being could ever own or have dominion over me.

The pretender turns to the earth, hoping to deceive it,[8] and repeats the same argument in the name of causality and in the language of mere naturalism: "I see that you roam about idly in the universe. Certainly you

---

7 In fact, the texture is animated, continuously giving the signs of life in a regular fashion. Its embroideries are renewed continuously with perfect wisdom and order to display the various, ever-differing manifestations of its Weaver's Names.

8 Briefly, beginning with the atom, each thing visited referred the pretender to the next level: from the atom to the red blood corpuscle, the cell, the body, humanity, the earth's outer garment, the earth as a globe, the sun, and the stars, respectively. Each said: "Be off! If you can subjugate the next one up from me, do so, and then return and seek to master me. If you cannot subjugate that level, you also cannot subjugate me!" Thus one whose authority does not embrace stars can have no acceptable claim to mastery over a single atom.

can have no master, and so I claim you." Upon hearing this, the earth roars like thunder in the name of truth and in the language of reality:

> Do not be foolish! How can I roam about without a master? Have you ever seen any disorder, lack of wisdom or skill, in the making of my dress or in any little point or fabric of it, that you dare to say that I roam about idly? Do you presume to own my orbit, which would take some twenty-five thousand years to traverse at a human being's pace but which I complete in my annual round with perfect discipline and precision?[9] Do you claim to own my ten fellow planets, which carry on their appointed tasks along their individual orbits as I do? Do you claim to have the unlimited science and power to create and control the sun, which gathers and focuses our orbits, orbits to which we are bound through the gravitation of mercy, and to make me and other planets revolve around it?
>
> Since you cannot plausibly make such a claim, leave me, for I have work to do. Our awesome circling, purposeful submission, and magnificent discipline show that our Maker is a Being to Whom all entities submit, and submit perfectly—as a dutiful soldier submits to his superior's orders. He is the Wise and Absolute Ruler of Majesty, Who holds the sun and planets in their proper order as easily as He adorns each tree with its proper fruit.

Having failed to find a place in governing the earth, the pretender turns to the sun in the expectation that he or she can open a path there. Since the sun is so great an entity, he or she hopes to use it to gain control of the earth. Addressing the sun in the name of the way of associating partners with God Almighty and in the language of satanic philosophy, as sun-worshippers do, the pretender says: "You are a monarch. You are your own master. You do whatever you will."

The sun answers in the name of truth and reality and in the language of Divine Wisdom:

> No, indeed! How can you utter such an untruth! I am but an obedient officer, no more than a candle in my Master's guest-house. I could not own and master so much as a fly, even its wing, for even such a small thing has such immaterial faculties and fine, exquisite works of art as its eye and ear that I do not have their like in any of my workshops. I cannot make even the smallest of them.

---

9   If half the diameter of a circle is roughly 180 million kilometers, the circle covers a distance of roughly 25,000 years [to cover on foot, provided one covers five kilometers (less than 3 miles) an hour and walks for 6 hours a day.]

Though rebuked by the sun, the pretender argues in the manner of Pharaohs, arrogant creatures who promote themselves as deities: "I claim you as mine in the name of causality, since you are not your own master but merely a servant." The sun replies in the name of truth and in the language of obedience to its Creator: "I can belong only to that Being Who has created me and all resplendent stars like me, Who, having fixed them in their stations with perfect wisdom, rotates them in glory and adorns the wide heavens thereby."

The pretender then comes among the stars and thinks: "Perhaps I can find some clients here." Talking to them in the name of causality and its partners and in the language of corrupt philosophy as star-worshippers do, he says: "You must be under the control of many different rulers, seeing that you are situated at such vast distances from each other." Upon this, one star, speaking for all others, answers him:

> How senseless and mindless you must be, not to see or understand the signs of the Creator's Oneness and the stamp of His Uniqueness in our nature. Do you not know how absolute is our organization, how secure the laws we obey? You think we have no order. In fact, we are the handiwork and servants of a Unique One of Unity that He holds the sky (our sea), the universe (our tree), and the vastness of space (our wide, maneuvering field) in His control. Like the many-colored lamps indicating human festivities, we are luminous witnesses of His perfect Dominion, brilliant evidence blazing across boundless space, of His Kingdom and Lordship.
>
> Each group of us are shining servants displaying His Majesty, near and far, in this world and the next, and in the many worlds beyond, within the infinitude of His Creation. Each of us is a miracle of the Power of the Unique One of Unity, a perfectly ordered fruit on the tree of creation, a bright evidence of God's Unity, a home and mount and mosque for His angels, a sun or a lamp of higher worlds, a witness of Divine Lordship, an ornament, a flower, a palace of the celestial sphere, a luminescent fish in the heavenly ocean, and each a beautiful eye set in the face of the heavens.[10] Throughout our vast community there exists profound silence amidst tranquility, movement in

---

[10] That is, we are pointers beholding the wonders of the Almighty's creation and pointing others to behold them also. The heavens observe the wonders of the earth's Divine artistry with innumerable eyes. As angels do in the skies, stars observe the earth, a display hall of wonders, and their doing so urges conscious beings to observe it attentively.

wisdom, shining ornament with majestic grandeur, the most varied beauty in perfect harmony, and the highest art in absolute balance.

While we therefore proclaim in innumerable tongues the Unity of our All-Majestic Maker and His being the Eternally-Besought, together with His Attributes of perfection, grace, and beauty, you accuse us of disorder and of having no duty and no master. Since you accuse us, who are infinitely pure and obedient servants, you merit a slap in the face in payment for your absurd effrontery!

A star strikes the pretender's face in a gesture like the stoning of the devil, and hurls him from the stars' domain to the bottom of Hell. It also hurls natural philosophy[11] into the valleys of delusion, and chance into the well of non-existence. It hurls all who arrogate to themselves some portion in the One God's Dominion into the utter darkness of improbability and impossibility, and every argument against true religion into the lowest of the low. Then the stars together recite the holy decree: *Had there been in the heavens and the earth any deities other than God, both (of those realms) would certainly have fallen into ruin* (21:22), and affirm: "There is no place for any partner with God, from a fly's wing to the heavens' lamps."

> All-Glorified are You! We have no knowledge save what You have taught us. Surely You are the All-Knowing, the All-Wise.
>
> O God, bestow peace and blessings on our master Muhammad, the lamp of Your Unity amidst the multiplicity of Your creatures, and the herald of Your Oneness in the display hall of Your universe, and on his Family and Companions altogether.

A Short Addendum

Listen to the following verse:

> Do they not observe the sky above them how We have constructed it and adorned it. (50:6)

---

[11] After its lapse, nature repented. Understanding that its proper purpose and duty is not to be active and cause effects, but rather to receive and to be acted upon, it realized that it is a sort of notebook of Divine Destiny, susceptible to mutation and change; a sort of program of the Lord's Power, analogous to the corpus of rules of creation instituted by the All-Powerful of Majesty, an assemblage of His laws. It assumed its duty of worship in perfect submission, admitting its absolute powerlessness and therein achieved the title of God's creation and the Lord's handiwork.

Look at the sky's face, where you see a silence in restful serenity; a wise, purposive motion; radiance in majesty; a smile in adornment; all combined in creation's orderliness and art's symmetry. Its candle's brilliance, its lamp's dazzle, and its stars' glitter manifest infinite Sovereignty for those with insight and sound reasoning.

The following expounds the lines above in interpreting the verse (50:6):

The verse draws attention to the sky's adorned and beautiful face. People who observe it with care must notice the silence in the extraordinary calmness and apparent rest observed there, and conclude that the sky has assumed that form through an Absolutely Powerful One's order and subjugation. If the heavenly bodies roamed at random, with their enormous size and speed of motion, the resulting noise would deafen everybody. They also would cause such tumult and confusion that the universe would collapse. If twenty buffaloes move together in the same area, you can guess what great uproar and confusion they would cause. However, according to astronomy, some moving stars are a thousand times larger than the earth and move at a speed seventy times faster than a cannonball. Given this, from the silence of the heavenly bodies in calmness and rest, you may understand the extent of the Power of the All-Majestic Maker, the All-Powerful One of Perfection, as well as the degree of His subjugation and the degree of the stars' submission and obedience to Him.

A wise, purposive motion: The verse orders us to see the purposive motion in the sky. That extremely strange and mighty motion takes place in absolute dependence on an extraordinarily subtle and comprehensive purpose. The immensity and order of a factory whose wheels and machinery turn and toil in wisdom, in perfect order and for wise purposes, show to what extent its engineer is learned and skillful. In the same way, with the sun in the center and mighty planets revolving around it in a perfect, subtle order for many wise purposes, the solar system shows the extent of the All-Powerful One's Power and Wisdom.

Radiance in majesty and a smile in adornment: The sky manifests a radiance of such majesty and a smile of such adornment that it shows how magnificent Sovereignty and how beautiful Art the All-Majestic Maker has. In the same way as innumerable illuminations used on special occasions to show the king's majesty and his country's advanced civilization, the vast

heavens, with their majestic glittering stars, show to attentive eyes the perfection of the All-Majestic Maker's Sovereignty and the beauty of His Art.

All combined in the orderliness of creation and the symmetry of art: The
verse says: See the order and subtle balance of the objects in the sky and
know how powerful and wise their Maker is. When you see someone turning numerous different objects one round the other or directing numerous
animals in a perfect order and with a special, delicate balance for many
wise purposes, you may guess how wise, powerful, and skillful that one is.
Likewise, together with their numberless stars of awesome size and speed,
the vast heavens in their tremendous immensity have performed their
duties for billions of years according to an established measure and with a
certain, sensitive balance. They have never transgressed their limits, and
have never caused even the slightest disorder. This shows to attentive eyes
just how sensitive and exact is the measure according to which their All-
Majestic Maker exercises His Lordship. Like similar verses in *Suratu'n-
Naba'*, among others, the verse indicates that the All-Majestic Creator has
subjugated the sun, moon, and other heavenly bodies.

*Its candle's brilliance, its lamp's dazzle, and its stars' glitter manifest the infi-
nite Sovereignty for those with insight and sound reasoning:* Almighty God has
hung on the world's adorned roof a lamp—the sun—that gives heat and
light. He uses this as a "pot" of light to write the Eternally Besought's "letters" on the lines of day and night on the pages of the seasons.

Like the phosphorescent hour-hands of a clock in a tall tower, He has
made the moon in heaven's dome the hour-hand of the largest clock of
time. He causes it to move through its mansions according to a perfect measure and fine calculations, as if He leaves a different crescent to each night
and then folds all of them in itself (making it invisible). Furthermore, He
has gilded the sky's beautiful face with stars that glitter and smile in that
dome. All this points to His Lordship's infinite Sovereignty and His Divinity's magnificence and invites thinking people to believe in His Existence
and Unity.

> Look at the colorful page of the book of the universe,
> and see how the golden Pen of the Power has inscribed it!
> No point has been left dark for those
> who can see with the eyes of their hearts.
> It is as if God has written His signs with light.
> See what an astounding miracle of wisdom the universe is!

See how tremendous a spectacle the space of the universe is!
Listen to the stars and heed their beautiful sermons.
See what Wisdom has written in these luminous missives of It.
They are all delivering this discourse with the tongue of truth:
"Each of us is a radiant proof for the majestic Sovereignty
of an All-Powerful One of Glory.
We are light-diffusing witnesses to the Existence of the Maker,
and also to His Unity and Power.
We are His subtle miracles gilding the face of the skies,
for the angels to make excursions on.
We are the innumerable discerning eyes of the heavens
directed to Paradise, and overseeing the earth.
We are the exquisite fruits attached to the heavenly branch
of the Tree of Creation; and to the twigs of the Milky Way,
attached by the hand of wisdom of
the All-Gracious One of Majesty.
For the inhabitants of the heavens, we are traveling mosques,
revolving houses and exalted homes,
light-diffusing lamps, mighty ships, and planes.
We are miracles of the Power of the All-Powerful One of Perfection,
the All-Wise One of Majesty.
Each of us is a wonder of His creative Art, a rarity of His Wisdom,
a marvel of His creation, a world of light.
To the people who are truly human, we present
countless proofs in countless tongues;
The eyes of the materialists, may they be blind,
never see our faces, nor do their ears hear our speech;
we are signs that speak the truth.
On us is the same stamp and seal. We obey and glorify our Lord,
and mention Him in worship.
We are ecstatic lovers in the widest circle of the Milky Way,
the circle reciting our Lord's Names.

The Third Proof: On Nature or Refuting Naturalistic Atheism

A REMINDER: The way of disbelieving naturalists is extremely irrational and based on superstitious beliefs. But why are such famous, intelligent naturalist philosophers able to accept such an obviously superstitious way of thought? The fact is that they cannot discern the
reality of their way, which cannot help but yield such superstitious
beliefs, although it is impossible to arrive at them reasonably or to accept them. They violently attack the Qur'an and the truths and es-

sentials of belief, condemning whatever they cannot grasp as super-stitious, and base their unbelief on nature. The Qur'anic verse, *Their Messengers said: "Can there be any doubt about God, the Originator of the heavens and the earth?"* (14: 10), which declares the existence and Oneness of God, is in fact too obvious to require discussion. There-fore, I will try to show why this is so and why it is impossible to rea-sonably infer the results the naturalist philosophers have arrived at with their methods. However, since numerous proofs for the exis-tence and Oneness of God have been elaborated in certain parts of the *Risale-i Nur*, I will offer here some other proofs and make a brief mention of some different proofs where necessary.

Introduction

O human! There are certain monstrous phrases uttered by people that imply unbelief. Some believers also use them without realizing what they actually mean. I will explain three of the most important of these.

THE FIRST: "The causes have brought it about."

THE SECOND: "Things have formed by themselves."

THE THIRD: "It is natural; nature necessitates and creates it."

Indeed, since things undeniably exist, and, as clearly observed, each thing comes into existence with great artistry and many wise purposes, and since nothing is eternal or without beginning, and everything comes into existence within time, then, O unbeliever, either things, for example, that animal, have been invented by lifeless, unconscious, deaf, and blind mate-rial causes coming together in a way requiring universal knowledge, con-sciousness, and will, or they form by themselves, or nature, or what you call natural powers, has caused it to exist. There is a fourth alternative that com-bined with absolute Knowledge and Will, the Power of an All-Powerful One of Majesty has invented it. Since there is no other way to explain the existence of things other than these four, if the first three can decisively be proven to be impossible, the fourth way, which is the way of Divine One-ness, will necessarily and undoubtedly be proven true.

The First Way

This is the theory that things come into existence by the coming together of material causes. Out of numerous arguments that show the falsity and impossibility of such a stance, I will mention only three.

THE FIRST IMPOSSIBILITY

Suppose there are hundreds of jars full of quite different substances in a pharmacy. We want to make some sort of liquid medicine or ointment out of them. So we go to the pharmacy and find out what the necessary ingredients are and what amount of each we should use. We see that an extremely precise amount should be taken from every ingredient. If the minutest amount more or less is taken, both medicine and ointment will lose their special properties and be of no use.

Is it at all possible or conceivable that those jars could be knocked over by a storm and exactly the required amount from each ingredient should come together to form the medicine and ointment demanded? Can there be something more superstitious or absurd than seeing such a coincidental formation as possible?

In this example we should think of each thing, particularly each living thing, as an animate ointment and each plant a living medicine. They are composed of numerous substances taken from a great variety of things in extremely precise amounts. Their attribution to the coincidental coming together of physical causes is much more impossible and inconceivable than the formation of any ointment or medicine as a result of the accidental coming together of substances in precisely required amounts, pouring from the jars as in the example.

In short, it is only by an all-comprehensive, limitless Wisdom, an infinite Knowledge, and an all-encompassing Will that any living thing in this vast pharmacy of the universe can be formed from the ingredients taken from substances in extremely precise amounts and measured on the scales of Divine Destiny or Determining and Decree. One who claims that they are the work of blind, deaf, and ignorant "natural causes and powers," or elements like floods, is more stupid than the one who asserts that the medicine in the example is self-formed as the result of the jars being knocked over.

THE SECOND IMPOSSIBILITY

If everything is attributed to "natural causes," not to the All-Powerful One of Majesty, the One and Unique, this means that many of the physical elements and causes should be present and work in the body of every living thing or being. However, that so many different and conflicting causes and elements come together of their own accord in perfect order and extremely precise measurements in the body of even the smallest of creatures, like a tiny fly, is so obviously inconceivable that one with even the smallest bit of consciousness could say, "This is inconceivable; it cannot occur." Indeed, the tiny body of a fly has a relationship and connection with most of the elements and causes in the universe; in fact, it is a summary or index of them. If it is not attributed to the Eternal, Powerful One, those elements and physical causes should be present and operate in it of their own accord. It is even required that they should be present and work in each of the cells of its eyes, which are tiny samples of its body. For if the causes or agents responsible for something's existence are of physical nature, they should be present in the immediate vicinity of, rather, inside their result. Therefore, attributing a fly to "natural" causes and elements requires that those causes and elements should be present and work in each of its cells. Even the most foolish of the people of sophistry would be ashamed of such an assumption.

THE THIRD IMPOSSIBILITY

It is an established rule that "a single, unique thing of particular individuality can only have issued from a single, unique source." If, in particular, a thing is a living one with a perfectly ordered and most sensitively balanced life, it will self-evidently display that it has not issued from numerous, different hands, which would be certain to cause great confusion and conflict, but rather it has issued from the Hand of a single All-Powerful, All-Wise One. Furthermore, the random coming together of innumerable inanimate, ignorant, unrestricted, unconscious, blind, and deaf "natural" causes and elements for the existence of something would only cause the increase of their blindness and deafness amidst the limitless probabilities. Therefore, attributing any being, which has a unique, particular individuality formed of innumerable elements in perfect order and a most sensitively balanced way, to such causes would be as unreasonable as accepting numberless impossibilities all at once.

Ignoring these impossibilities, physical causes or agents or powers affect something through direct contact. However, they have contact only with the exteriors of things or beings. But we see that the interiors of living beings, in particular, where the hands of physical or "natural" causes or agents have no contact, are ten times better ordered, more delicate, and

artistic than their exteriors. The tiniest living things, the minutest creatures, which the hands of physical or "natural" causes and agents cannot
reach and with which they do not have direct contact, not even with their
exteriors, are more strange and wonderful in art and more amazing in creation than the largest creatures. This being the case, only one who is a
hundred times more deaf and blind than the inanimate, ignorant, crude,
distant, and conflicting causes and elements can attribute these creatures
to those causes and elements.

The Second Way

This is the claim that things are formed by themselves. This is equally
inconceivable and impossible in numerous ways. As examples, we will
explain three of them.

THE FIRST IMPOSSIBILITY

O denier of the Creator! You can accept something that is impossible as
possible in numerous ways. For you exist and are not a simple, inanimate,
or unchanging substance. Rather, you are like a perfectly well-ordered and
continuously renewed factory or a like a wonderful palace that undergoes
continuous change and renewal. Innumerable particles are ceaselessly
working in your body, which has connections and mutual relations with
the universe, particularly in respect of the provision and permanence of
your species. The particles in your body are careful not to destroy those
connections and relations. It is as if they consider the entire universe from
the perspective of your relations with it and assume their positions accordingly. Therefore, if you do not accept that the particles in your body are not
tiny officials moving in accordance with the law of the Eternal, All-Powerful One, or the soldiers of one of His hosts, or the nibs of the Pen of Divine
Destiny, or the points of the Pen of the Divine Power, then each particle
working in your eye would have to have an eye capable of seeing the whole
of your body together with the whole of the universe, with which your body
is connected and related. You would also have to ascribe to each particle an
intelligence equivalent to that of a hundred geniuses; it would have to have
the capacity to know your whole past and future, your ancestors and descendants, the origins of the elements that form your body, and the sources of

your sustenance. Attributing the consciousness and knowledge of a thousand Platos to an unintelligent particle is obviously misguided.

THE SECOND IMPOSSIBILITY

Your body also resembles a wonderful palace that has a thousand domes kept in suspense with the stones all supporting one another. Rather, your body is a thousand times more wonderful than any palace. For that palace of your body is constantly renewed in perfect order. Even if we ignore your spirit, your heart, and other immaterial faculties, each of which is extremely wonderful, each member of your body is like a domed mansion. Supporting one another in perfect order and balance, your atoms form miracles of Art and Power, such as the eyes and the tongue. If those atoms were not officials working in perfect obedience to the orders of the Builder of that universe, then each of them would have to both dominate and be dominated by all the other atoms of the body, and be the origin of many Attributes that belong to the Necessarily Existent One exclusively, yet be both absolutely independent and dependent at the same time. Therefore, attributing any existent being, which has a unique individuality because of being a work of the Single One of Unity and Uniqueness, to the innumerable atoms that form it, is an obvious, hundred-fold impossibility.

THE THIRD IMPOSSIBILITY

If your body had not been "written" by the Pen of the Eternal All-Powerful One, Who is One and Unique, and were rather a work of nature or "natural" causes, then there would have to be as many printing-blocks or molds of nature as the number of its cells and the compounds they form in your body contained one within the other. For example, this book in your hand has either been written by a single scribe based on his knowledge, or if you claim that it has been formed by itself or nature, then there would have to be as many keys as the number of its letters. There are as many iron letters in a printing press as the number of the letters in the alphabet. They have to be arranged one by one in order to write a word, and therefore it can be said that as many iron letters as there are letters of a book are required for a book to produce itself. Furthermore, there is a kind of calligraphy consisting of only one large letter, yet, in which, for example, a whole Qur'anic *sura* of five or six pages can be written. This means that in order to write a single letter in a printing press, we need thousands of iron letters. Similarly, each living thing or being is like such a letter. It contains almost everything that exists in the universe. So, just as the attribution of a book to itself or to its iron letters requires those letters to come together by themselves in a conscious, meaningful way in a printing press, if we attribute a living thing or being to itself, then we would have to accept that all of the atoms or innumerable samples of the universe have come together consciously to form it. Even if we were to accept this ridiculous idea, which involves as many impossibilities as the particles of a living being, even of the universe, it is infinitely far from explaining life and its origin, or the many immaterial faculties of a conscious living being, such as reason, consciousness, and willpower.

The Third Way

This is the claim that "It is natural; nature necessitates it and has created it." This claim also involves numerous impossibilities, only three of which follow:

THE FIRST IMPOSSIBILITY

If the art and creativity observed in living beings that display infinite knowledge, wisdom, and willpower are attributed not to the Pen of the Determining and the Power of the Eternal Sun but to blind, deaf, and unconscious nature and "natural powers," this means that we accept that either nature should have present innumerable machines or printing presses in every being to invent it or nature should include in every being enough knowledge, will, power, and wisdom to create and administer the universe.

Consider that we see a reflection of the sun in every transparent thing, in every piece of glass or bubble of water. If we do not attribute the suns appearing in every transparent thing to the one and single sun in the sky, then we have to accept that in every thing, even in those that are so small that they cannot contain a match-head, there is a miniature sun that possesses all the qualities of the sun in the sky. In addition, we would also have to accept that there are as many suns as there are reflections of the sun in every piece of glass or every bubble in the oceans, rivers, or lakes, and so on.

In exactly the same way, if all existent things, animate or inanimate, are not attributed to the manifestations of the Names of the Eternal Sun, then we would have to accept that every thing, particularly every living thing or being, has in itself a nature or a power or, quite simply, a deity, that possesses infinite knowledge, will, power, and wisdom. Such an idea is the most false and superstitious of the impossibilities in the universe. One who ascribes the Art of the Creator of the universe to unconscious nature or certain nominal powers lacks consciousness more than any other being.

THE SECOND IMPOSSIBILITY

If all those perfectly ordered, and most artistically and wisely fashioned things and beings were attributed not to an infinitely Powerful and Wise One, but to nature, this would mean that nature should have in every bit of soil as many factories and printing presses as exist in Europe so that each bit of soil can be the means for the formation and growth of the flowers and fruit-bearing trees which grow there. For a pot of soil displays the actual capacity to give shape and form to the many different flowers whose seeds are buried in it. So, if those flowers are not attributed to the All-Powerful One of Majesty, then there would have to be a different machine for each flower in the soil.

Like sperms and eggs, all seeds are formed of the same elements. Each is a composition of oxygen, hydrogen, carbon and nitrogen, and is exposed to the effects of such unconscious things as air, water, heat, and light. But we see that each flower has a particular shape, smell, and color, and is completely different from others. Therefore, this requires that in that soil there should be as many factories as there are in Europe so that all those different living fabrics, thousands of various embroidered textiles, could be woven.

Thus, you can see how unreasonableness are the naturalists' and materialists' claims, and how unscientific and superstitious is attributing creativity to nature or causes or to things themselves.

IF YOU ASK: How do the difficulties that arise from the attribution of existence to nature disappear when existence is attributed to the Unique, Eternally Besought-of-All? How does existence, which is inconceivable when attributed to nature, become easy and necessary when attributed to God, the One and Unique?

THE ANSWER: We have seen when explaining the existence of a sun in every transparent thing on the earth, including every drop or bubble of water in the oceans that it is inconceivable and impossible for there to be as many suns as there appears to be. But if we attribute those (reflected) suns to the single sun in the sky, it is extremely easy to explain their existence. (It can even be said that the existence of the sun makes the existence of innumerable reflected sun necessary and inevitable.) Likewise, attributing all existent things to a Unique, Eternally Besought-of-All makes their existence so easy that we cannot help but think that their existence is necessary and inevitable. A connection between them and that Unique One is enough for their existence. But if this connection is cut off, with each thing being left to nature or to itself, then we would have to accept that in order to create a tiny creature like a fly, which is a miniature sample of the universe, blind and deaf nature should have enough knowledge, power, and wisdom to create and govern the entire universe. This is thousands-fold impossibility.

In short, just as it is inconceivable and impossible that the Necessarily-Existent One should have any partner or like in His Divine Essence, so too is the participation or interference of others in His creation and Lordship over His creation inconceivable and impossible.

As for the second part of the question, as stated in many other parts of the *Risale-i Nur*, when existence is attributed to the Single One of Uniqueness, then the being of all things becomes as easy as that of a single thing. But if it is attributed to "natural" causes or nature, it becomes as difficult for each thing to exist as it is for all things.

When a person joins the military or is connected to the state as an official, that person can be the means for the fulfillment of duties that exceed their own individual power and influence by a hundred thousand times. They can even take a king captive in the name of the state. Yet this person does not, nor are they compelled to, carry the equipment and power necessary to fulfill all the duties in which they play a part. By reason of their connection, the army, which is their point of support, carries such necessities. Therefore, any duties this one person carries out may be as great as those of the army or state. It is just like an ant being able to destroy the palace of the Pharaoh as an official of God, or a fly killing Nimrod, or a pine seed, the size of a grain of wheat, producing all the parts of a huge pine tree.[12] If the connection of the

---

[12] Due to its connection with the Creator, that seed works under the command of Divine Destiny or Determining and is the means for the fulfillment of many extraordinary duties. If that connection is cut off, the creation of the seed requires more capacity, equipment, and

person with the army is severed, leaving them to their own devices, then either their power will be restricted to themselves, or they will have to carry all the equipment belonging to the army and possess its power if they are required to carry out the same duties as they do as a member of the army. Even the clowns who invent stories and fantasies to make people laugh would be too ashamed to relate the second case.

To cut it short, when attributed to the Necessarily Existent One, the existence of all things is so easy as to be regarded as necessary and inevitable. But when attributed to nature, the existence of all things is unreasonable, impossible, and inconceivable.

THE THIRD IMPOSSIBILITY

The following two comparisons, which are mentioned in some other parts of the *Risale-i Nur*, explain this impossibility:

THE FIRST COMPARISON: A wild, uneducated man enters a palace which has been built in a vast desert and decorated with all the fruits of civilization. Having examined all the thousands of marvelous, artistically made objects, as there is no one in the palace and due to his ignorance and lack of sufficient intelligence, he thinks that one of the objects in the palace must have made the palace with whatever there is in it. But whichever object he examines, he cannot convince even his crude and uneducated intellect that that object has built the palace.

Later, he finds a notebook in which there is written the detailed plan of the palace, a list of its contents, and the rules of its management. It is also impossible for the notebook, which has no hands, eyes, or tools, to have built and decorated the palace. However, having not encountered anything visible to which he can attribute the existence of the palace, and since in comparison with the other objects the notebook, which contains the rules of the palace's construction, decoration, and management, seems to be more able to explain its existence, the man feels obliged to say, "It is this notebook which designed and built the palace, and decorated it with

---

skill than it takes to create a huge pine tree. For all the parts of the pine tree, which is a work of Divine Power, would be present in the potential tree—the seed, which is a work of Divine Destiny. The factory that produces a tree is a seed. The tree encapsulated in the seed by Destiny grows into a tree with that Power.

all those objects, which it had made and set in this palace." Is this not sheer stupidity and nonsense?

As in this comparison, a naturalist who denies God enters this palace of the universe, which is infinitely more well-ordered and more perfect than the palace in the above-mentioned comparison, and which is decorated with miracles of Wisdom throughout. Not thinking that it is the work of the Necessarily Existent Being's Art, Who is beyond the sphere of contingency, and evading that thought, he focuses on what they wrongly call "nature." Nature is, in fact, a board of Divine Destiny or Determining in the sphere of contingency. Divine Destiny or Determining uses it for inscribing and erasing Its judgments. From another perspective, nature is an ever-changing notebook of the titles or laws of the Divine Power's regular acts, and an index of the works of His Art as the Lord of the worlds. However, the naturalist who enters the palace of the universe says: "All these things require a cause for their existence. There is nothing visible that is more apt than this 'notebook' to attribute it to. Even though it is completely unreasonable to accept this blind, unconscious, ignorant, and powerless 'notebook' as the creator of the palace of the universe, which clearly requires an infinite knowledge and power for its existence, since I do not admit the existence of the Eternal Maker, I had better say that this 'notebook' has made this palace." To which we reply:

> O foolish one! Lift your head out of the swamp of naturalism, and turn round! You will see the Maker of Majesty, to Whom all things, from atoms to galaxies, testify, each with its own tongue, and at Whom they point, each with its own finger. Behold the manifestation of the Eternal Designer, Who has made that palace and written its program in that "notebook"! Lend an ear to His Book—the Qur'an—and be saved from your nonsensical words!

THE SECOND COMPARISON: An extremely rough, uneducated man enters a magnificent barracks. He watches the disciplined actions of a marvelously ordered army carrying out its drill. A regiment, a battalion, and an army corps sit down, stand up, march, and take up and put down arms as though they were a single private. Since his crude mind cannot understand this and thus denies that the army is working under the orders of a commander acting according to the laws of the state, he imagines that all the soldiers are tied to one another with strings. He thinks what a wonderful string this must be, and is astonished.

Later on Friday, he goes and enters a magnificent mosque, for example Ayasofya (Haghia Sophia). He observes that the congregation of Muslims performing the Friday congregational Prayer rises, bows, prostrates, and sits at the voice of one man. Since he does not know the Shari'a, which is the collection of sacred Divine laws and principles that guide the lives and worship of Muslims, he imagines that the members of the congregation are bound to one another with strings which control them and make them move like puppets. With this most ridiculous idea in his mind, he leaves the mosque.

Like this comparison, a naturalist denier of God enters this world, which is, in one respect, a splendid barracks of the Sovereign of eternity for His numerous hosts, and, in another respect, a well-ordered mosque of the Eternal, All-Worshipped One for His servants. He fancies that the laws which the Eternal Sovereign's Wisdom has established for the order and operation of the universe—the laws which have only nominal existence and are in fact the titles of His acts in the administration of the universe—have a physical existence and have enough knowledge and power to govern the entire universe. Instead of attributing these to the Divine Power, he attributes the existence and operation of the universe to these laws of nominal existence which he calls "nature"—and which have no power, knowledge, wisdom, consciousness, and will—and to what he calls "natural forces," which are in truth a manifestation of Divine Power. He regards these forces as an independent power that is able to direct the universe. This is a thousand times greater abasing ignorance than the ignorance of the man in the above-mentioned comparison.

In short, if the thing which naturalists call "nature" has an external reality, it can, at the very most, be a work of art, not an artist; it can be a design, not a designer; a set of decrees, not an issuer of decrees; a set of the laws of the creation and operation of the universe, not a lawgiver; a created veil before God's Dignity, not a creator; something originated according to God's way of acting, not an originator; only a law, not an independent, conscious power or a powerful one; and a set of lines to inscribe on, not a source or origin or an author.

To conclude, since things and beings exist and, as stated in the "introduction" of this treatise, there can be no other way to explain their existence than the four mentioned above, and since the first three of these ways have been proven to be invalid because of the impossibilities elucidated, then necessarily and self-evidently, the fourth way is clearly the only valid way. It is the way of Divine Existence and Unity. It is indicated by the verse quoted at the beginning, *"Can there be any doubt about God, the Originator of the heavens and the earth?"* (14: 10), which clearly and undoubtedly states that there can be do doubt about the Existence or Unity of God, and that everything issues directly from His Hand of Power, and the heavens and the earth are under His Grasp of supreme control and direction.

O one who attributes creativity to "nature" and "natural" causes! The nature of everything, like the things themselves, is created, for it is full of art, original, and particular to itself. In addition, like everything itself, which is the result of a cause, its apparent cause is also created. In addition, the existence of everything depends on the existence of numerous "instruments." Therefore, there must be an Absolutely Powerful One Who creates both the things and their nature and causes, and the instruments required. And what need does that All-Powerful One have to share impotent causes in His creativity and Lordship over existence? God forbid such a thought! Rather, He creates things together with their causes so that He displays the manifestations of His Names and His Wisdom. By so doing, He establishes an apparent, ordered cause-and-effect relationship, and makes the apparent causes a veil in people's sight between His Dignity and what people may see as being defective or incompatible with mercy in things and events.

Which is easier and more reasonable for a watchmaker? Making the cogs of a clock and then arranging them to form the clock, or inserting a wonderful machine inside the cogs and then leaving the making of the watch to the lifeless hands of the machine? Is the second alternative easier and more reasonable or inconceivable and impossible? Use your reason to be the judge!

Or a scribe readies a pen, a piece of paper, and ink to write a book. Is it easier and more reasonable for him to write the book by himself, or to invent a machine inside the pen, the piece of paper, and the ink, more artistic and more troublesome than the book itself, and then tell that unconscious machine to write the book, while he does not interfere? Is not the second alternative a hundred times more difficult than the first?

If you say: It is true that inventing a machine to write a book is a hundred times more difficult than writing it. But there is also an ease in this because numerous copies of the same book can be produced with that machine.

The answer: By ever-renewing the limitless manifestations and effects of His Names through His boundless Power in order to exhibit them in ever-differing fashions, the Eternal Designer and Inscriber creates things with such particular identities and features that none of the missives of the Eternally Besought-of-All and the books of the Lord are the same as others. In order to display different meanings, each thing must have a different identity and features particular to itself.

If you have eyes, look at the human countenance: you will see that although from the time of Adam all human faces have had the same structure and organs, each has particular features distinguishing it from all others. Therefore, each human face is a different, particular book. Creating each with its particular features requires a different writing-set and a different composition. In order to collect the necessary materials for each and establish each exactly in its place, there must be a completely different workshop. Even if we, supposing what is impossible to be possible, think of nature as a printing press, in addition to making a new arrangement of the iron keys of letters for every piece of writing, all the particles required for the existence of each body must be collected from all corners of "nature" in exact amounts and specific proportions and arranged in it in perfect order; this is a hundred times more difficult than arranging the iron keys of letters for every piece of writing. In order to do all these things, there is still an absolute need for the all-encompassing Knowledge, Will and Power of the absolutely Powerful One. Therefore, this hypothesis of a machine is a totally meaningless fantasy.

Like these comparisons of the watch and book, the Maker of Majesty, the All-Powerful One creates both the causes and their effects together, and out of His Wisdom makes the existence of the effects dependent on their causes. He has an assembly of laws for the creation and operation of the universe, which are in fact the titles of His acts of creation and direction. By His Will, He has appointed a nature for each thing as a mirror to those acts or laws, and by His Power He creates each thing according to its nature. Therefore, is it easier to accept this truth, which, being completely reasonable and the conclusion of innumerable rational proofs, leaves us no other alternative but to accept it, or to assume that what you call nature and natural causes, which are blind, unconscious, contained in time and space, mortal, and devoid of any knowledge or will, have the limitless equipment required for the existence of each and every thing, and are able to carry out such deeds as the creation and direction of a whole universe, which require infinite knowledge, wisdom and discernment? Is this second alternative not beyond all possibility, even inconceivable?

The disbelieving naturalist replies: Even if in the light of your explanations I admit that the way of thought I have adopted to date is beyond reason and unacceptable, and believe in the 'Necessarily Existent One' as the Creator of all things, saying 'All praise be to God for belief,' still I have one doubt. Although we accept that God is the Creator, what harm can there be in some insignificant causes playing a certain role in the creation of some things in respect to the sovereignty of God's Lordship? Does this imply a defect on the part of His Sovereignty?

The answer: As clearly explained is some parts of the *Risale-i Nur*, by its very nature, sovereignty rejects interference. Even an insignificant director or official does not tolerate the interference of even his own child with his authority. The fact that in history some religious rulers have killed their innocent sons in fear that the sons might attempt to interfere in their rule demonstrates how fundamental this "law of rejection of interference" is in rulership. The "law of prevention of others' participation," which the independence of sovereignty demands, rejects the existence of two sovereigns at the same time in the same place, whether it be a country or town. This has shown its great force through upheavals in human history.

Thus, if the sense of relative and transient rulership and sovereignty in humanity, which is powerless and in need of help, rejects the interference and participation of others, and seeks to preserve its independence in its position so jealously, then, if you can, compare how indispensable the rejection of interference and prevention of participation is to the All-Majestic One, Whose absolute sovereignty is based on or arises from His absolute Lordship over creation, Whose absolute rulership arises from His Divinity, Whose absolute independence arises from His absolute Oneness and Uniqueness, and Whose absolute self-sufficiency arises from His absolute Power.

As for the second part of your doubt, *which is:* If certain parts in the creation and control of some insignificant things is attributed to some insignificant causes, and those things assign some part of their worship to those causes, what harm does this cause in the worship of all beings from particles to galaxies, which is dedicated to the Necessarily Existent Being, Who is the Absolute Object of Worship?

The answer: The All-Wise Creator of the universe has made the universe like a tree with conscious beings as its most perfect fruit, and humanity as the most comprehensive fruit among conscious beings. Should that Absolute Sovereign and All-Independent Ruler, that Single One of Uniqueness, Who has created the universe so that He could be known and loved, allow others to own humanity, the fruit of the whole universe? Would He also allow humanity's thanks and worship, for which it has been created, and which are therefore its most elevated fruit, to be dedicated to others? Would He, totally contrary to His Wisdom, make the result of creation and the fruit of the universe futile and in vain? God forbid such a thought!

Also, would He give consent to the worship of creatures being dedicated to others, which would mean a denial of His Wisdom and Lordship? While He demonstrates through His acts that He wills to be known and loved to a boundless degree, would He cause Himself to be forgotten and His most elevated purposes for the existence of the universe to be denied by allowing the thankfulness, love, and worship of all creatures to be directed towards anything else other than Him?

O friend who has given up naturalism! Now it is your turn to speak! He replies:

> All praise be to God, these two doubts of mine have been resolved. You have convincingly explained God's absolute Oneness and why He is only the True Object of Worship, and that nothing else other than Him has the right to be worshipped and is not worthy of worship. Therefore, the denial of this truth would mean arrogance to the extent of denying the sun and the daytime.

Conclusion

The person who has renounced naturalism and accepted belief in God said, "All praise be to God; I no longer have any doubts concerning God's existence and Oneness, but still I have a few questions."

THE FIRST QUESTION

We hear many people who are idle in performing the daily Prayers ask: What need does God Almighty have for our worship? Why in the Qur'an does He severely reprimand those who do not worship and threaten them with such a terrible punishment as Hell? How does it behoove the moderate, mild, and balanced style of the Qur'an to display such severity in the face of an insignificant fault?

THE ANSWER: Truly, God Almighty has no need at all for your worship, nor indeed for anything else. But you need to worship, for in truth you are spiritually ill. We have indicated in many parts of the *Risale-i Nur* that worship is a cure for many spiritual wounds of humanity. If a patient responds to a compassionate doctor who insists that he should take the medicines prescribed for his illness, saying, "What need do you have for the medicine? Why are you insisting in this way?", you can understand how foolish this would be.

As for the severe threats of the Qur'an against the non-fulfillment of the duty of worship with terrible punishments, it is like this: In order to protect his subjects' rights, a monarch punishes an ordinary man in accordance to the extent that he violates those rights. Likewise, one who does not worship, including in particular the Prayer, is seriously violating the rights of the creatures, who are like subjects of the Absolute Sovereign of eternity. For the perfection of creatures displays itself through glorification and other kinds of worship manifested by their relationship with the Maker. One who does not worship does not, indeed cannot, see their worship, and even denies it. By reducing the creatures from their position of each being a missive of the Eternally Besought-of-All and a mirror to His Names by reason of their worship to the degree of being insignificant, inanimate, meaningless, aimless, and randomly existent things, this person has insulted them, and denies their perfections.

Indeed, everyone sees the universe in their own mirror. God Almighty has created humanity as a measure and scale for the universe. He has given each person a particular, private world out of the universe. The particular world of each person takes on the color of his or her heart. For example, a desperate, weeping person sees creatures as weeping and in despair, while a cheerful, optimistic one sees them as also cheerful and smiling. One who worships God Almighty in a serious, reflective manner can discern to certain degree the actual worship and glorifications of creatures, while a person who does not worship, due to either heedlessness or denial, thinks of creatures in a manner devoid of any truth and completely contrary to their actual perfections, and thus violates their rights.

Furthermore, no one is their own creator and owner; everyone is a servant of God Almighty. Therefore, those who do not perform the prescribed Prayers, defeated by their carnal, evil-commanding soul, wrong themselves, although they are servants of their Master and Owner. So, their Owner makes severe threats in order to protect His servant's rights against the evil-commanding soul, and to restore them. In addition, one who does not worship, which is God's purpose for His creation or the ultimate reason for a person's existence, is transgressing the Divine Will and Wisdom, and therefore deserves punishment.

In short, those who do not worship both wrong themselves, the servants of God Almighty owned by Him, and wrong and transgress the rights of creatures that arise from the perfections they share as worshipping servants of God. Just as unbelief is an insult to creatures, so too is the non-fulfillment of the duty of worship a denial of the perfections shared by creatures. Likewise, it is a transgression against Divine Wisdom and this deserves severe threats and punishment. It is in order to express this truth that the Qur'an of miraculous expression has chosen the severe style under discussion, which, in complete conformity with eloquence, corresponds to the requirements of the situation.

THE SECOND QUESTION

The person who has renounced naturalism and has come to believe next asks: It is astonishing that with whatever it has and whatever it does, and in every aspect, everything totally depends on Divine Will and Power. The infinite abundance, which we clearly see in existence, and the limitless ease in the creation of things that arise from their being created by One God, and which is demonstrated by such Qur'anic verses as

> Your creation and your resurrection are but as (the creation and resurrection) of a single soul (31: 28), and

> The matter of the Hour (of Doom) is (in relation with the Divine Power) but the twinkling of an eye, or even quicker (16: 77),

show that this supreme, astonishing fact is completely acceptable and rational. However, we cannot comprehend this supreme, astonishing fact. How do you explain this ease?"

THE ANSWER: It was explained clearly and in a convincing way while commenting on, *He is powerful over all things*, which is the Tenth Phrase of the Twentieth Letter. In particular, it was explained even more clearly in the Addendum to that Letter that when all things are attributed to One, Single Maker, their existence becomes as easy as the existence of a single thing. If they are not attributed to a Single One of Uniqueness, the existence of a single thing becomes as difficult as the existence of all things; indeed, the existence of a seed becomes as difficult as the existence of a tree. But if all things are attributed to their true Maker, the existence of the universe becomes as easy as the existence of a tree, and the existence of a tree as that of a seed, and the existence of Paradise as that of spring, and the existence of spring as that of a flower. In some parts of the *Risale-i Nur*, we have mentioned many reasons for and several instances of wisdom behind the limitless value of things despite the infinite abundance in existence, and the perfect artistry in everything despite the infinite facility and speed in things coming into existence. We will briefly point out only a few of them as follows:

For example, if the command of a hundred privates is given to one officer, their command will be a hundred times easier than the command of a single private by a hundred officers. Likewise, the equipping of an army by a single center or factory or government is as easy as the equipping of a single soldier, while the equipping of a single soldier by many different centers of command or factories is as difficult as that of a whole army. For there would have to be as many factories as there is equipment for an army.

It is observed that by reason of growing from a single seed and on one root and of growing and feeding through a single law, the growth of a tree that yields thousands of fruits is as easy as a single fruit. But if a tree were dependent on multiple sources for its growth, with the result that all the necessities vital for each fruit were to be provided from different places, then each fruit would become as difficult to produce as a tree. To produce even a single seed, which is a sample and index of the tree, would be as difficult as the production of the tree. For all the substances for the growth and life of a tree are also necessary for the seed.

Thus, there are hundreds of examples like these which show that it is easier for thousands of things that are dependent on a single source to come into existence than for a single thing depending on multiple sources to come into existence. Referring you to some other parts of the *Risale-i Nur* for a detailed explanation of this fact, we will here explain only a significant aspect of it that is related to Divine Knowledge, Power, and Destiny. It is as follows:

You are an existent being. If you attribute yourself to the Eternal, All-Powerful One, you will understand how He has created you with a single command out of nothing, like striking a match. However, if you do not attribute yourself to Him, but rather to physical causes and nature, then since you are a well-ordered summary, a fruit, and a miniature index of the universe, in order to make you, all the substances necessary for the formation of your body would have to be finely sieved from the universe and collected from all its corners in precise measures. For material substances are only used for formation or composition, and physical causes may serve only as means for their collection. Every sensible person knows and admits that they cannot create out of nothing what they themselves do not have. Therefore, they would have to collect all the particles of substances necessary for the body of even a minute living being from all corners of the universe.

Now understand what ease there is in Divine Unity and attributing everything to Him, and what difficulties lie in misguidance, in associating partners with God!

Secondly, when everything is attributed to a Single Creator, existence is infinitely easy from the perspective of there being Divine Knowledge as well. It is as follows:

Destiny is identical with Knowledge in one respect. It appoints a certain measure for each thing, which can be regarded as its particular, immaterial mold. That measure or mold appointed by Destiny serves as a model for its existence. When Divine Power creates, It does so with extreme ease according to that appointed measure. Now, if that being is not attributed to the All-Powerful One of Majesty with an unlimited, all-encompassing, eternal Knowledge, not only do thousands of difficulties appear, but its existence would be a hundred times more inconceivable. For if it were not for the measure appointed by Divine Destiny or Knowledge, thousands of material molds made in the physical world would have to be used in the body of a minute organism.

So, understand why there is infinite ease in attributing everything to a single Source, and why there are endless difficulties in accepting multiple sources or associating partners with God. Also, realize what an objective, undeniable, clear, and elevated truth is stated by the verse, *The matter of the Hour (of Doom) is (in relation with the Divine Power) but the twinkling of an eye, or even quicker* (16: 77).

THE THIRD QUESTION

The friend who has found the right guidance asks: Those most renowned among philosophers claim that nothing is invented out of nothing, and nothing goes into absolute extinction. The factory of the universe runs on the cycle of composition and decomposition. Is this so?

THE ANSWER: Those most renowned among the philosophers who do not view creation in the light of the Qur'an see the formation and existence of creatures by nature and physical causes as inconceivably difficult and they are divided into two groups. One group is the Sophists. Abdicating reason, which is exclusive to humanity, they find it easier to deny the existence of the universe, including their own, than to follow the way of misguidance which attributes creativity to nature and physical causes. Denying, therefore, both their own and the universe's existence, they descend into absolute ignorance.

The second group is aware of the fact that ascribing creativity to nature and physical causes incurs endless difficulties even for the existence of so tiny a creature as a fly or a seed, and is therefore irrational. This leads them to deny the act of creation, and claim that nothing can exist out of nothing, and annihilation is impossible. They fancy that everything consists in the cycle of composition, decomposition, and re-composition, as dependent on the random motion of atoms and the winds of coincidence.

Now, see the ignorance of those who consider themselves to be the most intelligent of all, and understand to what points of intellectual poverty misguidance can drag people!

Consider an Eternal Power Which created the universe in six days, and shows Itself in the simultaneous creation and re-creation of hundreds of thousands of species on the earth every year, and replaces the world every spring in six weeks with a new one more full of art and wisdom than the former! Like applying a chemical to invisible writing to make it visible, this Power gives external existence to the archetypes of things and beings already determined and identified in the Divine Knowledge by the Divine Destiny. Therefore, it would be more foolish and ignorant than the Sophists to deny this Power the capacity of creation and reject the act of creation. Since both these two groups of unfortunate ones, who are absolutely impotent in themselves and have nothing more than a partial willpower at their disposal, yet are more proud and refractory than Pharaoh, and nature and physical causes, on which they rely, are unable to make something out of nothing and annihilate it utterly, they claim that nothing exists out of nothing, and something existent does not go into non-existence, thus denying the Absolutely All-Powerful One creation and sending into non-existence.

The All-Powerful One of Majesty has two kinds of creating. One is origination and invention. That is to say, He brings a being into existence out of nothing together with whatever is necessary for it. The other is making and composing. That is, in order to demonstrate the perfection of His Wisdom and numerous subtle instances of It, such as displaying manifestations of many of His Names, He makes certain things out of the elements of the universe. Being the All-Providing, He also dispatches to them atoms and substances, subservient to His command, and makes them operate within.

Thus, bringing into existence out of non-existence and sending into non-existence are two constant, infinitely easy practices of the Absolutely All-Powerful One, Who both invents or originates and makes or composes. One who makes the claim that a Power Which each spring creates out of nothing the forms and attributes of hundreds of thousands of living species together with all their conditions and states cannot give existence to what does not exist deserves non-existence.

The one who abandons naturalism and accepts the truth concludes: Praise and thanks be to God the All-Mighty, I have attained perfect belief to the number of the particles of existence, and have been saved from groundless suppositions and misguidance. And not one of my doubts remains.

All praise be to God for the Religion of Islam and perfection in belief!

All-Glorified are You. We have no knowledge save what You have taught us. Surely You are the All-Knowing, the All-Wise.

The Fourth Proof:
The Divine Name the All-Just

There is not a thing but the stores (for its life and sustenance) are
with Us, and We do not send it down except in due, determined measure. (15: 21)

One aspect of the meaning of the above-mentioned verse and one manifestation of the Divine Name the All-Just, which is one of the Divine Names
that have all-encompassing manifestations or one of the six lights of the
All-Encompassing Name of God, appeared to me from afar while in
Eskişehir Prison. In order to make it understandable, again by means of a
comparison, we say the following:

The universe is such a palace that in it is a city which is being continuously shaken by destruction and repair. And in the city there is a "country"
which is incessantly surging up in war and emigration. And within the country is a "world" which is constantly revolving amidst death and life. But such
an astonishing balance, equilibrium and act of ordering prevail in the palace, city, country, and world that it obviously proves that all the changes,
incomings, and outgoings which occur in these innumerable beings are measured and weighed on the scales of a Single Being Who every moment sees
and supervises the whole universe. For, considering that, for example, a single fish lays a thousand eggs at one time and a single flower like a poppy produces twenty thousand seeds, if causes—all creatures—were free and unre-
strained, being ever able to destroy the balance and overrun everything
through the onslaught of incessant changes and the elements flowing in
floods; or if they were under the control of aimless, purposeless "chance,"
anarchic blind forces, or unconscious dark nature; then the balance in beings
or the balance of the whole universe would have been so utterly destroyed
that within a year, indeed within a day, there would have been chaos. The
seas would have been filled with things in total disorder and confusion and
would have become putrid; the atmosphere would have been poisoned with
noxious gases and the earth would have turned into a refuse heap, slaughter-
house, or swamp. The world would have suffocated.

Thus, everything in the universe from the cells of an animate body, the
red and white corpuscles in the blood, the motions and transformations of
atoms, and the proportion and relationship among the body's organs, to the

incomings and outgoings of the seas, and the income and expenditure of springs under the earth, the birth and death of animals and plants, the destruction of autumn and the reconstruction of spring, the duties and motion of the universal elements and the stars, and the alternations, struggles and clashes of death and life, light and darkness, and heat and cold, is ordered and weighed with such a sensitive balance, so fine a measure that the human mind can nowhere see any waste or futility, just as human science witnesses the most perfect order and beautiful balance everywhere. Indeed, human science is a manifestation and interpreter of that order and balance.

So, come and consider the balanced relationship between the sun and its twelve planets. Does it not indicate as clearly as the sun the All-Majestic One Who is the All-Just and All-Powerful? And in particular our ship, that is, the earth, which is one of the planets, travels an orbit of about eighty thousand years in human distances in one year. Despite that extraordinary speed, it does not scatter or shake the things heaped or arranged on its face, nor does it throw them off into space. If its speed had been less or more to a certain degree, it would have thrown its inhabitants off into space and scattered them. And if the balance in its movement and placement were to be destroyed for a minute, or even a second, this would destroy the world. Indeed, it would crash with another body and cause overall destruction.

In particular, the compassionate balance on the earth in the births, deaths, livelihoods, and lives of hundreds of thousands of plant and animal species shows a single All-Just and All-Compassionate One as clearly as light shows the sun.

And in particular the organs, faculties, and senses of just one of the innumerable members of those species are related to one another in such a sensitive balance that it self-evidently indicates an All-Wise and All-Just Maker.

And in particular, the cells and blood vessels in the bodies of animals, and the corpuscles in the blood, and the particles in the corpuscles are so sensitively balanced and have such a fine relationship with one another that it clearly proves that they are being maintained and administered through the balance, law, and order of a single All-Just and All-Wise Creator, Who has in His hands the reins of all things, and the key to all things, and directs all things as easily as a single thing without the direction of one thing impeding the direction of others.

If someone who, deeming it unlikely, does not believe that the deeds of jinn and humans will be weighed upon His supreme scales of Justice at the Last Judgment notes carefully this vast balance which they can see in this world with their own eyes, they will surely no longer consider it unlikely.

O wasteful, unjust, dirty one, disrespectful of economy, justice, and cleanliness! Since you oppose the whole universe by not observing economy, cleanliness, or justice, which the whole universe and all other beings observe as basic principles in their acts, you have become the object of their anger and disgust. On what are you based and on what do you rely that you make all beings angry through your wrongdoing, disequilibrium, wastefulness and uncleanliness?

Indeed, the universal wisdom in the universe, which proceeds from the most comprehensive manifestation of the Divine Name the All-Wise, observes economy and lack of waste, and orders economy. And the all-embracing justice in the universe that issues from the most comprehensive manifestation of the Name the All-Just administers the balance of all things and orders humanity justice. The word "balance" is mentioned four times in the following verses of *Suratu'r-Rahman*:

> And the heaven—He has made it high (above the earth), and He has set up the balance, so you must not go beyond (the limits with respect to) the balance; and observe the balance with full equity, and do not fall short in the balance. (55: 7–9)

This indicates four degrees and four types of balance, showing its supreme importance in the universe. Just as there is no wastefulness in anything, there is no disorder or imbalance in it either. Likewise, the act of cleansing and cleanliness that issue from the Name the All-Holy cleans and makes beautiful all the beings in the universe. Unless the polluting hand of humanity interferes, there is no uncleanness or ugliness in anything in the true sense of the word.

You may therefore understand from this how fundamental the principles of justice, economy, and cleanliness are to human life; these are truths of the Qur'an and of Islamic principles. And know how closely interconnected with the universe the commandments of the Qur'an are; they have spread their firm roots everywhere and enveloped and permeated all its corners. Know that it is impossible to destroy these truths in the same way that it is impossible to destroy the universe or change its form.

Moreover, like these three most comprehensive lights, hundreds of other comprehensive realities, such as mercy, munificence, and recording and preserving, require the Resurrection and the Hereafter. Is it therefore possible that the Resurrection will not happen and the Hereafter will not be established, and so all these powerful and comprehensive realities, namely mercy, munificence, justice, wisdom, economy, and cleanliness, which prevail not only in the universe but also with all beings, change into mercilessness, injustice, a lack of wisdom, wastefulness, uncleanness, and futility?

God forbid, a hundred thousand times, God forbid! Would a mercy and wisdom which compassionately preserve the rights to life of a fly violate the endless rights to life of all conscious beings or the boundless rights of numberless other beings by not bringing about the Resurrection? And if it is permissible to say so, would the Majesty and Magnificence of a Lordship Which shows infinite sensitivity and care concerning mercy, compassion, justice, and wisdom, and the Sovereignty of a Divinity Which adorns the universe with its countless wonderful arts and bounties in order to display Its perfections and make Itself known and loved, allow the non-occurrence of the Resurrection, which would reduce to nothing all the creatures and perfections of this universe, causing the denial of these perfections? God forbid! An absolute Beauty and Grace such as that clearly would not allow such absolute ugliness.

Indeed, one who attempts to deny the Hereafter must first deny the entire world with all its realities. Otherwise, with all its realities, the world would contradict them with a hundred thousand voices, proving that they are liars a hundred thousand times over. The Tenth Word (included in *The Words*) proves with certain proofs that the existence of the Hereafter is as certain and indubitable as the existence of this world.

The Fifth Proof:
The Divine Name the All-Wise

Call to the way of your Lord with wisdom (16: 125).

One aspect of the meaning of the above-mentioned verse and one manifestation of the Divine Name the All-Wise, which is one of the Divine Names that have all-encompassing manifestations or one of the six lights of the All-

Encompassing Name of God appeared to me in the holy month of Ramadan. In order to indicate it, the following five points have been written in haste.

The First Point

As pointed out in The Tenth Word, the all-embracing manifestation of the Divine Name the All-Wise has made the universe into such a book that hundreds of books have been written on every page of it, and hundreds of pages have been included in every line of it, and there are hundreds of lines in every word of it, and every letter of it contains hundreds of words, and a short index of the book is to be found in every point. The book's pages and lines, down to the very points, demonstrate its Inscriber and Author in hundreds of respects with such clarity that an observation of that book of the universe establishes the Existence and Unity of its Scribe to a degree that is hundreds of times greater than the proof of the book's own existence. For if a single letter exhibits its own existence to the extent of a letter, the same letter exhibits its Scribe to the extent of a line.

One page of this macro-book is the face of the earth. As many books as there are plant and animal species can be seen to be written on this page in the spring one within the other, together, at the same time, without error, and in the most perfect form.

One line of the page is a garden. We see with our eyes that on this page well-composed odes to the number of flowers, trees, and animals in the garden are written all together, one within the other, and without error.

One word of the line is a tree which has blossomed and put forth its leaves in order to yield its fruit. This word comprises meaningful passages that laud and praise the All-Wise One of Majesty to the number of its orderly, well-proportioned, adorned leaves, flowers, and fruit. It is as if, like all other trees, this tree too is a well-composed ode, singing the praises of its Inscriber.

It is also as though the All-Wise One of Majesty wants to look with thousands of eyes on His wonderful, venerable works, thus displaying them in the exhibition of the earth.

And it is as though the bejeweled gifts, decorations, and uniforms accorded to the tree by that Eternal Monarch have been made with such incredibly adorned, well-proportioned, orderly, and meaningful forms in order that they might be presented to His view in the spring, the tree's particular festival and parade, that each of these gifts, decorations, and uniforms—the flowers, leaves, and fruits—bear witness to the Existence and Names of the Inscriber in numerous ways and with many proofs, one within the other.

For example, each blossom or fruit displays a perfect organization and balance. The balance is maintained through an unceasing and ever-re-newed act of ordering; the act of ordering follows perfect art and decora-tion, and this art and decoration is combined with exceptional scents and purposeful tastes. Thus, each blossom indicates the All-Wise One of Majes-ty to the number of the blossoms on the tree.

The tree, which itself is a word, grows from a seed, which is a letter. This letter is a small coffer containing the future content and program of the entire tree. And so on. To continue the same analogy, the manifesta-tion of the Name the All-Wise not only makes every page of the book of the universe, but it also creates its lines, words, letters, and points, as mira-cles; thus even if all the causes—living or non-living—should gather together, they would not make the like of a single point, nor could they dare to compete with it.

Since each of the creational signs of this mighty Qur'an of the universe displays miracles to the number of its points and letters, then surely, pur-poseless chance, blind force, aimless, anarchic, unconscious nature can in no way interfere with that wise, insightful, and particular balance or most sensitive order. If they were able to interfere, some traces of confusion would certainly have been apparent. However, no trace of disorder is to be observed anywhere.

The Second Point

This consists of two matters.

THE FIRST MATTER: As expounded in The Tenth Word, it is "natural" and "inevitable" that an infinitely perfect beauty and infinitely beautiful perfection tend to observe and manifest themselves. It is because of this basic universal rule or tendency that the Eternal Inscriber of the mighty book of the universe makes Himself known with His Grace and Perfections, and makes Himself loved through the universe, through all its pages, lines and even letters and full stops.

So, O heedless human! While the All-Wise One of Majesty and Grace wants to make Himself known to you and loved by you through each of His creatures in such brilliant and endless ways, if, in return, you do not recognize Him with belief or you do not make yourself loved by Him with your worship, you should know just what a bottomless, compounded ignorance this is and what a loss it will be; so, come to your senses!

THE SECOND MATTER: There is no room for partnership in the dominion of the All-Powerful and All-Wise Maker of the universe. For, as an infinitely perfect order prevails in everything, it cannot admit partners. For, if many hands intervene in one matter, they will confuse it. If there are two kings in a country, two governors in a town, or two headmen in a village, disorder will reign in all matters in the country, town, or village. Moreover, the fact that even the most minor official does not accept the interference of others in his duties shows us that the most essential characteristic of dominion and sovereignty is independence. This means that order necessitates unity, and sovereignty requires independence.

If such a temporary shadow of sovereignty, manifested on powerless humans who are needy for assistance, rejects interference, then certainly absolute sovereignty, enjoyed by an absolutely Powerful One at the degree of Lordship over the entire universe, will certainly reject interference with all its might. If there were even the most minuscule interference, the order would be spoilt.

However, the universe has been so created that the creation of a seed requires as much power as is needed to create the entire tree. And in order to create a tree, there must be as great power as there is to create the entire universe. And if there were a partner who interfered in the universe, they would have to have a part in the existence of the tiniest seed. For the seed is a sample of the universe. So, two different Lordships, for which there is not the least room in this vast universe, would have to find room for themselves in a seed, or even in a minute particle. This is the most inconceivable and meaningless of impossibilities and false conceptions. Unbelief and associating partners with God mean attributing impotence to the absolutely Powerful One, Who holds and maintains the entire universe in all its states and circumstances, in the balance of His Justice and the order of His Wisdom, even down to the creation of a single seed. Know from this what an infinitely compounded opposition to the truth, (what and unforgivable) error, and (what monstrous) falsehood are unbelief and associating partners with God, and what an infinitely compounded truth and reality is Divine Oneness and belief in it. Know this and say, "All praise and thanks be to God for belief!"

The Third Point

Through His Name the All-Wise, the All-Powerful Maker has included thousands of well-ordered worlds in this world. Among those worlds, He has created humanity as a center and pivot in which His instances of Wisdom and the purposes behind the existence of the universe are concentrated. The most important of these instances of wisdom and purposes relate to humanity; He has made provision the focal point of the human sphere. Most of the purposes that are followed and the instances of wisdom in the human world relate to provision and are manifested through it. Consciousness in humanity and the pleasure provision gives display a manifestation of the Name the All-Wise in a brilliant fashion. And each of the hundreds of sciences invented by means of human consciousness describes one manifestation of the Name the All-Wise in one aspect of existence.

For example, if the science of medicine was to be asked, "What is the universe?" it would certainly reply: "It is an extraordinarily orderly and perfect vast pharmacy. All remedies are prepared and stored in it in the best and most proper way."

And if the science of chemistry was asked, "What is the earth?" it would answer: "It is a perfect, exceptionally ordered chemist's shop."

And the science of engineering would reply: "It is perfect factory with no faults."

And the science of agriculture would reply: "It is an infinitely productive, well-ordered field and garden which produces all kinds of crops just in time."

The science of trade would reply: "It is an extremely well-arranged exhibition, orderly market, and shop full of the most artistic wares."

The science of economics would reply: "It is an outstandingly well-ordered warehouse containing every kind of goods."

The science of dietetics would reply: "It is a kitchen built and prepared by the Lord and a cauldron made and filled by the All-Merciful in which hundreds of thousands of the most delicious types of food are cooked all together in the most orderly fashion."

The science of military affairs would reply: "The earth is a military camp. Although every spring in that army there are hundreds of thousands of different nations newly armed with their tents pitched on the earth, they are given their rations, uniforms, weapons, training, and discharges, all different and particular for each nation, in perfect order, with no confusion and none being forgotten, through the command, power, and compassion of a single Commander in Chief, from His treasury; they are all administered in the most regular fashion."

And if the science of electricity was to be asked, "What is this world?" it would certainly reply: "The roof of this magnificent palace of the universe has been adorned with innumerable, exceptionally well-made and arranged electric lamps. There is such an extraordinary order and balance in their composition and arrangement that although all these heavenly lamps, primarily the sun, which is a thousand times larger than the earth, unceasingly burn, they do not spoil their balance, nor do they explode or cause fires. Their expenditure is boundless, so where does their income or fuel come from? Why do they not consume their source? Why is the balance in their burning not destroyed? A small lamp goes out if it is not tended regularly. Consider the Wisdom and Power of the All-Wise One of Majesty, Who makes the sun, which astronomy tells us hundreds of thousands of times is larger than the earth and hundreds of millions of years older, continuously burn without being extinguished,[13] and say, "All-Glorious God is!" Say to the number of the seconds of the sun's age, "What wonders God wills! Whatever and however He wills is! How well God does it, and how blessed and supreme He is! There is no deity but He!" and reflect: These heavenly lamps are in a wonderful order, and they are tended with the greatest care. It is as though the boiler of these huge, numerous masses of fire, these light-diffusing lamps, is a Hell whose heat is never exhausted; it supplies them with lightless heat. While the machinery and central factory of those electric lamps is an everlasting Paradise; it supplies them with light;

---

[13] Let it be reckoned just how much fuel would be necessary for the stove or lamp of the sun, which heats and illuminates the palace of the world. According to astronomy, piles of wood equal to a million earths and thousands of oceans of oil would be required for it to burn every day. Now think and say, "All-Glorious is God! What wonders God wills! Whatever and however He wills is! How well God does it, and how blessed and supreme He is! to the number of the sun's particles in the face of the Majesty, Wisdom, and Power of the All-Powerful One of Majesty, Who makes it give light continuously.

and through the broadest manifestation of the Name the All-Wise they continue to burn in orderliness."

And so on. As hundreds of sciences like these certainly testify, the universe has been adorned with innumerable instances of wisdom and usefulness, and purposes within a faultless, perfect order. And through His all-encompassing Wisdom, He pursues the same instances of order and wisdom as He has pursued for the whole of the universe in seeds and the tiniest living creatures in small measures. It is obvious that there is a purposeful choice or will and intention in pursuing certain aims, purposes, instances of wisdom, or benefits. Therefore, these intended purposes, instances of wisdom, and blessings can never be the work of unconscious causes or nature, which lack will, choice, and purpose; neither can they interfere in them.

Consequently, it cannot be described how most ridiculously ignorant it is not to recognize or how foolish it is to deny that the All-Wise Maker, the One Who does whatever He wills, and Whom the universe requires and demonstrates with all the endless instances of order and wisdom observed in all the creatures it contains. Indeed, if there is anything that we can say is the most shocking thing in the world, it is such denial. For while the most perfect order and endless instances of wisdom in all the creatures of the universe testify to His existence and Unity, even the most infinite in ignorance and blindness understand what blindness and ignorance it is not to see or recognize Him. I might even say that among the people of unbelief, the Sophists, who are regarded as foolish because they denied the universe's existence, are the most intelligent. For since they saw that it was not possible to explain the existence of the universe without believing in the Existence of God, the Creator of the universe, they denied the universe's existence. They denied themselves as well. Claiming, "There is nothing that exists," they abdicated their intelligence, and saved themselves from the boundless irrationality—under the guise of rationalism—of the other deniers; in one sense they drew close to rationality.

The Fourth Point

As pointed out in The Tenth Word, no one with consciousness can accept that a wise master builder carefully pursues hundreds of instances of wisdom in each stone of the palace he builds, but then he fails to construct the palace's roof, allowing it to fall into ruin and thus losing all the innumerable purposes and instances of wisdom. Similarly, it is not possible for an exceptionally wise one to pursue hundreds of benefits and purposes in a tiny seed and then to allow all the expenditure they have made on the tree to go waste by obtaining a single fruit from it, thus following a completely wasteful way that is contrary to wisdom.

In just the same way, the All-Wise Maker attaches hundreds of instances of wisdom to each of the beings in the palace of the universe, and equips them with hundreds of duties, assigning every tree instances of wisdom and duties to the number of its fruits and blossoms. So, His not bringing about the Resurrection would mean rendering countless instances of wisdom and duties as meaningless, useless or fruitless and allowing them all to go to waste, thus imputing absolute impotence to His absolute, perfect Power, infinite futility and purposelessness to His perfect Wisdom, total ugliness to His absolute and perfect Beauty and Grace, and boundless injustice to His Justice. This would be paramount to simply denying the wisdom, mercy, and justice which everyone observes in the universe. This is the most bizarre inconceivability, containing endless fallacies. So, let the people of misguidance come and see just what a terrifying darkness there is in their misguidance and what kind of nest of vipers and scorpions it is, exactly as their graves will be. So, let them know that belief in the Hereafter is a way that is as beautiful and luminous as Paradise, and thus embrace belief.

The Fifth Point

This consists of two matters.

THE FIRST MATTER: As a manifestation of His Name the All-Wise, the All-Majestic Maker follows the lightest way, the shortest path, the easiest fashion, the most beneficial form in everything. This shows that there is no wastefulness, futility, or absence of benefits in the nature of things. As wastefulness is contrary to the Divine Name the All-Wise, the manifestation of this Name requires economy, which is one of its fundamental principles.

O wasteful human! Know how contrarily to the truth you act by not following economy, which is one of the most basic principles in the universe! And understand what an essential, comprehensive principle is taught by the verse, *Eat and drink, but do not be wasteful* (7: 31).

THE SECOND MATTER: The Name the All-Wise obviously points to and necessitates the Messengership of the noblest Messenger, upon him be peace and blessings.

Indeed, since a most meaningful book requires a teacher to teach it, and an exquisite beauty requires a mirror to see and reflect itself, and a most perfect art requires a herald to announce it, certainly there will be a perfect guide, a supreme teacher among humankind, which is addressed by the mighty book of the universe, in every letter of which there are hundreds of meanings and instances of wisdom. This teacher will show and teach the sacred and true wisdom the book contains, and he will be the means of the appearance, or even the realization, of the Lord's purposes for the creation of the universe. He will also mirror and make known the perfect art of the Creator and the beauty of His Names, which He particularly wills to be displayed throughout the universe.

And since the Creator wants to make Himself loved through all His creatures and wills His conscious creatures to respond with love and worship, one from among them will certainly respond with comprehensive worship in the name of all of them in the face of the manifestations of the all-encompassing Lordship. Through a resounding manner of making known and glorification, which will bring the land and sea to ecstasy and cause the heavens and earth to reverberate, he will also turn the gazes of these conscious creatures to the Maker of all these creatures that are full of art. Again, He will turn the attention of all beings with reason to Him through a sacred instruction and teaching. The noblest Messenger, upon him be peace and blessings, did all this through the Qur'an of mighty stature, as well as demonstrating in the best way the purposes of that All-Wise Maker (for the existence of the universe and humanity). He responded in the most perfect way to the manifestations of all His instances of wisdom and of His Grace and Majesty. In short, the existence of such a one is as necessary, as essential for the universe as the existence of the sun. This being the reality, all the wisdom in the universe necessitates the Messengership of Muhammad, upon him be peace and blessings, as much as the sun necessitates light, and the light, the day.

Just as through their most comprehensive manifestations, the Name the All-Wise necessitates the Messengership of Muhammad, upon him be peace and blessings, to the maximum degree, so too, through their broadest manifestations observed in the universe, do many of the All-Beautiful

Names like God, the All-Merciful, the All-Compassionate, the All-Loving, the Bestower of bounties, the All-Munificent, the All-Gracious, and the Lord necessitate the Messengership of Muhammad, upon him be peace and blessings, to the maximum degree and with absolute certainty.

For example, the all-embracing mercy which is the manifestation of the Name the All-Merciful manifests itself, first of all, through the one who was sent as "a mercy to all the worlds," upon him be peace and blessings. And God Almighty's will to make Himself known and loved as a manifestation of the Name the All-Loving gives fruit through that Beloved of the Lord of All the worlds, and finds response in him. And all instances of beauty, which are the manifestation of the Name the All-Beautiful and Gracious, that is, the beauty of the Divine Essence, the beauty of the Divine Names, the beauty of His Art, and the beauty of creatures, are seen and displayed in the mirror of Muhammad, upon him be peace and blessings. And the manifestations of the magnificence of the Lordship and sovereignty of Divinity are known, become visible and understood, and are confirmed through the Messengership of Muhammad, the herald of the dominion of Lordship, upon him be peace and blessings. And so on. Like these examples, each of the majority of the All-Beautiful Names is a shining proof for the Messengership of Muhammad, upon him be peace and blessings.

To sum up: Since the universe exists and cannot be denied, then surely, observable realities such as wisdom, munificence, mercy, beauty, order, balance, and adornment, which are in effect the colors, embellishments, lights, arts, lives, and bonds of the universe, can in no way be denied. Since denying these attributes and acts is not possible, certainly the Necessarily Existent One, the All-Wise, the All-Munificent, the All-Compassionate, the All-Beautiful and Gracious, and the All-Just, the One Who is signified by these attributes, and Who is the Performer of these deeds, and the Sun and Source of these lights, can in no way be denied. And certainly the Messengership of Muhammad, upon him be peace and blessings, who is the supreme guide, the most perfect teacher, the most eminent herald, the solver of the enigma of existence, the mirror of the Eternally Besought-of-All, the beloved of the All-Merciful, and the means of these attributes and acts being manifested, indeed of their perfection, and even of their being realized, can in no way be denied. Like the lights of the world of reality and of the reality of the universe, his Messengership is the most brilliant light of the universe.

Blessings and peace be upon him and his Family and Companions to the number of seconds of the days and the particles of the creatures.

All-Glorified are You. We have no knowledge save what You have taught us. Surely You are the All-Knowing, the All-Wise.

The Sixth Proof:
God's Being the All-Living and One Who Causes to Die

God revives this vast earth when it is dead and dry, thereby displaying His Power via resurrecting countless species of creation, each as extraordinary as the promised resurrection of humanity. He shows His all-embracing Knowledge in these creatures' infinite distinctions and differentiations within their complex intermingling. Also, He turns His servants' attention toward eternal happiness by promising their resurrection in His heavenly decrees, and displays the splendor of His Lordship by causing all His creatures to help and cooperate with each other and directing them within the orbit of His Command and Will. Furthermore, He shows the value His gives to us by creating us as the Tree of Creation's most comprehensive, subtlest, worthiest, and most valued, fruit; by addressing us directly; and by subjugating all things to us. So, could an All-Powerful and Compassionate, the All-Knowing and Wise, One Who does all these, not (or be unable to) bring about the Resurrection? Could He not institute His Supreme Court and create Paradise and Hell? Such ideas are inconceivable.

Indeed, the Almighty Disposer of this world's affairs continually creates on this finite, transient earth numerous signs, examples, and indications of the Supreme Gathering and the Plain of Resurrection. Each spring we see countless animal and plant species resurrected in a few days. All tree and plant roots, as well as certain animals, are revived and restored exactly as they were. Other animals are re-created in nearly identical forms. Seeds that appear so alike quickly grow into distinct and differentiated entities, after being brought to full vigor with extraordinary rapidity and ease, in absolute orderliness and harmony. How could anything be difficult for the One Who does this? How could He create the heavens and the earth in six days and yet be unable to resurrect humanity with a single blast?

Suppose a gifted writer could rewrite in an hour countless books whose letters were confused or effaced on a sheet of paper without error or omission, fully and in the best style. If someone then told you that he could rewrite in a minute from memory a book which he had written and had fallen into water, how could you say that he could not do so? Or think of a king who, to show his power or warn or for recreation, removes mountains with a command, turns his kingdom about, and transforms the sea into dry land. Then you see that a great boulder blocks the path of guests going to his reception. If someone says that the king will remove the boulder with a command, would you say that he could not do so? Or imagine someone assembles a great army in a day, and you are told that he will re-assemble it in battalions by a trumpet blast after dismissing them to rest, would you respond with disbelief? If you did, your error would be enormous.

Now, see how the Eternal Designer closes winter's white page and opens spring's and summer's green pages before our eyes. With the Pen of Power and Destiny, He inscribes infinite species on the page of the earth in a most beautiful style. They are all intermingled but he inscribes them without confusion and error, giving each its distinct form. Inscribing one does not hinder the inscription of another. Is it reasonable to ask concerning the All-Wise and All-Preserving, Who compacts a great tree's being into a dot-sized seed, how He preserves the spirits of those who die; how the All-Powerful One, Who spins the earth like a pebble in a sling, will remove the earth from the path of His guests travelling to the Hereafter?

Is it reasonable to ask concerning the All-Majestic One, Who installs the atoms of all living beings in their respective bodies with perfect orderliness with the command of Be! and it is, and thus creates disciplined, well-organized armies—is it reasonable to ask how He can re-assemble these atoms and bodily members, which have already known each other in perfectly organized battalions of bodies, after they have dispersed?

You see with your own eyes the numerous designs made by God as signs, similitudes, and analogies of the Resurrection. He displays them in every era, the alternation of day and night, even in the coming and going of clouds. If you imagine yourself 1,000 years in the past and then compare past and future, you will see as many examples and analogies of the Resurrection as there are centuries and days past. If, after this, you still consider bodily Resurrection improbable and unacceptable to reason, there is something seriously wrong with your powers of reasoning.

Concerning this truth, the Supreme Decree says:

Look upon the imprints of God's Mercy, how He revives the earth after its death. He it is Who will revive the dead [in a similar way]. He
has full power over everything. (30:50)

In short, there is nothing which makes the Resurrection impossible,
and there is much necessitates it.

The glorious and eternal Lordship, the all-mighty and all-embracing
Sovereignty, of the One Who gives life and death to this wide and wonderful earth as if it were a single organism; Who has made it as a pleasing cradle
and handsome craft for humanity and animals; Who has made the sun a lamp
that gives it both its light and heat; Who has made the planets transports for
His angels—such Lordship and Sovereignty cannot be confined to a mutable,
transitory, unstable, slight, and imperfect world. Thus there is another realm,
one worthy of Him, immutable, permanent, stable, great, and perfect. He
causes us to work for this realm and summons us to it. Those who have penetrated from outward appearances to truth, who have been ennobled by proximity to the Divine Presence, all spiritual "poles" endowed with light-filled
hearts, and those with enlightened minds, testify that He will transfer us to
that other kingdom. They teach us that He has prepared a reward and a
requital for us there, and that He gives us His firm promises and stern warnings thereof.

Breaking a promise is base humiliation and therefore irreconcilable with
His Sanctity's glory. Failure to carry out a threat can arise either from forgiveness or impotence (ignorance). Unbelief is an unforgivable crime.[14] The All-
Powerful is exempt from and far above all impotence. All who teach this
and bear witness to it are all agreed on this fundamental, even though they
follow different paths of thought and approach. Their testimony has the
authority of learned consensus. Each of them is a guiding light of humanity, the cherished one of a people and the object of their veneration. In

---

[14] Unbelief is an insult to the whole creation as it degrades it, alleging it to be with no meaning and worth. It is also a disrespect to the Divine Names because it denies their manifestations in the mirrors of creatures. It also rejects the witness borne to the Unity of God
by all beings, and so gives them the lies. Therefore, unbelief so corrupts our potentialities
that we cannot reform and become unreceptive to good. It is also an act of absolute injustice, a transgression against the rights of God's Names and creation. The defense of those
rights, and an unbeliever's irredeemable state, require that unbelief be unpardonable. The
Divine declaration, *Associating partners with God is truly a tremendous wrong* (31:13), expresses this.

importance, each is an expert and authority on this matter. In any art or science, two experts are preferred to thousands of non-experts, and two positive affirmers are preferred to thousands of negators in a report's transmission. For example, the testimony of two competent men that they have sighted the crescent moon marking the beginning of Ramadan nullifies the negation of thousands of deniers.

In short, this world contains no truer report, firmer claim, or more evident truth than this. The world is a field, and the Resurrection is a threshing-floor, a harvesting-ground for grain that will be stored in Paradise or Hell.

The Seventh Proof:
The Testimony of the Heavens and the Earth to God

Surely in the heavens and the earth are signs for believers. (45:3)

Consider the following points:

- During spring and summer we see in the creation of things an infinite generosity and absolute liberality, which could be expected to cause disorder and confusion, within an infinite order and harmony. See all the plants adorning the earth's face.

- The absolute speed in creating things, which normally would result in imbalance and loss of decorum, is observed within a perfect equilibrium and proportion. See all the fruits decorating the earth's face.

- The absolute multiplicity and variety, which normally would bring about triviality and even ugliness, is apparent within art's perfect beauty. See all the flowers gilding the earth's face.

- The absolute ease in creating things, which normally would cause simplicity and lack of art, is seen within an art, skill, and attention of infinite degree. See all the seeds, which are like tiny containers and programs of all plants and trees, and also like small cases containing their life-histories.

- The great distances, which normally would necessitate difference and diversity, appear within an absolute correspondence and conformity. See all the varieties of cereal grains sown throughout the world.

- The utter intermingling, which normally would cause confusion and mess, is seen within perfect differentiation and separation. Consider how seeds, cast into the ground all mixed together and resembling each other with regard to their substance, are perfectly differentiated when they are about to sprout. See how the various substances entering trees are separated perfectly for leaves, blossoms, and fruits, and how the foods entering the stomach all mixed together are separated perfectly for the body's members and cells. Consider all this and see the perfect power within perfect wisdom.

- The infinite abundance and profusion, which normally would cause triviality and worthlessness, are seen to be most valuable and most worthwhile in regard to the earth's creatures and art. Among all those innumerable wonders of art, consider only the varieties of mulberry, those sweets of Divine Power, on the table of the All-Merciful One on the earth, and observe the perfect mercy combined with the perfect art.

Just as daytime shows light and light shows the sun, the great value despite infinite profusion; within infinite profusion, the infinite differentiation and separation despite boundless intermingling; within infinite differentiation and separation, the infinite conformity and resemblance despite the great distances; within infinite resemblance, the infinite care and attention in the making despite infinite ease and facility; within the most beautiful making, the infinite equilibrium, balance, and lack of waste despite absolute speed and rapidity; within the utmost lack of waste, the highest degree of beauty of art despite the utmost abundance and multiplicity; within the highest degree of art, the absolute order and harmony despite the utmost liberality—all of these bear witness to the necessary Existence, Unity, and Oneness of an All-Powerful One of Majesty, an All-Wise One of Perfection, an All-Compassionate One of Grace and Beauty, and His Power's perfection and His Lordship's grace and beauty. They demonstrate the meaning of: *His are the All-Beautiful Names* (20:8).

So, unfortunate, obstinate, and heedless one! How can you interpret this mighty truth or explain this infinitely miraculous and wonderful state of affairs? To what can you attribute these truly extraordinary arts? What veil of heedlessness can you draw across this window as broad as the earth and then close it? Where is your chance and coincidence? Where is your unconscious companion on which you rely and call "nature," your friend and support in misguidance? Is it not utterly impossible for chance and coincidence to have a hand in these affairs? Is it not inconceivable to attribute to nature even a minute fraction of ordering these things? Or does lifeless, ignorant, unconscious nature have machines and printing presses within each thing, made from each, and equal in quantity to the number of individual things?

The Eighth Proof:
A supplication

This treatise proves decisively the most important of the fundamentals of belief, such as the necessary Existence of God, His Unity and Oneness, the magnificence of His Lordship, the immensity of His Power, the comprehensiveness of His Mercy, the universality of His Sovereignty, the all-inclusiveness of His Knowledge and the all-encompassing nature of His Wisdom. Its indications of the Resurrection, especially those emphasized at the end, are also powerful.

Each of the introductory passages of this proof of belief arrives at eight conclusions, together with the evidences used to prove them.

In the Name of God, the All-Merciful, the All-Compassionate.

Surely in the creation of the heavens and the earth, and the alternation of night and day (with their periods of shortening and lengthening); and in the vessels which sail the seas and bring people profit; and the water which God sends down from the sky, therewith reviving the earth after its death and dispersing therein all kinds of living creatures; and in His disposal of the winds and the subjugation of the clouds between the earth and the sky—surely in all of these there are signs (demonstrating that He is the One God deserving of worship, and the sole Refuge and Helper) for all those people who reason and understand. (2:164)

O God, O my Lord!

I see through the eye of belief, the instruction and light of the Qur'an, the teaching of God's noblest Messenger, upon him be peace and blessings, and the guidance of the Divine Name the All-Wise that:

There is not a single movement in the heavens but it indicates Your Existence through its orderliness;

There is not a single heavenly body but it indicates or testifies to Your Lordship and Unity by performing its duties in silence and standing without any visible support;

There is not a single star but it demonstrates or bears witness to Your Unity or the magnificence of Your Divinity through its most proportionate structure, its precisely ordered position, its bright countenance, and the stamp of its resemblance to all other stars;

There is not one of the twelve planets but it testifies to Your absolutely necessary Existence and indicates the dominion of Your Divinity through its wise movement, its subjugation to Your law, its orderly duties, and through the satellites which orbit them.

Indeed, just as each of the heavens testifies to Your absolutely necessary Existence, so too, O the Creator of the heavens and earth, all of the heavens, as a totality, clearly bear witness with utter certainty to the absolute necessity of Your Existence. O You Who govern all atoms together with the compounds they form and Who have subjugated all the planets to Your command, making them revolve with their satellites, all of these testify to Your Unity and Oneness so powerfully that the shining proofs to the number of the stars in the heavens confirm their testimony.

With their extraordinarily large bodies, which move at amazing speeds, these unblemished heavens resemble an orderly army or a royal celebration illuminated by numerous electric lamps. They indicate most clearly the magnificence of Your Lordship and the grandeur of Your Power, Which has created all things; they indicate the limitless expanse of Your Dominion, Which dominates the heavens, and of Your Mercy, Which embraces all living creatures. They testify, with utmost certainty, to the all-encompassing nature of Your Knowledge, Which penetrates and orders all of the acts and states of the heavenly creatures, and to the comprehensiveness of Your Wisdom. This testimony and indication are so clear that it is as if the stars were the words of testimony of the heavens and their embodied luminous proofs.

As for the stars, which are like obedient soldiers, orderly ships, extraordinary planes, and astonishing lamps, they exhibit the splendor of the dominion of Your Divinity. As we can see from the sun, which is a soldier in the army of stars, and the duties that it performs with respect to our earth and the other planets under its sway, some of the companion stars of the sun have a relationship with the world of the Hereafter, and may in fact be the suns of the eternal worlds.

O the Necessarily Existent One, O the Single, Unique One!

These wonderful stars, these breathtaking suns and moons have been subjugated, ordered, and entrusted with various duties in Your domain and in Your heavens through Your Command, Power, Rule, and Management. All those celestial bodies glorify the sole Creator, Who has created them, Who administers them, and Who makes them revolve; they magnify Him, and say with the tongue of their disposition, "All-Glorified are You!," and "God is the All-Great." I too declare You to be the All-Holy through their glorifications.

O the All-Powerful One of Majesty, hidden because of the intensity of His manifestation and veiled on account of His Grandeur!

I have understood through the teachings of the Qur'an and the instruction of God's noblest Messenger, upon him be peace and blessings, that:

Just as the heavens with all their stars bear witness to Your Existence and Unity, the atmosphere also testifies to your absolutely necessary Existence and Unity through its clouds, its lightning, its thunder, wind, and rain.

Indeed, it is only by Your Mercy and Wisdom that the lifeless and unconscious clouds send rain, the water of life, to the aid of living creatures, which are in need of it: chance has not the least part in this.

Also, being the brightest and most powerful form of electricity, urging us to benefit from it on account of its illuminating quality, lightning sheds light on Your power in the heavens.

In addition, the thunder, which gives the glad tidings of the coming of rain, makes the vast heavens speak, and the roaring voice of whose glorification resounds in the sky, declares with the tongue of its disposition that You are the All-Sacred One and testifies to Your being the Lord of the whole creation.

Again, entrusted with many duties, such as bringing living beings their vital sustenance and causing them to respire and refresh themselves, winds transform the atmosphere into a kind of "tablet for effacing and confirming or writing and erasing" on account of certain Divine purposes, thus indicating the activities of Your Power and testifying to Your Existence.

Also, through its orderly words of drops milked from clouds and sent to living beings through Your Mercy, rain, which is the embodiment of Your mercy for living beings, bears witness to the comprehensiveness of Your Mercy and Your extensive Affection.

O the Ever-Active One Who controls everything; O the All-Transcending Bestower of abundant bounties!

While the clouds, lightning, thunder, wind, and rain testify individually to the absolute necessity of Your Existence, as a whole, they provide a powerful indication of Your Unity and Oneness through the fact that, despite their differences in nature, they exist and work together in harmony and help each other with their tasks. They also testify to the magnificence of Your Lordship, Which makes the vast atmosphere an exhibition of wonders and frequently fills and empties it; and to the greatness and comprehensiveness of Your Power, Which uses the atmosphere as though it were a tablet of "writing and erasing," and a sponge by means of which You water the garden of the earth. They also testify to the inconceivably vast and all-encompassing nature of Your Mercy and Dominion, Which embrace and maintain all creatures under the veil of the atmosphere.

Also, the employment of the air in so many wise duties and the employment of the clouds and rain for so many benefits which require an all-embracing knowledge, make it quite clear that were it not for an all-embracing Wisdom and an all-encompassing Knowledge, they could not be thus employed.

O He Who does whatever He wills!

Your Power, Which performs actions such as continuously displaying samples of the Resurrection in the atmosphere, and changing summer into winter and vice versa and bringing forth a new world while sending another into the Realm of the Unseen, all within an hour, gives an indication that It will change this world into the Hereafter and demonstrate unending activity therein.

O the All-Powerful One of Majesty!

Air, clouds, rain, lightning, and thunder in the atmosphere are subservient and dutiful in Your domain, through Your Command and by Your Power. These atmospheric creatures, which differ in nature, sanctify their Commander and Sovereign, Who makes them obey immediate commands with rapidity, and they praise Your Mercy.

O the All-Majestic Creator of the heavens and the earth!

Through the instruction of Your wise Qur'an and the teachings of the noblest Messenger, upon him be peace and blessings, I have come to believe in and understand what follows:

In the same way that the heavens, through their stars, and the atmosphere, through its elements, testify to the absolute necessity of Your Existence and Your Oneness, the earth also bears witness to Your Existence and Oneness through all its creatures and circumstances to the number of the existent beings it contains.

There are no transformations on the earth, nor any changes—be they universal or particular—in its plants, trees, and animals, such as the donning of new garments every year, but they bear witness to Your Existence and Oneness.

There is not a single animal but it bears witness to Your Existence and Oneness through the sustenance that is given to it compassionately and in proportion to its needs and weaknesses, and through being wisely equipped with the things that it needs to exist.

Also, there is not a single plant or animal that is resurrected or originated before our eyes every spring but it makes You known through its remarkable art, its fine component parts, its distinguishing features, and the perfect order and proportion in its composition and life.

All these plants and animals that fill the face of the earth as miracles of Your Power are created with perfect differentiation and rich adornment, and with absolutely no faults or flaws, from eggs or seeds that resemble one another and which are made up of almost the same substances. Thus, their testimony to the Existence, Oneness, Wisdom, and boundless Power of their All-Wise Maker is such that this testimony is more powerful and brilliant than the light which bears witness to the existence of the sun.

Also, there is no element in creation, such as air, water, light, fire, or soil but it bears witness to Your Existence and Oneness by performing perfect tasks that require consciousness in spite of their inanimateness, and by bringing perfectly formed fruits and crops of all kinds from the treasury of the Unseen, despite their simplicity and their seemingly random distribution over a vast area.

O the All-Powerful Originator, O the All-Knowing Opener, O the Ever-Acting Creator!

Just as together with all its inhabitants the earth testifies to the absolutely necessary Existence of their Creator, so too, O the Single and Unique One, O the All-Kind and All-Benevolent One, and O the All-Bestowing and All-Providing One, through the stamp on its face and the stamps on the faces of its inhabitants, and through their harmonious co-existence and mutual assistance despite being distributed widely, and through Your Names and Acts Which relate to them as Your being their Lord being the same, the earth clearly testifies to Your Unity and Oneness to the number of the creatures on it.

Also, the fact that the earth is like an army encampment, an exhibition, a place of instructions and drill, and that the hundreds of thousands of plant and animal divisions which form this global army are provided in perfect order with the exact component parts or equipment they need, demonstrates the magnificence of Your Lordship and shows that Your Power commands everything at the same time. Similarly, the fact that innumerable living creatures are compassionately and munificently provided with their sustenance at precisely the right time from simple soil, and that all of them obey the orders of Your Lordship with the utmost subservience, indicates the all-encompassing nature of Your Mercy and Dominion.

Moreover, it is only by virtue of an all-encompassing knowledge and an all-administering wisdom that it is possible for the endless convoys of creatures and all instances of life and death to follow one another on the earth in such perfect order, and for all the plants, trees, and animals to be administered with such perfection and regularity. This obviously indicates the all-encompassing nature of Your Knowledge and Wisdom.

Also, although humanity is entrusted with limitless duties, including the stewardship of all other creatures on earth, and although they are provided with capacities and potentialities so vast that it would take an eternity on earth to fulfill them, the sojourn of the human being on earth is actually a very brief one. One must therefore conclude that the importance given to humanity, the limitless expenditure provided for them, the boundless manifestations of Divine Lordship bestowed on them as the addressee of the All-Glorified One, and the infinite amount of Divine bounties showered upon them—none of these can be intended solely for this brief, fleeting, painful, and calamity-stricken life in this training-ground of the world, this temporary military encampment of the earth, this transient exhibition. Rather, since these things can only be intended for another, eternal life, an everlasting realm of happiness, they indicate, even testify to, the otherworldly bounties in the realm of Hereafter.

O *the Creator of all things!*

All the creatures of the earth are subservient to and administered by Your Strength, Power, Knowledge, Will, and Wisdom on this earth, which is Your property. And Your Lordship—Your acts of creation, maintenance, provision, nurturing, and administration—which can be observed on the earth, display such vastness and comprehensiveness, and the administration, provision, and nurturing within this Lordship are so perfect and sensitive, and Its actions and operations are replete with such unity, uniformity, and coordination that Your Lordship is clearly universal and indivisible. Also, the earth, together with all its inhabitants and through countless tongues that are more articulate than the speech of humanity, glorifies its Creator and declares Him to be the All-Sacred; through the tongue of His limitless bounties the earth praises and extols its All-Providing One of Majesty.

O *the All-Sacred One, Who is hidden because of the intensity of His manifestation and veiled on account of His Grandeur!*

With all the earth's glorifications of You and its declarations of You as the All-Sacred, I too declare that You are absolutely exalted above any faults, impotence, or the ascription of partners, and I praise You and offer thanks to You with all their praises.

O *the Lord of the land and the sea!*

I have understood through the instructions of the Qur'an and the teachings of the noblest Messenger, upon him be peace and blessings, that, just as the earth, the atmosphere, and the heavens bear witness to Your Existence and Oneness, the rivers, springs, and streams also testify clearly to the absolute necessity of Your Existence and Your Oneness.

Indeed, there is not a single creature, indeed, not a single drop of water in the seas, which are in effect our globe's steam boilers and the source of countless marvels, but it makes its Creator known through its existence, orderliness, position, and benefits.

There is not a single one of these amazing creatures, the sustenance of which is provided through simple sand or water, not one of these sea animals, each of which is created in an extremely orderly fashion, not one of the myriad kinds of fish, each laying a million or more eggs, but it indicates its Creator and testifies to its Provider through its creation, its duties, and the way it is administered, provided for, and maintained.

Also, there is not one single precious, ornamented substance or jewel in the sea with distinguishing features but it makes You known through its subtle creation, fascinating composition, and beneficial qualities.

All of these aforementioned creatures testify to You individually. Also, although they exist in extremely great varieties and numbers, and although all are mixed with one another, the facility with which they are brought into being and the stamp of unity displayed by their creation bear witness to Your Unity. Furthermore, the earth remains suspended in space and revolves around the sun at great speed without its lands or seas mixing with one another or its seas invading the lands. Also, all of its minerals and other substances, and all of its terrestrial and marine life are well-formed and extremely varied: created from simple water or soil, all these creatures are administered and nurtured with perfect orderliness. Moreover, despite their extremely abundant existence and the fact that everyday countless numbers of them die, none of their corpses remains on the earth or in the sea for long, with the result that both the face of the earth and the seas are always clean and pure. So, the earth bears witness to Your Existence and to the fact that You are the Necessarily Existent Being to the number of its creatures. In the same way that all these creatures clearly indicate the splendor of Your Lordship and the immensity of Your all-encompassing Power, they also indicate the boundless comprehensiveness of Your Mercy and Dominion, Which embrace everything—from the extremely large stars in the heavens above to the tiny fish at the bottom of the oceans. Also, through their perfect organization and ordered existence, through the benefits they give and the instances of wisdom they display, and through their well-proportioned structure and composition, they indicate Your all-encompassing Knowledge and your all-embracing Wisdom.

You have pools of mercy for the travelers in this guesthouse of the world and You have subjugated these pools for their benefit and for their ship so that they may travel. This indicates that the One Who offers such innumerable gifts from the sea to His guests of one night in a sideway inn— the world—must certainly have eternal oceans of Mercy at His eternal domain of sovereignty, and those here are but their tiny, transient samples.

Thus, the way in which the seas skirt the land in such an extraordinary fashion, and the wonderful sustaining and nurturing of the creatures that inhabit their depths all demonstrate self-evidently that they are subservient to Your Command in Your domain through Your Will, Power, and Administration. Through the language of all these facts, they declare You to be their All-Sacred Creator, saying "God is the All-Great."

O the All-Powerful One of Majesty, Who has made mountains as treasure-filled masts for the ship of the earth!

I have understood from the instruction of God's noblest Messenger, upon him be peace and blessings, and from the teachings of the Qur'an that just as the seas recognize You and make You known through their marvels, the mountains also recognize You and make You known through the instances of wisdom in their existence and the benefits they provide. For example, they serve the earth, keeping it solid and unperturbed by the invasion of the seas, and preserving its stability in spite of quakes and the stormy movements within it. They also purify the air of harmful gases, store and preserve water, and function as vast treasure-troves of minerals and metals that are necessary for living beings.

Indeed, there is not a single rock or precious stone in the mountains, there is not a single one of the innumerable kinds of substance that are used as ingredients for medication, there is not a single one of the extremely diverse kinds of minerals or metals that are vital for living beings in general and humankind in particular, there is not a single one from among the countless varieties of plants and trees that adorn the mountains, plains and fields with their flowers, making them prosperous with their fruits—there is not a single one of these but it testifies with utmost clarity to the absolute necessity of the Existence of an infinitely Powerful, Compassionate, and Munificent Maker through their instances of wisdom, their subtle arrangement and composition, their fine creation, their numerous benefits, and the extreme diversity of their tastes and natures, however similar they may appear to be on the surface. Also, in addition to bearing witness to the Maker through their great variety of blossoms and fruits, which show extreme variety despite the fact that they all grow in simple, uniform soil and are nurtured with the same, simple water, trees and flowers also testify to His Unity and Oneness through the similarity of their administration, maintenance, origin, habitat, creation and artistry. They also point to His Unity and Oneness through their abundance and the speed and facility with which they are created, even though each one is a unique work of art and of inestimable value.

Also, the fact that the all of the world's mountains have almost the same composition and that all species of beings are made perfectly, without the slightest flaw, in the same way, in the shortest time imaginable, and without the creation and sustenance of one individual and species being confused with or impeding another—all of this indicates the magnificence of Your Lordship and the immensity of Your Power, for Which nothing is difficult. In addition, the mountains hold many different varieties of plants, trees, and minerals to meet the endless needs, tastes, and appetites of innumerable kinds of living creatures; they also provide the necessary medications for countless kinds of illnesses. All of this indicates the boundless extent of Your Mercy and the infinite vastness of Your Dominion. Although the minerals and the seeds of all these plants and trees lie hidden and intermingled under the ground in darkness, they are grown and prepared with perfect order by virtue of a vast knowledge and an all-encompassing sight. All of these facts indicate the comprehensiveness of Your Knowledge, Which encompasses everything, and the all-embracing nature of Your Wisdom, Which arranges everything perfectly. In addition, through the preparation of medicinal substances and the depositing of minerals and metals in them, mountains obviously indicate the beauties of Your Lordship's compassionate and munificent arrangement and providence and the precautionary subtleties of Your Benevolence.

Again, Your creation of these huge mountains as well-made warehouses of supplies for the future needs of Your guests in this earthly caravanserai and as the perfectly arranged stores of the infinite treasures that are of vital importance for the lives of these guests testify indubitably to the fact that a Maker Who is this munificent and hospitable, this wise and caring, and this powerful and nurturing has most certainly prepared treasures of everlasting bounties for these beloved guests in an eternal world. The stars there will perform the duties of the mountains here in the world.

O the One Who has absolute power over all things!

The mountains are subjugated to the service of humanity in Your domain by Your Power, Knowledge, and Wisdom, as are the creatures that reside in and on them. They glorify and declare to be the All-Sacred their Creator, Who has made them subservient and dutiful in this manner.

O the All-Merciful Creator and All-Compassionate Lord!

I have understood from the instruction of God's noblest Messenger, upon him be peace and blessings, and the teaching of the wise Qur'an that just as the heavens, the earth, the seas, and the mountains, with all their creatures and contents, recognize you and make You known, so do all of the plants and trees on the earth, together with their leaves, flowers, and fruits, also know You and Make You known clearly.

Each leaf of all plants and trees, which commemorates its Maker through its enraptured movements, together with every flower, which describes and defines its Maker through its adornments, and every fruit, which smiles joyously on account of the manifestation of His Mercy, testifies with utmost certainty to the absolute necessity of the Existence of an infinitely Compassionate and Munificent Maker through its perfect and extraordinarily artistic formation, which is utterly impossible to ascribe to chance; it does this also through the perfect balance and proportion in its formation, and the adornment that accompanies that balance and proportion, and through the embroideries that contribute to its adornment, and the many beautiful scents and tastes that are added to its embellishments. As a totality these bear clear witness to the Unity (*Wahidiya*) and Oneness (*Ahadiya*) of the necessarily existent Maker. They do this through their mutual resemblance all over the world and their similarities in their creation, through the relationship between their growth and the way they are provided for, through the interconnectedness of the Divine Names and Acts Which relate to their existence and maintenance, and through the administration and nurturing of the countless individual members of the hundreds of thousands of varieties without flaw or confusion.

In the same way that these testify to the absolute necessity of Your Existence and Your Unity, the perfect and distinctive maintenance of countless members of the hosts of living beings on the earth, formed of hundreds of thousands of "nations," indicates the splendor and uniqueness of Your Lordship and the immensity of Your Power, Which encompasses everything and creates spring as easily as it does a flower. Furthermore, the preparation of countless varieties of food for the innumerable animals and human beings distributed throughout the earth indicates the boundless comprehensiveness of Your Mercy. Moreover, the perfect order in the performance of all these acts of providing, administering, and nurturing, together with the subservience and obedience of everything, down to the tiniest particle or atom, to

Your Acts and Commands, provides clear evidence of the all-encompassing nature of Your Dominion. Similarly, the fact that whatever relates to the existence, growth, and nurturing of every leaf, flower, fruit, root, branch or twig is based on certain knowledge and insight, with many wise purposes and benefits in mind, they each point clearly to the all-encompassing nature of Your Knowledge and Wisdom. With innumerable tongues, all of these also praise and extol the beauty of Your infinitely perfect Art and the perfection of Your infinitely beautiful Bountifulness.

In addition, through the hands of the trees and plants in this temporary guesthouse, such invaluable bounties and gifts are offered, such extraordinary expenditure is laid out, and such wonderful munificence is displayed that they clearly indicate, indeed, bear witness to this fact: the Powerful and Munificent All-Compassionate One has prepared, out of His eternal treasure of Mercy, a host of fruit-bearing trees and blossoming plants which are suited to the perpetual Gardens of Paradise, for the servants whom He will favor with eternal life in an everlasting realm. This He does because, in accordance with His will to make Himself known and loved through the bounties He bestows, He does not want His loving friends to complain, saying: "He has given us a taste of them and has now dispatched us to eternal non-existence without being able to enjoy them to the full." Nor does He will to reduce the infinite value of the dominion of His Divinity or cause His loving friends to deny His endless Mercy, thus transforming their love to enmity. All the fruit-bearing trees and blossoming plants in this world are but examples of their eternal counterparts, and are here in this world merely on display for those who would "buy" them for all eternity.

Just as the trees and plants glorify and praise You, and declare You to be the All-Sacred through their words of leaves, flowers, and fruits, each one of these words too proclaims Your absolute sacredness. The glorifications offered by the fruits through the mute eloquence of their disposition—that is, through their attractive shapes, their many different and fascinating colors, their edible parts of infinite variety and their marvelous seeds, and through being offered to the guests of this earthly caravanserai from the hands of the trees or plants—manifest themselves as though spoken words. All of them are subjugated in Your domain through Your Power, Will, Benevolence, Mercy, and Wisdom, and they are perfectly obedient to all of Your commands.

O the All-Wise Maker and All-Compassionate Creator, Who is hidden because of the intensity of His manifestation and veiled on account of His Grandeur!

With the voices of all trees and plants, together with their leaves, flowers, and fruits, and to the number of all of them I praise and exalt You and declare You to be absolutely exalted above and free from defect, impotence, and having partners.

O the All-Powerful Originator, the All-Wise Administrator, the All-Compassionate Nurturer!

I have understood from the instruction of God's noblest Messenger, upon him be peace and blessings, and from the teaching of the wise Qur'an, and I believe that just as plants and trees recognize You and make known Your sacred Attributes and All-Beautiful Names, there too is not a single animal or human but it testifies to the absolute necessity of Your Existence and to Your Attributes. They bear witness through their perfectly and artistically made bodies, equipped as they are with extremely delicate and well-functioning "instruments" that possess the finest order and equilibrium; they give evidence through all of their internal and external organs, which are made to operate with perfect sensitivity and orderliness, and through their members and senses that are arranged in their bodies with perfect balance and for extremely important purposes. For it is absolutely impossible that any random force, unconscious "nature," or blind chance should contribute to an artistry that is so delicate and wise, or to a wisdom that requires such care and consciousness, or to a perfect balance that is so sensitive and purposeful.

As for the notion that they form themselves; well, this is a hundred times more impossible and inconceivable. For their self-formation would require each of their particles or atoms to have God-like knowledge and power. Otherwise, how would each one be able to know itself perfectly and bring itself into existence, particularly since it would also have to create all of the other atoms with which it interconnects and has relations, together with all the other elements in the universe which have a part in its existence and operation?

The observable unity in their administration and maintenance as a whole, the perfect similarities among the members of each species, as well as between the species themselves, the stamp of unity that can be observed in their creation and nurturing, and the fact that each of them has eyes, ears, mouths, and so on, and is each directed toward similar goals—all of these and similar other instances of unity bear most decisive witness to Your absolute Unity. And just as all of Your Names are manifested in the universe as a whole, thus indicating Your Unity (*Wahidiya*), they are also manifested in each of the beings in the universe, thus displaying Your Oneness or Uniqueness (*Ahadiya*).

Also, like humankind, hundreds of thousands of animal species that are distributed throughout the world are equipped, trained, and obedient, like a well-organized army, and the commands of Your Lordship operate with perfect order in their kingdom. While this indicates the magnificence of Your Lordship, their extreme value despite their abundance, their perfect composition and organization despite their rapid origination, and the perfect, peerless art they contain despite the facility with which they have been created, all indicate the grandeur of Your Power. From microbes, which exist in all four corners of the globe, to rhinoceroses, and from the tiniest flies to the largest birds, the precision with which they are provided for and nurtured clearly indicates the endless comprehensiveness of Your Mercy. And each of them performs its vital duties without any shortcomings, while the earth, functioning as the parade ground for their mobilization in spring and for their demobilization in fall and winter, indicates the boundlessness of Your Dominion.

Also, every animal is like a sample in miniature of the universe. It is originated through an extremely profound knowledge and fine wisdom, without any confusion in the appointment or placement of any of its atoms, compounds or organs, one within the other, and in their complex relationships with one another. Again, every animal is given a different form and distinguishing features that have no defects, confusions, or faults. As these facts indicate Your all-encompassing Knowledge and Your all-embracing Wisdom to the number of animals in existence, the creation of each one with such artistry and beauty as a miracle of art and a marvel of wisdom also indicates the perfect beauty of Your Lordship's Art, Which you love and will to be displayed. Again, through their delicate nourishment and the gratification of their needs and desires, all of them, and in particular their young, indicate endlessly the sublime beauty of Your Benevolence.

O the All-Merciful, the All-Compassionate, O He Who is absolutely true to His promise, and O the Master of Judgment Day!

I have understood from the instructions of Your noblest Messenger, upon him be peace and blessings, and the teaching of Your wise Qur'an the following:

Since the ultimate result of the universe is life, and the ultimate result of life is the spirit, and since the most elevated among beings with spirit are those with consciousness, and the most comprehensive among those with consciousness is humanity, and since the whole universe serves life, and living beings are sent to the world to serve those among them with spirit, and since beings with spirit are put in the service of humankind, and since human beings have a strong innate love for their Creator, Who both loves and makes Himself loved by them by every means, and since the capacities and immaterial faculties given to humanity are directed primarily toward the eternal life, and their heart and consciousness desire eternity with all their might, and their tongues entreat their Creator with never-ending prayers for everlasting life—since all this is self-evidently true, then it is clear that the One Who loves and is much loved will never distress humankind, whom He has created for eternity, by making them die only to fail to revive them again, which would thus transform their love for Him into eternal enmity. For humanity has been sent to this world to strive for and earn an eternal life of happiness in another, eternal realm. There we will be favored with the eternal manifestations of the Divine Names, Which we mirror in this short and transient life. Indeed, the faithful friend of the Eternal One will be eternal; the conscious mirror of the Everlasting One must be everlasting.

As can be understood both from authentic Prophetic Traditions and as is required by the truth of Divine Wisdom, Mercy, and Lordship, the spirits of animals will also endure permanently. Moreover, certain members of them, such as the hoopoe which served Prophet Solomon, upon him be peace, and the ant found in the narratives concerning him, as well as the she-camel of Prophet Salih, upon him be peace, and the dog of the People of the Cave will go to the eternal world with their bodies and spirits, while each animal species will continue to exist as a single, representative body for occasional employment.[15]

---

[15] They must be employed by the people of Paradise. For the relevant Prophetic narrations, see, al-Baghawi, *Ma'alimu't-Tenzil*, 3:154; al-Alusi, *Ruhu'l-Ma'ani*, 15:226.

O All-Powerful and Self-Subsistent One by Whom all subsist!

All living creatures, all beings with spirit and all beings with conscious-ness have been made subservient to the commands of Your Lordship and entrusted with duties according to their nature in Your domain through Your Power, Will, Administration, Mercy, and Wisdom. Some of them have been put in the service of humankind—not because of any power or dominance on the part of humanity, but, rather, because of human innate weakness and impotence. By glorifying their Maker and declaring Him to be absolutely exalted above having defects, faults, or partners, and by prais-ing and thanking Him for His bounties, both verbally and through the mute eloquence of their natures and dispositions, each performs its own particu-lar form of worship.

O the All-Sacred One, hidden because of the intensity of His manifestation and veiled on account of His Grandeur!

With the intention of declaring You to be the All-Sacred through the glorifications of all beings who possess spirits, I say: All-Glorified are You, O He Who has made every living thing from water!

O the Lord of all the worlds! O the Deity of all those who have already come to this world and of all those who are destined to come in the future! O the Lord of the heavens and the globes!

From the instruction of God's noblest Messenger, upon him be peace and blessings, and the teaching of the wise Qur'an, I have come to under-stand and believe the following:

In the same way that the heavens and the earth, the atmosphere, the land, and sea, the trees, plants, and animals, with all their organs, component parts and atoms, recognize You and testify to Your Existence and Oneness, so too do living beings, which are the essence of the universe, bear witness to the absolute necessity of Your Existence, Your Unity, and Your Oneness. And in the heart of this witnessing stands humanity, the essence of living beings; among humanity are the saints, the purified scholars, and the Proph-ets, all of whom testify to Your Unity through the observations and unveil-ings of their intellects and hearts, and through their inspirations and spiritual discoveries. Indeed, their testimony has the certainty of the consensus of hundreds of different groups of scholars with true and expert knowledge, and hundreds of chains of transmitters of knowledge, whose truthfulness and reli-ability cannot be doubted. Furthermore, they also substantiate the informa-tion they provide with their miracles, wonders, and decisive proofs.

Not a single thing occurs to a sound heart but it draws the attention to the One Who inspires it from behind the veil of the Unseen, and testifies to the absolute necessity of His Existence, as well as to His Attributes, Unity, and Oneness. Similarly, there is not a single instance of true inspiration that focuses attention on the One Who inspires but it bears witness in the same way. Also, there is no certain creed that discovers Your sacred Attributes and All-Beautiful Names with a certainty based on experience but it testifies in a similar fashion, nor is there a pure, illuminated heart such as belongs to the Prophets and saints and which observes the lights of the Necessarily Existent One with piercing clarity, but it bears the same witness. And there is not a single enlightened intellect, such as is possessed by the truthful, pure, and saintly scholars, but it confirms with certain knowledge the signs of the necessary Existence and Oneness of the Creator of all things. Indeed, there is no occurrence, no true inspiration, no certain creed, no pure and illuminated heart, no enlightened intellect, in fact, there is nothing but it indicates or testifies to the absolute necessity of Your Existence, Your sacred Attributes, Your Unity, Your Oneness, and Your All-Beautiful Names.

In particular, there is not a single clear miracle of the noblest Messenger, upon him be peace and blessings, who is the leader and essence of all the Prophets, saints, purified scholars, and those who are most advanced in truthfulness, which confirms the glad tidings he brought; there is not a single exalted truth of him which shows his absolute truthfulness; and there is not a single verse in the miraculous Qur'an, the essence of all sacred Scriptures and books of truth, which demonstrates Divine Unity; and there is not a single sacred matter or truth of belief contained in it—there is not a single one of these miracles, truths, verses, or matters but it indicates or bears witness to the absolute necessity of Your Existence, Your sacred Attributes, Your Unity, Your Oneness, and Your All-Beautiful Names.

Also, in the same way that these countless people of truth bear witness to Your Existence and Oneness with their miracles, wonder-working, and rational proofs, they also proclaim and prove with unanimity the magnificence of Your Lordship, Which has perfect knowledge of and control over all things in creation, however large or small—from the universal affairs connected with Your Supreme Throne to the most secret occurrences of the heart and its most hidden desires and prayers: they also proclaim the sublimity of Your Power, Which invents countless things simultaneously and instantly before our eyes, and accomplishes the greatest thing as easily as it does the smallest one, without one impeding the other.

With their miracles and other proofs, all these truthful ones also demonstrate and prove the limitless comprehensiveness of Your Mercy, Which has made this universe a perfect palace for beings which possess spirit, humanity in particular, and Which prepares Paradise and eternal happiness for the jinn and humanity, does not forget even the lowliest being, and gratifies the most powerless heart. These miracles and proofs also demonstrate and prove the infinite vastness of Your Dominion, Which has subjugated all kinds of creatures, from atoms to galaxies, and entrusted them with certain duties, causing them to obey Your Commands. Moreover, these miracles and proofs also testify, as one, to the all-encompassing nature of Your Knowledge, Which has made the universe a cosmic book that is composed of as many volumes as there are particles and compounds in the universe, and Which has recorded all that happens in the lives of all creatures in the Manifest Record and the Manifest Book, which are the registers of the Supreme Preserved Tablet. Your Knowledge has also inscribed completely and without error the contents and programs of all trees in each of their seeds, and the entire life histories of conscious beings in their memories. These miracles and proofs also bear witness, with utmost clarity, to the all-embracing nature of Your Wisdom, Which attaches to each creature numerous instances of wisdom, such as each tree yielding results to the number of its fruits, or placing in each living being as many benefits as it has members or, indeed, compounds and cells, or equipping the human tongue with abilities to the number of tastes it encounters, as well as entrusting it with many duties. Furthermore, these miracles and proofs unanimously bear witness to the fact that Your Names of Majesty and Grace, Whose exemplary manifestations are witnessed throughout the universe, will continue to manifest themselves in the abode of eternity in a more splendid way; that Your gifts and bounties, the compassionate manifestations and samples of which are observed in this fleeting world, will endure in the eternal realm of happiness in a more brilliant fashion; and that those who are fond of them and who discern them in this brief worldly life with pleasure and seek them in love will accompany them through all eternity.

Also, based on the countless proofs of their Prophethood, including their hundreds of evident miracles, and on hundreds of decisive evidences which exist in all the Scriptures You revealed, but primarily in the wise Qur'an, as well as on the promises and threats that You repeat in them frequently; and relying on Your all-sacred Attributes and essential Characteristics such as Power, Mercy, Favoring, Wisdom, Majesty and Grace, Which require Resurrection, and on the dignity of Your Majesty and the dominion of Your Lordship, all the Prophets with luminous spirits, including first and foremost God's noblest Messenger, upon him be peace and blessings, give both jinn and humankind the glad tidings of eternal happiness for the people of guidance, and they warn that Hell awaits the misguided, while themselves being the first to believe in and bear witness to these. And so do all the saints with illuminated hearts, who rely on their spiritual unveilings and visions, and the pure, saintly scholars with enlightened intellects, who are based on their convictions at the degree of certainty of knowledge.

O the All-Powerful and All-Wise! O the All-Merciful and All-Compassionate! O the All-Munificent Who is absolutely true to His promises! O the All-Overwhelming One of Dignity, Grandeur and Majesty!

Failure to bring about the Resurrection would mean contradicting so many truthful friends of Yours, breaking Your vehemently repeated threats and promises, and negating Your sacred Attributes and essential Characteristics, thereby leaving unfulfilled that which is required by the very nature of Your dominion as the Lord; it would mean rejecting and render futile the hopes and prayers for the Hereafter of Your innumerable servants whom You love, and who make themselves loved by You by confirming and obeying You; it would also mean confirming the people of unbelief and misguidance in their rejection of the Resurrection, who through unbelief and disobedience and by contradicting You in Your promises, insult Your Grandeur, attack the dignity of Your Majesty, offend the honor of Your Divinity and disparage your Lordship's compassion. Undoubtedly You are utterly exempt from and infinitely exalted above such a failure! I declare Your infinite Justice, Grace and Mercy to be absolutely free of such unlimited ugliness and unrighteousness. I wish to recite the verse, *All-Glorified is He, and absolutely exalted, immeasurably high above all that they say* (17: 43) as many times as there are particles in my body. Indeed, these numerous truthful Messengers of Yours and heralds of Your dominion are absolutely correct in their testimony to Your eternal treasures of Mercy and Benevolence and the extraordinarily exquisite manifestations of Your All-Beautiful Names in the world of permanence with certainty based on knowledge, and certainty based on vision, and certainty based on experience. They also believe and teach others that the greatest ray of Your Name the Ultimate Truth, Which is the origin, sun, and preserver of all truths, is this greatest truth of the Resurrection.

O the Lord of the Prophets and those most advanced in truthfulness after the Prophets!

All these beloved friends of Yours have been subjugated and dutiful to You in Your domain through Your Command, Power, Will, Administration, Knowledge, and Wisdom. Through their glorification, praise, and declarations of Your Oneness, and through their profession that You are absolutely exalted above having defects, faults, or partners, they have shown this world to be the most expansive house of remembrance and the universe to be the most expansive place of worship.

O my Lord, and the Lord of the heavens and the earth! O my Creator and the Creator of all things!

For the sake of Your Power, Will, Wisdom, Sovereignty, and Mercy, Which subjugate the heavens with their stars, the earth and all that is in it, and all creatures with all their states, make my carnal soul subservient to me and subjugate my desires to me. Subjugate people's hearts to the *Risale-i Nur* purely for the service of the Qur'an and belief. And bestow on me and my brothers and sisters perfect belief and a happy end. Subjugate hearts and intellects to the *Risale-i Nur*, just as You subjugated the sea to Prophet Moses, upon him be peace, the fire to Prophet Abraham, upon him be peace, the mountains and iron to Prophet David, upon him be peace, the jinn and humans to Prophet Solomon, upon him be peace, and the sun and the moon to Prophet Muhammad, upon him be peace and blessings. And preserve me and the students of the *Risale-i Nur* from the evil of the carnal soul and Satan and from the torments of the grave and Hellfire; make us happy in the highest realm of Paradise! Amin! Amin!

> All-Glorified are You! We have no knowledge save what You have taught us. Surely You are the All-Knowing, the All-Wise.

> And their invocation will close with "All praise and gratitude are for God, the Lord of the worlds!"

If I have erred by offering this lesson, which I have taken from *al-Jawshanu'l-Kabir* ("The Great Shield"), a supplication of God's Messenger, upon him be peace and blessings, to the Court of my All-Compassionate Lord as a reflective act of worship, O my Lord, I call upon Your Mercy to forgive me for the sake of the Qur'an and *al-Jawshanu'l-Kabir*.

Said Nursi

The Ninth Proof:
About the Resurrection and the Afterlife

In the Name of God, the All-Merciful, the All-Compassionate.

So glorify God when you enter the evening and when you enter the morning—and (proclaim that) all praise and gratitude in the heavens and on the earth are for Him—and in the afternoon, and when you enter the noon time. He brings forth the living out of the dead, and brings the dead out of the living, and revives the earth after its death. It is in this way that you will be brought forth from the dead. And among His signs is that He created you from earth; then, you have grown into a human population scattered widely. And among His signs is that He has created for you, from your selves, mates, that you may incline towards them and find rest in them, and He has engendered love and tenderness between you. Surely in this are signs for people who reflect. And among His signs are the creation of the heavens and the earth, and the diversity of your languages and colors. Surely in this are signs indeed for people who know. And among His signs is your sleeping at night and in the day, and your seeking (livelihoods) out of His bounty. Surely in this are signs for people who pay heed. And among His signs is His displaying before you the lightning, giving rise to both fear and hopeful expectation, and that He sends down water from the sky, and revives with it the earth after its death. Surely in this are signs for people who reason and understand. And among His signs is that the heaven and the earth stand firm by His Command. In the end, when He calls you forth from the earth, then (at once) you will come forth. To Him belongs all that is in the heavens and on the earth. All are obedient to Him in humble service. He it is Who originates creation in the first instance and then reproduces it, and will bring it back: and that is easier for Him. Whatever attribute of sublimity there is in the heavens and the earth, it is His in the highest degree, and He is the All-Glorious with irresistible might, the All-Wise. (30:17–27)

One most significant argument included in these sublime heavenly verses, which point to one pole of belief, in these exalted sacred proofs that establish the Resurrection's reality, will be explained in this Ray. It is a subtle Divine favor that at the end of *Muhakemat* ("The Reasonings"), which he wrote thirty years ago as an introduction to the Qur'anic commentary, the Old or Former Said wrote, "A Second Summation of Two Other General Proofs: This explains the two verses of the Qur'an which indicates the Resurrection. *In the Name of God, the All-Merciful, the All-Compassionate*"... and then put down his pen, unable to continue. Praise and thanks to my All-Compassionate Creator to the number of the signs and proofs of the bodily Resurrection, He has enabled me to resume that task.

Nine or ten years ago, God granted me The Tenth and Twenty-ninth Words, two works containing numerous strong proofs and interpretations of the Divine Decree—*Look upon the imprints of God's Mercy, how He revives the earth after its death. Certainly it is He Who will revive the dead (in a similar way), and He has full power over everything* (30:50). The Tenth and Twenty-ninth Words silenced those who denied the Resurrection. Now, a decade or so later, He has granted to me the interpretation of the supreme verses quoted above, unassailable fortresses of belief in the Resurrection. It consists of two points.

The First Point

We will relate only four of the many arguments for belief in the Hereafter as the very basis and bedrock of human social and individual life, and as the foundation of all happiness and achievement.

THE FIRST ARGUMENT: Children make up a third of humanity. They cannot endure death, which must seem to them an awful tragedy, unless it be tempered by the idea of Paradise, which gives spiritual strength to their weak and fragile spirits. It gives them the hope to live joyfully, despite the vulnerability of their nature. Keeping Paradise in mind, they may say: "My little sister has died and become a bird in Paradise. She is flying there and enjoying a better life than us." If they could not do this, their awareness of the deaths of those around them would overwhelm them: it would crush their powers of resistance and inner strength, causing their eyes and all inner faculties, heart, mind and spirit to weep, and transforming them into the most wretched and distraught of creatures.

THE SECOND ARGUMENT: The elderly make up another one-third of humanity. They can endure the grave, which is never far from them, only by believing in the afterlife; this consoles them to some extent in the face of what they see as the inevitable extinction of their lives, to which they are so attached, and the fact that their precious and lovable worlds have come to an end. Only the hope of eternal life allows them to counter the pain and despair which the anticipation of death and separation give rise to in their child-like, fragile temperament and spirit. Without such a hope, our venerable elders who are so worthy of compassion, those aged parents of ours who need a serene and steady heart, would become so distraught and distressed in heart and spirit that their world would seem to be a dark prison and their lives a ghastly torment.

THE THIRD ARGUMENT: Young people are the mainspring and foundation of social life. Only the thought of Hell enables them to control the stormy energy of their feelings and passions, their tempestuous, evil-commanding souls, from destructiveness and oppression, and divert them into serving the collective interest of society. Without this fear, and drunk on the energy of youth, they would follow the principle of "Might is right" and give free rein to their passions and caprices. This would turn the world into a hell for the weak and powerless; it would lower human life to the level of beasts.

THE FOURTH ARGUMENT: The family is the most important core of our worldly life; it is our most fundamental resource, and the paradise, home and citadel of our worldly happiness. Each person's home is his or her own miniature world. The vitality and happiness of our homes and families depend upon sincere and devoted respect, true kindness and self-denying compassion. All of this, in turn, depends upon eternal friendship and companionship; it depends on an immortal bond, as well as the belief that feelings and relations between parents and children, brothers and sisters, and husbands and wives will be everlasting.

For example, a man can say: "My wife will be my eternal companion in an eternal world. Even if she is now old and not as physically beautiful as before, her eternal beauty will show itself in the Hereafter. For the sake of that companionship in eternity, I will make every sacrifice and show her as much compassion as I can in this world." Thus he can regard his aged wife with love, care and compassion as though she were a beautiful *houri*. A relationship that ends in permanent separation after a few hours of physical proximity can only be slight, transient and insecure: it would produce only a superficial love and respect based on physical attraction and sexual desire. Eventually, other interests and powerful emotions would arise and, defeating that respect and concern, turn a worldly paradise into hell on earth.

One of the numerous benefits in the Resurrection and afterlife therefore relates to human social life. If many other related aspects and benefits are deduced by analogy with these four, it will be clear that the realization of the truth of the Resurrection and its occurrence are as certain as our own existence and our universal needs. It will be even more evident than the argument that the stomach's need for sustenance testifies to the existence of food. Were it not for the Resurrection and afterlife, then the lofty status of being human—a status so significant, exalted and vital within creation—would be reduced to that of a carcass fed upon by microbes. Let those concerned with humanity's orderly life, morals and society focus on this matter. If the Resurrection is denied, with what will they fill the resulting void and cure humanity's deep wounds?

The Second Point

Among innumerable proofs of the truth of the Resurrection, we set out succinctly the support offered by the other pillars of belief. It is as follows:

- All miracles which affirm the Messengership of Muhammad, upon him be peace and blessings, all proofs of his Prophethood, and all evidence of his truthfulness establish and bear witness to the realization of the truth of the Resurrection. For after the Unity of God Almighty, all the claims which that exalted person set forth during his life focused on the Resurrection.

- Also, all the miracles and proofs of all other Prophets that attest to their Prophethood and urge humanity to attest to the same bear witness to this same truth.

- In addition, all the signs and proofs which establish the Divine-authorship of all the Divine Scriptures and therefore make completely clear the testimony to the Messengers, bear witness to this truth also.

- All miracles and proofs which establish the reality and truth of the Qur'an also establish and prove the realization of the truth of the Resurrection. For about a third of the Qur'an deals with the Hereafter: most of its short *suras* begin with powerful verses evoking it, and its truth is expressed explicitly or implicitly in hundreds of verses. For example:

> When the sun is folded up. (81:1)

> O humankind, keep from disobedience to your Lord in piety; the violent convulsion of the Last Hour is an awesome thing. (22:1)

> When the earth quakes with a violent quaking destined for it. (99:1)

> When the heaven is cleft open. (82:1)

> When the heaven is split asunder. (84:1)

> What are they asking each other about? (78:1)

> Has the account of the overwhelming event come to you? (88:1)

Just as the initial verses of about twenty *suras* state that the truth of the Resurrection is a most important and essential reality of creation, many other verses affirm and provide other evidences of the same truth. Given that the truth of the Resurrection has been established in a manner as clear as the light of day by numerous arguments and proofs of the Qur'an—a Book every verse of which has yielded innumerable fruits in both the religious and the natural sciences—would denial of this truth not be similar to denial of the existence of the sun itself? Would such a thing not be absurd?

A sovereign sometimes sends his army into battle merely to prove the truth of one of his statements. Is it then conceivable that the truth of that most solemn and glorious sovereign's innumerable words, promises and threats stand contradicted? Is it possible that they should be false? A single indication from that glorious sovereign—namely the Qur'an—is enough to prove the truth of the Resurrection, particularly given that it has ruled over and educated countless spirits, intellects, hearts and souls in perfect truth and righteousness for more than thirteen centuries. Having demonstrated this truth with thousands of explicit proofs, what else can we say except that those who continue to deny this truth are deserving of punishment in Hellfire? Would that not be pure justice?

Furthermore, all Divine Scriptures and sacred Books other than the Qur'an, each of which was addressed to a specific age and time, accept the truth of the Resurrection—a truth which the Qur'an, addressing all times, explains and establishes in detail and with explicit arguments. Even their brief and sometimes allusive explanations affirm it so powerfully that they constitute an irrefragable endorsement of what the Qur'an teaches.

We offer here an argument drawn from The Treatise of Supplication, The Third Ray. This argument, which includes the testimony of belief in the Last Day by the other pillars of belief—in particular, belief in God's Messengers and Books—is forceful and may suffice to end all doubt. In this supplication, we say:

> O my All-Compassionate Lord! Through the teaching of the noblest Messenger and the instruction of the wise Qur'an I have understood that all Divine Books and Prophets—primarily the Qur'an and Your noble Messenger—assert and testify that all Your Names of Majesty and Grace, Whose exemplary manifestations are witnessed throughout the universe, will continue to manifest themselves in the abode of eternity in a more brilliant way; that Your bounties and blessings, the merciful manifestations and samples of which are observed in this fleeting world, will endure in the eternal realm of happiness in a more brilliant fashion; and that those who are fond of them and who discern them in this brief worldly life with pleasure and seek them in love will accompany them through all eternity.
>
> Also, based on the countless proofs of their Prophethood, including their hundreds of evident miracles, and on hundreds of decisive evidences which exist in all the Scriptures You revealed, but primarily in the wise Qur'an, as well as on the promises and threats that You repeat in them frequently; and relying on Your all-sacred Attributes and essential Characteristics such as Power, Mercy, Favoring, Wisdom, Majesty and Grace, Which require Resurrection, and on the dignity of Your Majesty and the dominion of Your Lordship; all the Prophets with luminous spirits, including first and foremost God's noblest Messenger, upon him be peace and blessings, and all the saints with illuminated hearts and the pure, saintly scholars with enlightened intellects, who rely on their spiritual unveilings and observations, along with their convictions at the degree of certainty of knowledge and certainty of vision or observation—all of these prominent members of humanity give both jinn and humankind the glad tidings of eternal happiness for the people of guidance, and they warn that Hell awaits the misguided, while themselves being the first to believe in and bear witness to this happiness and Hell.

O the All-Powerful and All-Wise! O the All-Merciful and All-Compassionate! O the All-Munificent Who is absolutely true to His promises! O the All-Overwhelming One of Dignity, Grandeur and Majesty!

Failure to bring about the Resurrection would mean contradicting so many truthful friends of Yours, breaking Your vehemently repeated threats and promises, and negating Your sacred Attributes and essential Characteristics, thereby leaving unfulfilled that which is required by the very nature of your dominion as the Lord; it would mean rejecting and render futile the hopes and prayers for the Hereafter of Your innumerable servants whom You love, and who make themselves loved by You by confirming and obeying You; it would also mean confirming the people of unbelief and misguidance in their rejection of the Resurrection, who through unbelief and disobedience and by contradicting You in Your promises, insult Your Grandeur, attack the dignity of Your Majesty, offend the honor of Your Divinity and disparage your Lordship's Compassion. Undoubtedly You are utterly exempt from and infinitely exalted above such a failure! I declare Your infinite Justice, Grace, and Mercy to be absolutely above such limitless ugliness and unrighteousness.

We believe with all our heart that all of the Prophets—those more than one hundred thousand truthful messengers of Yours and heralds of Your dominion—and saintly, purified scholars and saints are absolutely correct in their testimony to Your eternal treasures of Mercy and Benevolence and the extraordinarily exquisite manifestations of Your All-Beautiful Names in the world of permanence with certainty based on knowledge, and certainty based on vision, and certainty based on experience. What they have indicated is true and conforms with reality. They also believe and teach other servants of Yours that the greatest ray of Your Name the Ultimate Truth, Which is the origin, sun and preserver of all truths, is this greatest truth of Resurrection.

O Lord! For the sake of what they teach and in veneration of it, bestow on us and all students of the *Risale-i Nur* perfect belief and a happy end to our earthly lives. And allow us to receive their intercession. Amin!

All arguments and evidences which establish the veracity of the Qur'an and all other Divine Books, as well as the miracles and proofs establishing the Prophethood of Muhammad, the beloved of God, upon him be peace and blessings, and of all other Prophets also point to the truth and reality of the Hereafter; indeed, after the Unity of God, the reality of the Hereafter is the teaching which they emphasized the most. Similarly, most arguments and evidences for the Necessarily Existent Being's Existence and Unity also affirm the existence and appearance of the Abode of Happiness—that Realm of Eternity where God's Lordship and Divinity will be manifested most fully. For the Existence of the Necessarily Existent One, as well as most of His Names, and all His Attributes and His essential Characteristics such as Lordship, Divinity, Grace, Wisdom, and Justice necessitate most certainly the existence of an eternal realm—the Hereafter—and the resurrection of the dead for the meting out of just punishment and reward.

Since an All-Eternal God exists, most certainly there is a Hereafter, the everlasting pivot of His Divine Sovereignty. Since we see that a most magnificent, wise, caring, purposeful and absolute Lordship exists throughout the entire universe, there must certainly be an eternal realm of happiness to which admission is granted, so that the majesty of that Lordship is not extinguished, His Wisdom is rendered futile, and His Caring is not destroyed by betrayal and oppression.

Since these infinite visible bounties, blessings, kindnesses and instances of generosity and mercy show to hearts and minds that are not dead the fact that an All-Merciful and All-Compassionate Being exists beyond the veil of the Unseen, there must of necessity be an eternal life in an eternal world, for it is the existence of such a world which can show that His Divine bounties are not for nothing, that His Act of bestowing is not in truth an act of deceit, that His Favoring His servants is not something deserving only of enmity, that His Mercy is not in reality a torment, and that His generosity is not in actual fact an act of betrayal. In addition, eternity and everlastingness will allow all bounties and blessings to assume their true and perfect forms.

Also, each spring on the narrow page of the earth, a Pen of Power tirelessly inscribes before our eyes innumerable books one within the other without the slightest error. The Owner of that Pen has promised repeatedly: "I will write a beautiful, imperishable book in a place far more spacious than this and 'more easily' than this cramped and intermixed book of spring, which is written on such a narrow page, and I will allow you to read it." He mentions this book in all of His decrees. Given this, its draft has been written already, and it will be set down in writing with all its additions and footnotes on the Day of Resurrection. And all the records of people's deeds will be included in it.

Also, the earth has a special importance. For on account of the multiplicity of its inhabitants and the fact that it is the abode, origin, workshop, and place of display and resurrection of countless constantly changing species of living beings and beings with spirits, it is the very heart, center and core of the universe; indeed, it is the very reason for the creation of the universe. Despite its small size, the heavenly Decrees hold it equal to the vast heavens, describing God as the Lord of the heavens *and* the earth. And there is humanity, which dominates the earth. We have dominion over most of its creatures; we subordinate and gather around ourselves almost all animate beings, and order, display and ornament most of the creation according to our needs and desires. We catalogue and classify all things in their wonderful variety, each species in its own place, and in such a way that all people and jinn, all dwellers of the heavens and the universe, gaze upon it with appreciation; even the Lord of the universe bestows His appreciative glance upon it. We have thus a very high value and importance, and through our arts and sciences we show that we are the reason for the creation of the universe and its most important and valuable fruit. We have been chosen and appointed to administer the earth and develop it according to our Creator's laws. Since we demonstrate and arrange most excellently the miraculous works of our Maker in this world, we are given a respite here despite our rebellion and unbelief, and our punishment is postponed. On account of the services we perform, we are granted a temporary stay and are favored with success.

However, despite being endowed with such qualities, we are in reality extremely weak and impotent when it comes to fulfilling the demands of our nature and disposition: we have innumerable needs and are subject to innumerable pains. And yet a most powerful, wise and caring Ruler provides for us in a way altogether beyond our power and will. He makes the planet a storehouse stocked with every kind of mineral and food we need and with all the merchandise we desire. Thus does the Ruler nurture and take care of us and grant our wishes.

The Lord Who does all this loves us and makes Himself our beloved. He is eternal and has eternal worlds. He does all things with justice and wisdom. But the magnificence of this All-Eternal Ruler's Sovereignty and the eternality of His Rule cannot be encompassed within the transient life of this fleeting, temporary world. Furthermore, many of the enormous injustices which humanity commits, and which are hostile and contrary to the wise order, just balance and harmonious beauty of the universe, go unpunished in this world, as does much of the rebellion, betrayal, denial and unbelief of countless people with respect to their Benefactor and Provider. The cruel and the treacherous appear to live charmed lives, while the oppressed and downcast live in wretchedness. But the absolute justice, traces of which can be seen throughout the universe, is by its very nature totally at odds with the notion that the cruel and the treacherous—who die just like the oppressed and the desperate—should never be resurrected to account for their crimes at a supreme tribunal.

Since the Owner of the universe has chosen the earth out of the universe and humankind out of the earth, giving both a high rank and significance. Out of humankind, He has chosen the Prophets, saints, and pure, saintly scholars—true human beings who conform to His purposes as the Lord of creation and make themselves loved by Him through belief and submission. He has taken them as friends and addressees, ennobling them with miracles and Divine support, while punishing their opponents with wrathful blows from above. And out of these lovable and most valued friends He has chosen their leader and source of pride, Prophet Muhammad, upon him be peace and blessings. For long centuries He has illumined with his light the half of the globe and one-fifth of humanity. As though the universe were created solely for his sake, all of its exalted purposes become manifest through him, his Religion, and the Qur'an revealed through him. Although he was deserving of an infinite reward for the inestimable value of the services he rendered—services that would take ordinary people thousands of years to perform—he was granted a brief life of no more than sixty-three years spent in hardship and struggle. Is it then at all likely that he should not be resurrected, together with all his peers—the other Prophets—and Companions? Or that he should not, even now, be alive in the spirit? Or that they should die and disappear into eternal extinction? The entire universe and the truth on which it is based demand his being again, demand his life from the Owner of all that is.

Thirty-three powerful arguments in The Supreme Sign, The Seventh Ray, have established that the universe is the handiwork and property of a Single Being. They have also demonstrated self-evidently His Unity and Oneness, Which give rise to all His Perfections. Through His Unity and

Oneness all beings become His duty-bound soldiers and absolutely obedient officials. And by means of the Hereafter, His Perfections remain ever free of defect; thanks to the existence of the world to come, His Absolute Justice will never become reduced to absolute treachery, His universal Wisdom to foolish pointlessness, or His all-inclusive Mercy to frivolous tormenting. Thanks to the Hereafter, His all-dignified Power is saved from being reduced to impotence.

Without doubt, and as is necessitated by the universal truths discussed—the truths from among the many which arise from the cardinal truth of God's Existence and Unity—the Resurrection will occur. The dead will be resurrected and gathered together on the Place of the Supreme Gathering, and the realm of reward and punishment will open its gates. All this will occur so that the real significance and centrality of the earth, and the true significance and value of humanity may be truly realized. It will occur so that the Justice, Wisdom, Mercy and Sovereignty of the All-Wise Ruler, Who is the Creator and Lord of us and our planet, will be established wholly and eternally. It will occur so that all true friends and ardent lovers of the All-Permanent Lord may be delivered from eternal annihilation, and that the nearest and dearest of them, upon him be peace and blessings, may be rewarded for the sacred services with which he graced the world. And the All-Eternal Sovereign's Perfections will show themselves to be without defect, His Power will show Itself to be without incompetence, His Wisdom without foolishness and His Justice without oppression.

In sum, the Hereafter exists because God exists.

The three pillars of faith mentioned above—belief in the Existence and Unity of God, belief in Prophethood and belief in the Qur'an and other Divinely-revealed Scriptures—bear witness to the truth and reality of the Resurrection. Similarly, the remaining two pillars of faith—belief in angels and belief in Divine Decree and Destiny—also require the Resurrection and bear witness to the reality of that eternal realm. We will elucidate as follows:

All proofs which establish the existence of the angels and their duties of worship, as well as numberless human observations of them and conversations held with them, also attest to the existence of the world of spirits, the World of the Unseen, the Hereafter, the world of permanence and the abode of happiness and Hell, which in the future will be peopled by human beings and jinn. For the angels are able to see and enter these worlds by Divine leave. All the angels who are close to the Divine Throne and who communicate with humanity, such as Gabriel, are unanimous in reporting their existence and their travels in these abodes. Even if we ourselves have never been to America, for example, the reports of travelers returning from there leave us in no doubt as to its existence. Similarly, the reports given by angels, which have the authority of numerous undisputed narrations, should leave us in no doubt as to the existence of the eternal realm of the Hereafter and of Heaven and Hell.

All arguments contained in the Twenty-sixth Word (on Divine Decree and Destiny) which establish the pillar of faith also attest to the Resurrection, to the revealing in the world to come of all our recorded deeds in this world, and of their being weighed in a Supreme Balance. For the apparent order, regularity and balance in the universe provide an indication of the fact that the lives of all things were pre-recorded and lived out according to that eternal program.

Also, the life history of every animate being is inscribed in its memory or its seed, and other tablet-like forms; the deeds of every being endowed with spirit, especially human beings, are recorded on preserved tablets. Such an all-embracing determining, such wise and purposive ordaining, such detailed and precise recording and inscribing exist only to enable the meting out of permanent reward or punishment at the Supreme Tribunal on the Day of Judgment. Were this not the case, such comprehensive, meticulous recording and registering would have no purpose or meaning; it would be contrary to sense and reality. Moreover, if there were no Resurrection, all of the carefully established meanings inscribed by the Pen of Divine Destiny in the book of the universe would be annihilated. This would be tantamount to denying the existence of the universe itself.

In short, then, the five pillars or articles of faith and their proofs bear witness to and necessitate the Resurrection: they require that the Realm of the Hereafter appear and open its gates. It is because, in keeping with its vastness and sublimity, the truth of Resurrection has such firm and tremendous supports that approximately a third of the miraculous Qur'an is devoted to it. The Qur'an makes it—next to belief in God—the bedrock of all of its truths and constructs everything on its basis.

The Tenth Proof:
Belief in and Love of God and Worshipping Him

In His Name, All-Glorified is Him.
There is nothing but it glorifies Him with His praise.

In the Name of God, the All-Merciful, the All-Compassionate.

There is no deity but God, One having no partners; His is the Sovereignty and to Him belongs all praise; He alone gives life and causes to die; He is All-living and dies not; in His hand is all good. He has full power over everything, and to Him is the homecoming.

It is very meritorious to recite this affirmation of Divine Unity, which consists of eleven phrases, after the early morning and evening Prayers. Each phrase is equal in worth to God's Greatest Name, and conveys good tidings to humanity by displaying and manifesting a different aspect of the Lordship's Unity. This is equal to manifesting one of the Greatest Names, a ray of Divine Unity's magnificence, and a perfection of Divine Oneness. Referring the reader to *The Words*[16] for a full explanation of such a sublime truth, I summarize it below.

Introduction

Know with certainty that belief in God is creation's highest aim and most sublime result, and humanity's most exalted rank is knowledge of Him. The most radiant happiness and sweetest bounty for jinn and humanity is love of God contained within knowledge of God. The human spirit's purest joy and the human heart's sheerest delight is spiritual ecstasy contained within love of God. All true happiness, pure joy, sweet bounties, and unclouded pleasures are contained within knowledge and love of God. Those who truly know and love God can receive endless happiness, bounties, enlightenment, and mysteries. Those who do not are afflicted with endless spiritual and material misery, pain, and fear. If any person were allowed to rule this world, despite his or her being powerless, miserable, and unprotected amid other purposeless people in this world, what would its true worth be?

People who do not recognize their Owner and discover their Master are miserable and bewildered. But those who do, and then take refuge in His Mercy and rely on His Power, see this desolate world transformed into a place of rest and felicity, a place of exchange for the Hereafter.

---

[16] Said Nursi, *The Words*, Tughra books, New Jersey, 2010.

The Eleven Phrases

Each phrase affirming Divine Unity bears good tidings to believers. Each message offers a cure, and each cure contains a spiritual pleasure.

THE FIRST PHRASE: *There is no deity but God*

This provides an inexhaustible source of help for the human spirit, which is subject to innumerable needs and prey to countless attacks, by opening the door to a treasury of mercy that can meet its needs. The spirit finds therein a point of support that shows and makes known its Master and Owner, its Creator and True Object of Worship, Who secures it against its enemies' evil.

This phrase saves the heart from desolation and the spirit from suffering through constant uplift and continual felicity.

THE SECOND PHRASE: *(He is) One*

This implies that the human spirit, which is connected to most species in the universe and thereby overwhelmed with misery and confusion, finds therein a refuge and savior to deliver it from such misery and confusion.

For humanity, the phrase means: God is One, so do not tire yourself with other things. Do not demean yourself and feel obliged to them, or humiliate yourself before them for security. Do not trouble yourself by following them, and do not tremble before them, for the Sovereign of the universe is one and holds the key to and the reins of all things. His command resolves everything. Finding Him means that you obtain whatever you wish and are liberated from interminable indebtedness and innumerable fears.

THE THIRD PHRASE: *He has no partners*

This means that He is One and has no partners in His Divinity and Sovereignty, as well as in His Lordship, acts, and creating. In principle, a worldly king may have no partner in his sovereignty, but nevertheless his officials may be regarded as his partners in the execution of his sovereignty, as they act as intermediaries between him and his subjects. God, the eternal Sovereign, has no such need and therefore no partner in His Sovereignty. One thing can interfere with another only if He permits it. In addition, His Oneness rejects any intermediaries between Him and His creatures, and so everyone has direct access to Him regardless of time and place.

This phrase informs the human spirit that nothing can prevent any believer from entering the Presence of the Majestic, All-Gracious, All-Powerful One of Perfection, Who is the Eternal Owner of the treasuries of mercy and bliss, and presenting his or her petition. Finding His Mercy and relying upon His Power enables believers to attain perfect ease and happiness.

THE FOURTH PHRASE: *His is the Sovereignty*
This means that He owns the heavens and Earth—including you—and that you work in His Kingdom. It also implies: Do not imagine that you own yourself, for you cannot administer your own affairs. You cannot maintain your spirit and body by meeting their needs and securing them against calamity. You cannot avoid exhaustion and aging, because you are subject to time and other erosive factors. Therefore, do not suffer pain and torment without reason. Somebody All-Powerful and All-Compassionate owns everything. Rely on His Power and do not accuse His Compassion. Renounce grief and anxiety and accept relief. Be rid of your troubles and find serenity.

This phrase also means: This world that you love, to which you are connected and which you see in disorder and cannot put right, belongs to an All-Powerful and Compassionate One. So return it to its Owner and leave it to Him. Mind your own duty and do not interfere with His acts. Do not be troubled by what you cannot overcome. Be at ease, for its Owner controls it completely and administers it as He wills. He is All-Wise and All-Compassionate, and acts for a wise purpose. So whenever you are afraid, say like Ibrahim Haqqi of Erzurum[17]: "Let's see what the Master does—whatever He does is always best—and observe His acts with complete trust."

THE FIFTH PHRASE: *To Him belongs all praise*
This means that only God deserves praise and acclaim, that everything is indebted only to Him. All bounties are His, for they come from His infinite and inexhaustible treasury.

This phrase implies: The bounties (you now enjoy) will never cease, for His Mercy's treasury is inexhaustible. Your (current) enjoyment will never cease, for every enjoyment you are granted is the fruit of infinite Mercy. And the tree of that Mercy cannot die, for each exhausted fruit is

17 Ibrahim Haqqi of Erzurum (1703-1780) was one of the most outstanding figures in the Ottoman Turkey of the 18th century. He lived in Erzurum and Siirt in the Eastern Turkey. He was a prolific, encyclopedic Sufi guide and writer, who wrote in many subjects such as Theology, Morality, Mathematics, Astronomy, and Medicine. His *Ma'rifatname* ("The Book of Knowledge and Skills") is very famous and still being widely read. (Tr.)

replaced with a new one. Furthermore, offering thanks and praise for what you currently enjoy increases it a hundredfold, since every enjoyment is, in essence, a favor from the Divine Mercy and therefore 100 times more enjoyable than the enjoyment by itself. If a glorious king gives you an apple, your pleasure at such a royal favor will be superior to the material pleasure of 100 or even 1,000 apples.

Similarly, this phrase opens the door of a spiritual enjoyment 1,000 times sweeter, since it makes you consider the bestowal of bounty, which leads you to recognize the Bestower and reflect on His merciful favors that pour out continually.

THE SIXTH PHRASE: *He alone gives life*

This states that only He gives and sustains life and provides all its necessities, and that life's sublime aims and important results are related to Him.

This phrase calls out: Do not bother to shoulder life's heavy responsibilities, or feel unease because the world is transient, or let life's insignificant worldly fruits make you regret that you came to this world. Rather, the "life mechanism" of your being is like a vessel which belongs to the Ever-Living and Ever-Self-Subsistent One, Who fulfills all life's needs and expenditures. Further, life's innumerable aims direct it to many important results, nearly all of which are related to Him. You are just a helmsman on that ship, so perform your duty properly. Receive your wages and be content with the resulting enjoyment. Ponder that ship's preciousness and its valuable benefits, and consider the magnitude of its Owner's generosity and compassion. Rejoice and give thanks, for performing your duty righteously will cause your life's results to be recorded, in one respect, as good deeds securing your immortal life in eternity.

THE SEVENTH PHRASE: *...and causes to die*

This means that He discharges you from life's duty, changes your abode from this transient world to an eternal one, and releases you from the burden of service.

This phrase announces: Good news! Death is not annihilation or going to non-existence, not an eternal separation or a chance event without an author. Rather the All-Wise and All-Compassionate Author is discharging you from service, changing your abode, and sending you to the everlasting happiness that is your true home. Death is the door to union with the Intermediate World, where you will meet with 99 percent of your friends.

THE EIGHTH PHRASE: *He is All-living and dies not*

This means that the Undying Object of Worship and the Everlasting Beloved, One Whose Beauty, Perfection, and Benevolence are wholly superior to their counterparts in this world and that arouse the love of all creatures, has an eternal life. One manifestation of His Beauty replaces all other beloveds. His eternal life is free of any trace of cessation or ephemerality, and has no flaw or defect.

This phrase proclaims to all conscious beings, whether human or jinn, and to all lovers: The Eternal Beloved will heal the wounds caused by separation from your loved ones. Since He exists and is undying, do not worry about those others. You loved them because of their beauty and goodness, grace and perfection. But these are only dim, shadow-like manifestations of the Everlasting Beloved's Eternal Beauty, which has passed through many veils. So do not grieve when they disappear, for they are only mirrors. When the mirrors are changed, that Beauty's reflection is renewed and becomes more radiant. When you find Him, you find everything.

THE NINTH PHRASE: *In His hand is all good*

This means that only He possesses all good and guides you to do good. Also, He records on your behalf any good and righteous deed that you do.

This phrase announces: O helpless people and jinn, do not cry out when you die: "Alas, everything we owned is destroyed and our efforts have come to naught. We have left that wide, beautiful world and entered this narrow grave!" Everything is preserved, for all your deeds and services were recorded. The One of Majesty, in Whose Hand is all good and Who is able to do whatever is good, summons you to reward your service. He will keep you underground temporarily and then bring you to His Presence. How fortunate you are that you completed your duty and service, for your labor is over and you are on the way to ease and mercy. Having toiled, you now receive your wages.

The All-Powerful One of Majesty, Who preserves seeds and grains as records of last spring's activities and services and then unfolds and publishes them the following spring in the most dazzling, abundant, and benevolent manner, also preserves the results of your deeds. Thus He will reward your service most abundantly.

THE TENTH PHRASE: *He has full power over everything*

This means that He is One and Unique and has power over everything. As everything is therefore easy for Him, creating spring is as easy as creating a flower, and creating Paradise is as easy as creating spring. The countless creatures He continually brings into existence every instant bear witness with innumerable tongues to His limitless Power.

This phrase implies: O people, your service and worship are not lost. A world of reward, an abode of bliss, has been prepared for you. An everlasting Paradise awaits your arrival from the transitory world. Have belief and confidence in the Majestic Creator's promise, the One you know and worship, for He never breaks His promise. His Power contains no defect, and impotence does not interfere in His works. As He creates your small garden, He also can create Paradise for you. In fact, as He created it and promised it to you, He shall admit you to it.

Every year we watch Him speedily revive Earth with perfect order and ease despite countless animal and plant species and groups. Such an All-Powerful One of Majesty fulfills His promise. Furthermore, since He annually creates samples of Paradise, which He has promised through all His revealed Books; since all His acts and executions are performed with truth and seriousness; since the perfection of all His works point to and testify to His infinite Perfection, which contains no flaw or defect; and since breaking a promise, lying, falsehood, and deception are the ugliest of qualities, we can rest assured that the All-Powerful One of Majesty, the All-Wise One of Perfection, the All-Compassionate One of Grace will fulfill His promise. He will open the gate to eternal happiness and admit you, O people of belief, into Paradise, the original home of your forefather Adam (and foremother Eve).

THE ELEVENTH PHRASE: *And to Him is the homecoming*

This means that all people are sent to this world of trial and examination for specific purposes. After fulfilling these, they return to the Presence of the All-Munificent Master, Majestic Creator, Who sent them in the first place. Leaving this transient realm, they are delivered from the turbulence of cause-and-effect cycles and from the obscure veils of means and devices. After that, they will be honored in the eternal abode in their Compassionate Lord's Presence and meet with Him, without any veil, in His Everlasting Kingdom. Everyone will discover that their creator is the Worshipped

One, Lord, Master, and Owner. Thus this phrase implies the following news, much happier than all the rest:

O people, do you know where you are going, where you are being driven? You are going to the sphere of Mercy, to the peaceful Presence of the All-Beautiful One of Majesty. A happy life of 1,000 years in this world cannot be compared to an hour of life in Paradise, and 1,000 years of life in Paradise cannot be compared to an hour's vision of His Countenance of utmost beauty. All the loveliness and beauty seen in this world's creatures, including the loved ones that so fascinate and obsess you, are only shadows of one manifestation of His Beauty and the loveliness of His Names. Paradise and its charms are merely manifestations of His Mercy; all longing, love, and attraction are merely flashes from His Love's light. You are going into the Presence of the One Eternally Worshipped and Everlastingly Beloved, and are invited to Paradise, His eternal feasting place. So enter the grave with a smile.

This phrase also announces: O people, do not worry or think that you are going to extinction, non-existence, nothingness, darkness, oblivion, decay, and dissolution. In fact, you are going to permanence, eternal existence, and the world of His Light. You are returning to your true Owner, to the Eternal Sovereign's Seat. You will rest in the sphere of unity and not drown in multiplicity. You are bound for union and not separation.

The Eleventh Proof:
Arguments for Divine Existence and Unity

In the name of God, the All-Merciful, the All-Compassionate.

God sets forth parables for humanity in order that they may bear (them) in mind and take lessons (through them). (14:25)

Such parables do We set forth for humanity so that they may reflect. (59:21)

Once two people washed themselves in a pool and fell into a trance-like state. Upon awakening, they found themselves in an amazing land. With its perfect order and harmony, it was like a country, or rather a city, or a palace. They looked around in utmost amazement: from one point of view, it was a vast world; from another, a well-ordered country; from yet another, a splendid city. If it was looked from still another point of view, it was a palace though one it was in itself a magnificent world. They traveled and saw its creatures speaking a language they did not know. However, their gestures indicated that they were doing important work and carrying out significant duties.

One of them said: "This world must have an administrator, this well-ordered country a master, this splendid city an owner, and this skillfully made palace a master builder. We must try to know him, for it must be he who brought us here. If we do not, who will help us? What can we expect from those impotent creatures whose language we do not know and who ignore us? Moreover, one who has made a huge world in the form of a state, a city, or a palace and filled it with wonderful things, embellished it with every adornment, and decorated it with instructive miracles must have something he wants us and those who come here to do. We must know him and learn what he wants."

The other man objected: "I don't believe it, that there is such a being and he governs this world by himself." His friend replied: "If we do not recognize him and remain indifferent, we gain nothing and might face great harm. But if we try to recognize him, there is little hardship and the chance of great benefit. So, it is in no way reasonable to remain indifferent?" The other man insisted: "I find all my ease and enjoyment in not thinking of him. Besides, I am not to bother myself with things that make no sense to me. These are all confused things that are happening by chance or by themselves. They are none of my concern." His smart friend replied: "Such obstinacy will get us and many others in trouble. Sometimes a land is ruined because of one ill-mannered person."

The other person turned and said: "Either prove that what you say is true or leave me alone." At that, his friend said: "Since your obstinacy borders on insanity and will cause us to suffer a great calamity, I will demonstrate you twelve arguments that this palace-like world, this city-like state, has one master builder who administers it by himself and has no deficiency. He is invisible to us, but must see us and everything and also hear all voices. All his works seem miraculous. All these creatures whom we see but whose languages we do not understand must be his officials (working in his Name).

Twelve arguments

THE FIRST ARGUMENT

Look around! A hidden hand is working in everything, for something little and without strength like a seed is bearing loads weighing thousands of pounds.[18] Something without consciousness is doing much intelligent and purposive work.[19] As they therefore cannot be working on their own, a powerful, hidden one is causing them to work. If everything were happening on its own, all the work being done in this place must itself be a miracle, and everything a miracle-working marvel.

THE SECOND ARGUMENT

Look at the adornments of these plains, fields, and residences! Each are marks pointing to that hidden one. Like a seal or stamp, each gives news of him. Look at what he produces from a few grams of cotton.[20] See how many rolls of cloth, linen, and flowered material have come out of it; how much sweet food and other delights are being made. If thousands of people clothed themselves from these or ate of those, there would still be enough. Again, look. He has taken a handful of iron, soil, water, coal, copper, silver, and gold and made some living creature.[21] Look and see. These sorts of work are particular to one that holds this land together with all its parts under his miraculous power and all-submissive to his will.

THE THIRD ARGUMENT

Look at these priceless, moving works of art![22] Each has been fashioned as a miniature specimen of this huge palace. Whatever is in the palace is

---

[18] This refers to seeds, which bear trees on their heads.

[19] This refers to delicate plants like grapevines, which cannot rise by themselves or bear the weight of fruits, and so throw their delicate arms around other plants or trees and wind themselves around and load themselves onto them.

[20] For example, an atom-sized poppy seed, an apricot stone that weighs a few grams, or a melon seed each produce from Mercy's treasury woven leaves more beautiful than broadcloth, flowers whiter or yellower than linen, fruits sweeter than sugar, and finer and more delicious than jams, and offer them to us.

[21] This refers to the creation of animal bodies from elements and living creatures from sperm.

[22] This refers to animals and human beings. Since an animal is a tiny index of the world, and humanity is a miniature of the universe, whatever is in the universe has a sample that is contained within each human being.

found in these tiny moving machines. Who but the builder of this amazing palace could include all of it in a tiny machine? Could chance or something purposeless have intervened in this box-sized machine that contains a whole world? However many artistically fashioned machines you see, each is like a seal of that hidden one, like a herald or a proclamation. In their language of being, they announce: "We are the works of art of one who can make this entire world as easily as he made us."

The Fourth Argument

I will show you something even stranger. Look. All things in this land are changing. Each lifeless body and unfeeling "bone" has started to move toward certain purposes, as if each were ruling the others.

Look at this machine beside us.[23] It is as though it were issuing commands and all the materials necessary for its adornment and functioning were running to it from distant places. Look over there.

That seemingly lifeless body is as though beckoning, for it makes the biggest bodies serve it and work for it.[24] You may compare the rest with these.

Everything seems to have subjugated to itself all creatures in the world. If you do not accept the hidden one's existence, you must attribute all his skills, arts, and perfections to the stones, soil, animals, and creatures resembling people to the things themselves. In place of one miracle-working being, millions of miracle-workers like him have to exist, both opposed to and similar to each other at the same time, and one within the other, without causing any confusion and spoiling the order. But we know that when two rulers intervene in an affair, the result is confusion. When a village has two headmen, a town two governors, or a country two kings or governments, chaos arises. Given this, what would happen if there were an infinite number of absolute rulers in the same place and at the same time?

---

[23] This refers to fruit-bearing trees. As if bearing on their slender branches hundreds of looms and factories, they weave wonderful, richly adorned leaves, blossoms and fruits, and then cook these fruits and offer them to us. Such majestic trees like pines and cedars have set up their workbenches on hard, dry rock to work.

[24] This "body" signifies grains, seeds, and the eggs of flies. A fly leaves its eggs on an elm tree's leaves. Suddenly, the huge tree turns its leaves into a mother's womb, a cradle, a store full of honey-like food, as if it, although not fruit-bearing, produces animate fruit.

THE FIFTH ARGUMENT

Look carefully at the palace's ornaments and the city's adornments! See this land's orderliness and reflect on this world's artistry. If the pen of a hidden one with infinite miracles and skills is not working, or if all these ornaments are attributed to unconscious causes, blind chance and deaf nature, then even every stone and every blade of grass here would have to be a miracle-working decorator and a wonderful inscriber able to write a thousand books in a letter, and to display infinitely different forms of artistry in a single ornament.

Look at the inscriptions in these stones.[25] Each contains the inscriptions of the whole palace, the laws for the city's order, and the programs for organizing the state. Given this, making the inscriptions a stone contains is as wonderful as making the state. So each inscription and instance of art is a proclamation of that hidden one and one of his seals. As a letter indicates its writer, and an artistic inscription makes its inscriber known, how can then an inscriber, a designer, or a decorator, who inscribes a huge book in a single letter and displays a thousand ornaments in a single one, not be known through his inscriptions and ornaments?

THE SIXTH ARGUMENT

Come onto this vast plain![26] We will climb to the top of that huge mountain to see the surrounding area. We use these binoculars, for curious things are happening in this land. Every hour things are happening that we never imagined.

Look! These mountains, plains, and towns are suddenly changing so that millions of new things can replace them with perfect orderliness, one within and after the other. The most curious transformations are occurring, just as though innumerable kinds of cloths are being woven inside and among others. See, familiar flowery things have been replaced in an

---

[25] This refers to humanity, the fruit of the Tree of Creation, and to the fruit that bears the program of its tree and its index. For whatever the Pen of Divine Power has inscribed in the great Book of the Universe has been compressed in our creation. Whatever the Pen of Divine Destiny has written in a huge tree has been included in its fingernail-sized fruit.

[26] This signifies the earth's face in spring and summer, when innumerable individuals of countless species are brought into existence; they are "written" on the earth. They are recruited and may undergo changes without flaw and with perfect orderliness. Thousands of tables of the All-Merciful are laid out and then removed and replaced with fresh ones. All trees are like bearers of trays, and all gardens are like cauldrons.

orderly fashion with others of similar nature but different form. Everything is happening as if each plain and mountain is a page upon which infinite different books are being written without flaw or defect. It is utterly inconceivable that these things, which display infinite art, skill, and exactness, come about on their own. Rather, they show the artist who engenders them. The one who does all these things displays such miracles, for nothing is difficult for him. It is as easy for him to write a thousand books as to write one book.

Look around you! He puts everything in its proper place with such wisdom, pours his favor so generously on the needy and deserving, draws back and opens universal veils and doors so bountifully that all are satisfied, and lays out such munificent tables that a particular feast of bounties is given to each and every species of animate beings of this land. Indeed, each group and even each individual being is offered a table of bounties particular and suitable to it. Can there be anything more inconceivable than that any of these affairs could be attributable to chance, purposeless or vain, or have many hands behind it, and that their maker is powerful over everything, and everything is subjugated to him? So, my friend, what pretext can you find to persist in your denial?

THE SEVENTH ARGUMENT

Come, friend! Let's turn to the mutual interrelations of this amazing palace-like world's parts. Look! Universal things are being done and general revolutions are taking place with such perfect orderliness that as if all rocks, soil, and trees in this palace were obeying this world's general rules and were free to do whatever they will. Things that are most distant come to each other's aid. Look at that strange caravan[27] coming from the unseen on mounts resembling trees, plants, and mountains. Each member is carrying trays of food on its head and bringing it to the animals waiting on this side. Look at the mighty electric lamp in that dome.[28] It not only provides light, but also cooks their food wonderfully; the food to be cooked is attached to a string[29] by an unseen hand and held up before it. Also see

---

[27] It refers to "caravans" of plants and trees bearing the sustenance of all animals.

[28] An allusion to the sun.

[29] The string and its attached food denote a tree's slender branches and the delicious fruits thereon.

these impotent, weak, defenseless little animals. Over their heads are small, spring-like "pumps" full of delicate sustenance.[30] They only have to press their mouths against these pumps to be fed.

In short, all things in this world, as if positioned face-to-face, help each other. As though seeing each other, they cooperate with each other. To perfect each other's work, they support each other and work together. The wonders in this world cannot be counted. You can approach them in the light of the examples cited. All of this decisively proves that everything is subjugated to the builder of that wonderful palace, the real owner of this world. Everything works on his behalf, like an obedient soldier carrying out his commands. Everything takes place by his power, moves by his command, and is arranged through his wisdom. Everything helps the others by his munificence, and everything is made to hasten to the aid of others through his compassion. O my friend, can you object to this?

THE EIGHTH ARGUMENT

Come, O my friend who suppose yourself to be intelligent, as does my own selfhood! You do not want to recognize this magnificent palace's owner although everything points to him, shows him, and testifies to him. How can you deny such testimony? Given this, you have to deny the palace as well and say: "There is no world, no state." Deny your own existence, too, and disappear, or else come to your senses and listen to me.

In the palace are uniform elements and minerals that encompass the whole land.[31] It appears that everything is made from them. This means that whoever owns them owns everything made from them, for whoever owns the field owns its crops, and whoever owns the sea owns its contents. These textiles and decorated woven clothes are made from a single, similar basic thing. Obviously, the one who creates this thing both prepares it and makes it into yarn, for such a work does not allow the participation of others. Therefore, all of the things skillfully woven out of it are particular to him.

---

[30] The breasts of mothers.

[31] Elements and minerals denote the elements of air, water, light, and soil, which perform numerous systematic duties: By Divine permission, they hasten to help all needy beings, enter everywhere by Divine command and provide help, convey the necessities of life, and "suckle" living creatures. They also function as the source, origin, and cradle for the weaving and decoration of Divine artifacts.

All types of such woven things are found throughout the land. They are being made all together, one inside or among others, in the same way and at the same instant. Therefore, they can be the work only of one person who does everything with one command. Otherwise such correspondence and conformity as regards time, fashion, and quality would be impossible. So, each skillfully made thing proclaims that hidden one and points to him.

It is as if each kind of flowered cloth, skillfully made machine, and delicious morsel is a stamp, a seal, a sign of that miracle-working one, and proclaims in the language of its being: "Whoever owns me as a work of art also owns the boxes and shops in which I am found." Each decoration says: "Whoever embroidered me also wove the roll of cloth in which I am located." Each delicious morsel says: "Whoever cooked me also has the cooking pot in which I am located." Each machine says: "Whoever made me also makes all those like me that are found throughout the land. The one who raises us everywhere is also the same. As this same person owns the land and this palace, he also must own us." This is just as the real owner of, say, a cartridge-belt or a button belonging to the state, has to own the factories in which they are made. If someone ignorantly claims ownership of it, it will be taken away. Such people will be punished for pretending to own the state's property.

In short, just as each element in this land has permeated throughout it, so can their owner only be the one who owns all the land. Since the artistry throughout this land is of the same nature and works of art resemble each other, displaying the same stamp, whatever has spread throughout the land is evidently the work of a single being's art. And, that one rules over everything. Thus there is a sign of oneness, a stamp of unity in this magnificent palace-like land. Some things are uniform, unique, and of the same nature, yet all-encompassing. Other things, though various and abundant, display a unity of grouping since they resemble each other and are found everywhere. Such unity demonstrates the one of unity. That means that this land's builder, host, and owner must be one and the same.

Look attentively! See how a thick string has appeared from behind the veil of the Unseen.[32] See how thousands of strings hang down from it. See

---

[32] The "thick string" is a fruit-bearing tree, the strings are its branches, and the diamond decorations, favors, and gifts are the various flowers and fruits hung thereon.

their tips, to which have been attached diamonds, decorations, favors, and gifts. There is a gift particular to everyone. Can you be so foolish as not to recognize and thank the one who offers such wonderful favors and gifts from behind the veil of the Unseen? For if you do not recognize him, you must argue: "The strings themselves make and offer these diamonds and other gifts." In that case, you must attribute to each string the status and function of a king [who has a miraculous power and knowledge to do whatever he wishes]. Whereas, before our very eyes an unseen hand is making the strings and attaching gifts to them! Given this, everything in this palace points to that miracle-working one rather than to itself. If you do not recognize him, by denying what is occurring in the palace, you show a determined ignorance of a kind to which a truly human being must not sink.

THE NINTH ARGUMENT

Come, O friend! You neither recognize nor want to recognize the palace's owner because you deem his existence improbable. You deny because you cannot grasp his wonderful art and manner of acting. But how can all of these exquisite things, this wonderful existence, be explained without recognizing him? If we recognize him, all this palace and its abundant contents are as easy to understand as a single thing in it.

If we do not recognize him and if he did not exist, one thing would be as hard to explain as the whole palace, for everything is as skillfully made as the palace. Things would not be so abundant and economical. No one could have any of these things that we see. Look at the jar of conserve attached to that string.[33] If it had not been miraculously made in his hidden kitchen, we could not have bought it at any price. But now we buy it for a few cents.

Every kind of persistent difficulty and impossibility follows from not recognizing him. A tree is given life from one root, through one law, and in one center. Therefore, forming thousands of fruits is as easy as forming one fruit. If this depended on different, particular centers and roots and on separate, particular laws, each fruit would have been as hard to form as the tree. If an army's equipment is produced in one factory, through one law, and in one center, it is done as easily as equipping one soldier. But if each

---

[33] The jar of conserve denotes Mercy's gifts (melons, watermelons, pomegranates, and coconuts like tins of milk), each of which is a conserve of Divine Power.

soldier's equipment is procured from many places, then equipping one soldier would require as many factories as needed for the whole army.

This is also true in this well-organized palace, splendid city, progressive state, and magnificent world. If the invention of all these things is attributed to one being, it is easy to account for their infinite abundance, availability, and munificence. Otherwise everything would be so costly and hard that the whole world would not be enough to buy a single thing.

THE TENTH ARGUMENT

My friend, we have been here for 15 days.[34] If we still do not know and recognize this world's ruler and rules, we deserve punishment. We have no excuses, because for 15 days we have not been interfered with, as though given respite. But neither have we been left to ourselves. We cannot wander about and cause disorder among creatures so delicate, well-balanced, subtle, skillfully made, and instructive as these. The majestic lord's punishment must be severe.

How majestic and powerful he must be to have arranged this huge world like a palace and turn it as though a light wheel. He administers this vast country like a house, missing nothing. Like filling a container and then emptying it, he continuously fills this palace, this city, this land with perfect orderliness and then empties it with perfect wisdom. Also, like setting up a table and then removing it, he lays out throughout the land, as though with an unseen hand, diverse tables with a great variety of foods one after the other, and then clears them away to bring new ones.[35] Seeing this and using your reason, you will understand that an infinite munificence is inherent in that awesome majesty.

Just as all these things testify to that unseen being's unity and sovereignty, so these revolutions and changes occurring one after the other bear witness to his permanence. How so? For the causes of things disappear along with them, whereas the things we attribute to causes are repeated after them. So nothing can be attributed to causes; everything takes place as the work of an undying one. For example, sparkling bubbles on a river's

---

[34] An allusion to the age of 15, the age of responsibility.

[35] The tables denote the earth's face in summer, during which hundreds of the All-Merciful's tables are prepared fresh and different in the kitchens of Mercy, and then are laid down and removed continuously. Every garden is a cooking pot, and every tree is a tray-bearer.

surface come and go, but new ones coming after them also sparkle. Therefore, what makes them sparkle is something constant standing high above the river and having permanent light. Similarly, the quick changes in this world and the things that replace the disappearing ones, assuming the same attributes, show that they are manifestations, inscriptions, mirrors, and works of art of a permanent and undying one.

THE ELEVENTH ARGUMENT

Come, O friend! Now I will show you another decisive proof as powerful as the previous ten proofs put together. Let's board the ship[36] and sail to that peninsula over there, for the keys to this mysterious world are there. Moreover, everyone is looking to that peninsula, expecting something and receiving orders from there.

We have landed. Look at the huge meeting over there, as if all the country's important people have gathered. Look carefully, for this great community has a leader. Let's approach nearer to learn about him. See his brilliant decorations—more than a thousand.[37] How forcefully he speaks. How pleasant is his conversation. I have learned a little of what he says during these fifteen days, and you could learn the same from me. He is speaking about the country's glorious miracle-displaying sovereign, who has sent him to us. See, he is displaying such wonders that we have to admit that he is the special envoy of the sovereign.

Look carefully. Not only the peninsula's creatures are listening to him; he is making his voice heard in wonderful fashion by the whole country. Near and far, everyone is trying to listen to his discourse, even animals. Even the mountains are listening to the commandments he has brought so that they are stirring in their places. Those trees move to the place to which he points. He brings forth water wherever he wishes. He makes his fingers like an abundant spring and lets others drink from them.

---

[36] The ship refers to history, the peninsula to the place of Age of Happiness, the age of the Prophet. Taking off the dress of modern civilization on the dark shore of this age, we sail on the ship of history over the sea of time, land on the Arabian peninsula in the Age of Happiness, and visit the Pride of Creation as he is carrying out his mission. We know that he is a proof of Divine Unity so brilliant that he illuminates the whole earth and the two faces of time (past and future), and disperses the darkness of unbelief and misguidance.

[37] A thousand decorations signify the Prophet's miracles that, according to meticulous researchers, number around one thousand.

Look, that important lamp in the palace's dome splits into two at his gesture.[38] That means this whole land and its inhabitants recognize that he is an envoy. As though understanding that he is the most eminent and true translator of an unseen miracle-displaying one, the herald of his sovereignty, the discloser of his talisman, and a trustworthy envoy communicating his commandments, they heed and obey him. All around him, those who are sensible affirm whatever he says. By submitting to his commands and answering his beckoning, everything in this land, even the mountains, the trees, and the huge light that illuminates everywhere, affirm him.[39]

So, O friend, could there be any deception in the words of this most illustrious, magnificent, and serious of beings, who bears a thousand decorations from the king's royal treasury, about the miracle-displaying king and his attributes, and in the commands he communicates from him? He speaks with firmest conviction and is confirmed by all the country's notables. If you think they contain some deception, you must deny the existence and reality of this palace, those lamps, and this congregation. Your objections will be refuted by the proof's power.

The Twelfth Argument

Come, O friend who must have come to your senses a little. I will show you further proof as strong as the sum of the previous eleven proofs. Look at this illustrious decree,[40] which has descended from above and which everyone looks upon with full attention out of amazement or veneration. That being with a thousand decorations is explaining its meaning. The decree's brilliant style attracts everyone's admiration, and speaks of matters

---

[38] The important lamp is the moon, which split into two at his gesture. As Mawlana Jami remarked: "That unlettered one who never wrote, wrote with the pen of his finger an *alif* [ﺍ—the first letter of the Arabic alphabet] on the page of the skies, and made one forty into two fifties." In other words, before he split the moon, it resembled the Arabic letter *mim* (ﻡ), the mathematical value of which is forty. After splitting, it became two crescents resembling two *nuns* (ﻥ), the value of which is fifty.

[39] The author refers to the mountains and trees answering the Prophet's call. See The Nineteenth Letter's ninth through twelfth signs in Said Nursi, *The Letters* (NJ: The Light, Inc., 2007) (Tr.) The huge light is the sun. Once the Prophet was sleeping in 'Ali's arms, who did not wake him up out of deep love and respect for him. When the Prophet woke up, the sun was about to set, and 'Ali had not yet prayed the afternoon Prayer. Upon the Prophet's order, the earth revolved a little backwards and the sun appeared above the horizon so 'Ali could pray. This is one of the Prophet's famous miracles.

[40] The illustrious decree refers to the Qur'an, and the seal to its miraculousness.

so important and serious that everyone feels compelled to listen. It describes all the acts, attributes, and commands of the one who governs this land, who made this palace, and exhibits these wonders. There is a mighty seal on the decree, an inimitable seal on every line and sentence. The meanings, truths, commandments, and instances of wisdom it provides are in a style unique to him, which also functions like a stamp or seal.

In short, this supreme decree shows that supreme being as clearly as the sun, so that one who is not blind can "see" him. If you have come to your senses, friend, this is enough for now. Do you have more objections?

The stubborn man replied: "In the face of all these proofs I can only say: 'All praise and gratitude are for God,' for I have come to believe, in a way as bright as the sun and clear as daylight, that this land has a single Lord of Perfection, this world a single Owner of Majesty, and this palace a single Maker of Grace. May God be pleased with you for saving me from my former obstinacy and foolishness. Each proof was sufficient to demonstrate the truth. But since with each successive proof, clearer and finer, more pleasant, agreeable, and radiant levels of knowledge, scenes of recognition, and windows of love were opened and revealed, I waited and listened."

Index

A

Abdülmecid, 72

'Abdu'l-Qadr al-Jilani, 110

'Abdu'l-Qahir al-Jurjani, 113

Abdurrahman, 72

Abraham (Prophet), 57, 199

acquisition, 74; minor, 74

Adam (Prophet), 21, 32, 77, 111, 153, 217

Africa, 89

age; old, 8, 14, 37-38

Age of Happiness, 105, 111, 228

Age of Ignorance, 113

Alima Hanim, 72

America, 77, 211

Anatolia, ix

angels, 20, 28, 32-33, 37, 49, 54, 57, 65, 69-77, 94, 98-99, 102-103, 116, 119, 128, 136, 140, 177, 210-211; of Thunder, 25; of Thawr and Hut, 75; of Hell, 12, 43; questioning, 71; of Munkar and Nakir, 71

Archangel; of death, 69; Azra'il, 68-69, 73, 76; Gabriel, 68, 76, 98, 211; Israfil, 25, 68, 76, 111; Michael, 68, 76

annihilation, 10, 26, 35, 42, 63, 68, 119, 160, 210, 215

Arab, 117

Arabic, 66, 71, 113, 229

'Arafat, 46

astronomy, 170

atheism, xiii; naturalistic, 140

Ayasofya (Haghia Sophia), 151

B

Balance; Supreme, 211

belief, x-xiv, 5-6, 9-15, 18-20, 24, 32-40, 42, 44, 46, 48-52, 54-56, 60-62, 65, 68-73, 75-77, 81, 88, 92, 94-100, 106-108, 111, 117, 119, 141, 154-155, 161, 168-169, 172, 180, 196, 199, 201-203, 205-206, 209-212, 217; essence of, 44; fruits of, xiv, 42, 69, 71-72; in Divine Determining or Destiny, 54; in Divine Decree and Destiny, 210; in God, xi, 15, 50-52, 54-56, 61, 88, 94, 98, 155, 205, 211-212; in the Existence and Unity of God, 210; in Prophethood, 210; in the angels, 54, 69, 71, 73, 75-76; in the Hereafter, 6, 34-40, 42, 50-51, 55, 172, 201; in the Prophets, 52, 69; in the Qur'an and other Divinely-revealed Scriptures, 210; true, pain-free pleasure found in, 10; truth of, 10, 54, 88, 196

Books; Divinely-revealed, 33, 55

Bridge; Supreme, 54

C

capital; intellectual, 14; of life, 12

cause-and-effect relationship, 152

causes; as veils that cover the hand of Divine Power, 73; ascribing creativity to physical, 142-143, 159-161; "natural", 142-145, 148, 152-153

Index of God's Names and Attributes